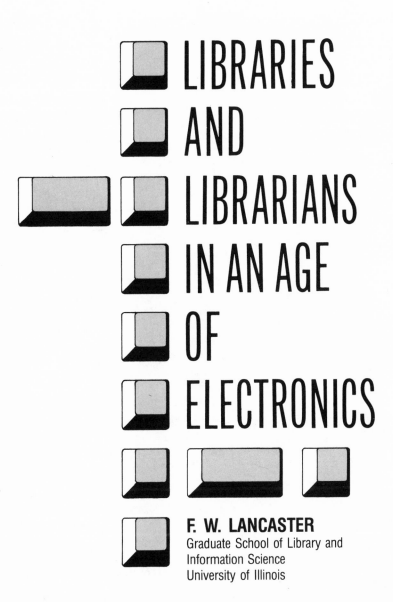

LIBRARIES
AND
LIBRARIANS
IN AN AGE
OF
ELECTRONICS

F. W. LANCASTER
Graduate School of Library and
Information Science
University of Illinois

I**R**P INFORMATION RESOURCES PRESS
Arlington, Va. 1982

Available from
Information Resources Press
1700 North Moore Street
Arlington, Virginia 22209

Library of Congress Catalog Card Number 82-081403
ISBN 0-87815-040-4

The Author

F. WILFRID LANCASTER is a Professor in the Graduate School of Library and Information Science, University of Illinois, where he teaches courses in information storage and retrieval, evaluation of information services, and content analysis and control of vocabularies.

Professor Lancaster is the author of approximately 30 papers and reports in his fields of specialization. One of his papers, "MEDLARS: Report on the Evaluation of Its Operating Efficiency," was judged the Best *American Documentation* Paper for 1969. He is also the author of numerous books, including *Information Retrieval Systems: Characteristics, Testing, and Evaluation*, 2nd Edition (Wiley, 1979), for which he received the American Society for Information Science Best Information Sciences Book Award in 1970 (1st Edition); *Vocabulary Control for Information Retrieval* (Information Resources Press, 1972); *Information Retrieval On-Line* (Melville, 1973), for which he received the 1975 American Society for Information Science Best Information Sciences Book Award; *The Measurement and Evaluation of Library Services* (Information Resources Press, 1977), for which he received the 1978 ALA Ralph R. Shaw Award for Outstanding Contribution to Library Literature; and *Toward Paperless Information Systems* (Academic Press, 1978), for which he received the 1979 American Society for Information Science Best Information Sciences Book Award. He is co-author with John Martyn of *Investigative Methods in Library and Information Science* (Information Resources Press, 1981).

In 1980, Professor Lancaster received the first Outstanding Information Science Teacher Award from the American Society for Information Science.

Preface

In the past several years, I have written extensively on an evolving paperless society and the implications of this evolution for libraries and librarians. *Libraries and Librarians in an Age of Electronics* represents an attempt to pull this and other material together and to present it as a coherent whole. My hope is that it will stimulate members of the library profession to reassess the role of the library as an institution and the role of the librarian as an information specialist in a time of extensive social and technological change.

Parts of this book have appeared in other forms. In particular, Chapters 6 and 9 are based heavily on my contributions to *Telecommunications and Libraries* (Knowledge Industry Publications, Inc. [1981]). Much of Chapter 7 is drawn from an article appearing in *Online Review* (Vol. 5, No. 4, 1981; reproduced by permission of the publisher); and a small part of Chapter 11 is based on an article appearing in *Aslib Proceedings* (Vol. 33, No. 1, 1981; reproduced by permission of Aslib).

I would like to thank Kathy Neff and Rashmi Mehrotra, my graduate assistants in 1980 and 1981, for their help in gathering materials and in the tedious job of checking references and quotations.

Contents

1   The Information Age

The future of library science cannot be considered in isolation. Rather, it must be viewed within the context of a pattern of change affecting society as a whole. Parker (1976) has claimed that the world is on the brink of a new social revolution—the information revolution—that will be as important as the industrial revolution. The term *information revolution* implies a transition from an industrial society to a society where information processing will dominate industrial production in the labor field. He predicts that economic progress will occur through the information sector rather than the production sector and that governments will, in the long run, gain more from investing in improved information processing than from investing in industrial productivity.

Parker points out that most of the service occupations are primarily information services:

Whether we look at trends in the distribution of the labor force, trends in the components of the National Income, or the trends in personal consumption, the same answer is obtained: The U.S. society is in the midst of a transition from an industrial society to an information society. (p. 95)

Bell (1973) uses the term *postindustrial society* to refer to a changing social structure where the economy evolves from goods-producing to service-oriented. From 1947 to 1968, employment in service activities increased 60 percent compared to an increase of less than 10 percent in the goods-producing industries. Porat (1977) states that, between 1970 and 1980, the information occupations formed the largest component of the work force, a trend that will likely continue.

Drucker (1980) calls for "reindustrialization" within developed countries, a need brought about by the second major demographic transition in the developed world in the twentieth century. The first such transition, cresting shortly after World War II, was the shift from agriculture to manufacturing. This gave rise to mass production industries and to the emergence of the semiskilled machine operator — the blue-collar worker. Drucker points out that farmers constituted 60 percent of the work force in the United States in 1900. Today they account for only 3–4 percent. In Japan, the transition has been greatly accelerated. As late as 1946, 60 percent of the work force was engaged in agriculture. This value is less than 10 percent today. The migration from farm to factory, however, did not cause a decline in agricultural productivity. In fact, productivity in this century has tripled or quadrupled through improved technology and the more efficient use of natural resources.

The second major demographic transition, in which developed countries now find themselves, is the large-scale move from manual labor to what Drucker calls "knowledge work," that is, some form of information processing:

Compared with 30 years ago, only half as many young people in the U.S. are coming into the labor force with the schooling, expectations and skills that will lead them into traditional blue-collar work. The squeeze will become even tighter when the "baby bust" children of the Sixties and Seventies reach working age: Only one-third to two-fifths as many potential blue-collar entrants will be available in 1990 as there were in 1950. (p. 10)

The reindustrialization that Drucker advocates does not mean a reversal of the trend toward knowledge work. On the contrary, the rapid decline in traditional blue-collar employment must be promoted if the developed economies are to maintain a competitive edge over economies now developing.

The less-developed countries (LDCs) are still in the midst of the first demographic transition — the movement of the labor force from rural, agricultural areas to urban manufacturing centers. As a result, these countries find themselves with a surplus of low-paid, poorly skilled workers. The developed countries, paying high wages to their semiskilled machine operators, can no longer compete effectively with the LDCs in labor-intensive approaches to manufacturing. Manufacturing technology must be reoriented to capitalize on the growing supply of "knowledge workers" and minimize dependence on the shrinking pool of blue-collar labor.

Discussing the situation in France, Nora and Minc (1980) suggest that the country is caught in a kind of industrial "pincers," facing trade competition, on the one hand, from the more computerized nations and, on the other, from under-industrialized economies with a cheap pool of labor.

Reindustrialization, then, means decreasing reliance on manual labor and increasing automation of the manufacturing industries. In particular, it calls for the increased application of computers to these industries. In a fully automated production environment, entire plants and processes are redesigned as "integrated flow systems" where manual labor is replaced by robots or by fully automated machine tools, each incorporating its own minicomputer or microprocessor. In such an environment, the blue-collar operator is transformed into a white-coated technician. He does not operate a machine tool but rather is primarily involved in processing information needed to control the operations of these tools or even a complete assembly line. The technician is engaged in knowledge work rather than manual labor. Moreover, some control of operations can be removed from the factory floor itself and performed by remote control.

The two demographic transitions that Drucker alludes to can also be examined in terms of the contribution of the three industries to total national income. Figure 1 shows that manufacturing overtook agriculture around 1880 and that the "knowledge industry" overtook agriculture by 1920 and manufacturing by 1970. Of course, the knowledge industry represents a fairly heterogeneous collection of activities, as Phillips (1975) has pointed out:

Exact description of this "knowledge industry" is difficult. Some of its component parts are obvious: the huge bureaucracies of government multiplied tenfold since the New Deal era, the colleges and universities now serving 10 million young Americans, the huge communications empires, the network of think-tank and charitable foundations, and the huge corporate giants of knowledge technology—IBM, Xerox, and so forth. The lesser fry include consultants on problems from poverty to banking, professionals—from doctors and lawyers to architects—and many others providing a variety of specialized services. Indirectly, many other forms of "commerce" are involved. Banks, insurance companies, and stock-brokerage houses are becoming more "knowledgified" as the corporate economy itself leans more toward computerization and information systems. Many large corporations are also moving toward the research and the "social awareness" outlook promoted by the knowledge sector. (p. 15)

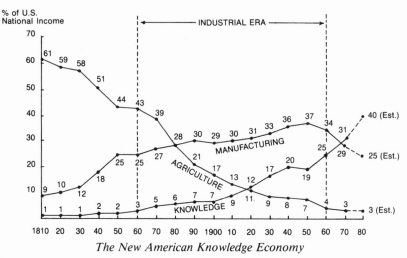

The New American Knowledge Economy

Notes:

1) Included in the manufacturing category (all manufacturing except categories excluded below) are public utilities, mining, and transportation, closely tied to the industrialization of the United States. These additions increase the post-1950 turndown in the manufacturing segment.

2) Data for early years (1810–30) are projections based on changes in agricultural/rural/farm employment/residence output and in value of coal produced and shipping carried.

3) Components of "knowledge" segment figure (capable of precise use only since 1929):

   a) Communications category—all

   b) Manufacturing category—printing, publishing, and allied industries, electrical machinery

   c) Services category—miscellaneous business services

            motion pictures

            amusement, recreation services

            medical, other health services

            legal services

            educational services

            non-profit membership organizations

            miscellaneous professional services

   d) Government, government enterprises category—general federal government general state government

N.B. While some of the above categories are not entirely knowledge industry in nature, some other categories not included (for example, finance, insurance, and real estate) have major knowledge industry components, so the above totals are reasonable.

Figure 1 The knowledge economy compared with agriculture and manufacturing. (Illustration from *Mediacracy*, by Kevin P. Phillips. Copyright © 1975 by Kevin P. Phillips. Reprinted by permission of Doubleday & Company, Inc.)

There is some cross-classification among the various categories. Clearly, IBM and Xerox are major contributors to the knowledge sector. Nevertheless, as manufacturers of equipment, they also contribute to manufacturing. Thus, the categorization is somewhat arbitrary.

The term *service economy* refers to the phenomenon of the increasing number of people providing services to others rather than producing material goods (Gershuny [1977]). In the developed world, the service occupations have changed radically; many of these services (e.g., domestic chores) are being replaced by labor-saving machines. The low-level service occupations (exemplified by domestic servants) have virtually disappeared as increasing numbers of workers moved into more highly paid jobs in the production industries. To some extent, then, the function of those employed in low-level service occupations has changed from providing a low level of manual labor (e.g., on the farm or in the home) to producing equipment capable of doing the jobs that they themselves had vacated.

The move from an agricultural society to an industrial society to a postindustrial society has been accompanied by greater affluence, more leisure time, and a longer life expectancy. This, in turn, promotes rapid growth of higher-level service occupations, such as in retail sales, education, banking, entertainment, insurance, travel, health care, social welfare, real estate, and law, as well as in a wide range of cultural activities and in the government bureaucracy needed to control a society of ever-increasing diversity and complexity. These services are becoming more dependent on computers and telecommunications, or what has become known as *compunications* or, alternatively, as *telematics* (Nora and Minc [1980]). Computer terminals are now abundant in airports, banks, travel agencies, car rental agencies, department stores, supermarkets, hospitals, and schools. They are in homes in the form of personal computers and domestic television receivers modified to allow two-way communication.

In addition to an increasing reliance on electronics, those involved in the service occupations have something else in common with the white-coated technicians of the automated manufacturing industry: Both groups are primarily involved in processing information. We are truly in an information age. Indeed, the Inner London Education

Authority (1980) says that "The ability to locate, retrieve, select, organize, evaluate and communicate information will increasingly become a major component of what we understand the term 'literacy' to mean; consequently such abilities will be crucial to each individual's quality of life."

The growth of information processing has been described by Drucker (1969) as follows:

The "knowledge industries" which produce and distribute ideas and information rather than goods and services, accounted in 1955 for one-quarter of the U.S. gross national product. This was already three times the proportion of the national product that the country had spent on the "knowledge sector" in 1900. Yet by 1965, ten years later, the knowledge sector was taking one-third of a much bigger national product. In the late 1970s it will account for one-half of the total national product. Every other dollar earned and spent in the American economy will be earned by producing and distributing ideas and information, and will be spent on procuring ideas and information. (p. 263)

Thus, the trend is toward more workers becoming involved largely in information handling activities and depending increasingly on electronic capabilities to process information more effectively. The move from manufacturing to information processing, together with the compunications revolution, may cause another important social change: a growing decentralization of professional activities. Before the industrial revolution, human labor was largely decentralized; people worked on the farm or in a cottage-industry situation. The industrial revolution brought about a centralizing effect; people were brought together to work in the factory or the mill and, at a later time, in "the office." Toffler (1970) has pointed out a direct analogy in education, where children are assembled in schools in much the same way that workers are assembled in factories.

Compunications can free us from centralization of activities (i.e., a fixed place of work) and allow at least a partial return to the cottage-industry type of work environment. The fact is that many information-processing activities do not need to be centralized. Rather, they can be performed wherever there is access to a computer terminal, electricity, and a telephone. Banking and many kinds of shopping are examples. Remote diagnosis of certain health problems is possible. Groups of people can confer via telecommunications networks. With educational television and computer-aided instruction, much classroom instruction could be transferred from the school to the home. Many of the service activities involving information processing could be performed in the home rather than the office.

This decentralized future has been predicted by Toffler (1970):

In the technological systems of tomorrow — fast, fluid and self-regulating — machines will deal with the flow of physical materials; men with the flow of information and insight. Machines will increasingly perform the routine tasks; men the intellectual and creative tasks. Machines and men both, instead of being concentrated in gigantic factories and factory cities, will be scattered across the globe, linked together by amazingly sensitive, near-instantaneous communications. Human work will move out of the factory and mass office into the community and the home. (p. 356)

Toffler (1980) later referred to this work-at-home environment as the "electronic cottage." The term *telecommuting* has recently been introduced to represent the same phenomenon.

These social changes will inevitably have a profound impact on libraries and librarians. Before this is examined, however, some further forecasts of technological developments and social change in the next two decades should be considered, with particular reference to developments that may alter the entire information-transfer environment in which libraries function.

The Next Two Decades

Progress has been dramatic in all segments of society during the past 20 years. Developments in the next two decades will be even more spectacular since, as time passes, the pace of change accelerates. This point was forcefully made by Toffler (1970) in the following example:

Year	Mode of Transportation	Speed (mph)
6000 B.C.	Camel caravan	8
1600 B.C.	Chariot	20
1784	Mail coach	10
1825	Steam locomotive	13
1880	Steam locomotive	100
1938	Airplane	400
1960	Rocket plane	4,000
1970	Space capsule	18,000

A more telling demonstration of the accelerative thrust is depicted by the "800th lifetime." As Toffler observes,

. . . if the last 50,000 years of man's existence were divided into lifetimes of approximately sixty-two years each, there have been about 800 such lifetimes. Of these 800, fully 650 were spent in caves.

Only during the last seventy lifetimes has it been possible to communicate effectively from one lifetime to another—as writing made it possible to do. Only during the last six lifetimes did masses of men ever see a printed word. Only during the last four has it been possible to measure time with any precision. Only in the last two has anyone anywhere used an electric motor. And the overwhelming majority of all the material goods we use in daily life today have been developed within the present, the 800th, lifetime. (p. 15)

Toffler (1980) also has referred to three waves of social change. The first, the agricultural revolution, occurred over thousands of years. The second, the industrial revolution, lasted only three hundred years. The third wave of change, in which we are now immersed, will complete itself in just a few decades:

Tearing our families apart, rocking our economy, paralyzing our political systems, shattering our values, the Third Wave affects everyone. It challenges all the old power relationships. . . . Third Wave brings with it a genuinely new way of life based on diversified renewable energy sources; on methods of production that make most factory assembly lines obsolete; on new, non-nuclear families; on a novel institution that might be called the "electronic cottage"; and on radically changed schools and corporations of the future. (p. 26)

A cursory examination of the many "futures" journals presently being published shows no lack of forecasts of what the future holds. In health care, breakthroughs are predicted in the treatment of many intractable diseases through an improved understanding of their underlying etiology. The use of transplants and artificial devices to replace malfunctioning organs will be increasingly successful. But not all progress in health care will come from dramatic scientific discoveries or technological inventions. Some forecasters expect to see continued strength in holistic medicine, which emphasizes preventive care, nutrition, and treatment of the whole person (Selim [1979]). Sobel (1979) views the future of health care as follows:

We are now at a frontier of health. The way forward lies not in an extrapolation of the present, nor in a resurrection of the past, but in a new synthesis—an integration of medical and nonmedical approaches to health, Western scientific medicine with alternative systems of healing, and physiochemical investigations with a scientific understanding of human behavior and psychosocial factors in health and disease. (p. 10)

The decentralization phenomenon discussed earlier is already affecting medicine. Midwives are assisting in more and more at-home births. Nurse practitioners and physician's assistants located in rural areas are using telecommunications to contact physicians. The use of health information services, offered by telephone, seems to be growing. It is reasonable to suppose that computers will soon be applied more extensively (and more successfully) to diagnosing diseases, recording patient histories, and searching for and analyzing patient records. Nora and Minc (1980) postulate that computerization will tend to break up medical specialties "by restoring to the general practitioner functions he was not able to perform in the past." The distinction between physician and medical aide will tend to blur.

Brennan (1979) believes that Americans will continue to rely predominantly on private automobiles for transportation in the year 2000 (although this clearly depends on the availability and cost of petroleum or alternative energy sources). Others, however, expect a continued migration to various forms of mass transportation (David [1979]). Of course, commuting could decline considerably as more and more activities are performed from the home and the need to travel for discussion purposes is greatly reduced by computer-conferencing networks (Hiltz and Turoff [1978]). A study by the Committee on Nuclear and Alternative Energy Systems, of the National Academy of Sciences, has predicted that by the year 2010, telecommunications could have reduced by 25 percent the amount of travel that would otherwise be necessary (Olson [1980]). As communication technology begins to replace transportation in the work environment, travel for pleasure may predominate travel for business purposes. Tourism may increase (Shackleford [1979] and Epstein [1976]). The decline in commuting for business purposes could mean that the "neighborhood" may reemerge as the focal point of activity, with neighborhood clusters serving as centers of human interaction (Kahn and Brown [1978]).

Barnes (1978) predicts that in education the book-centered approach will give way to the use of "unlimited learning resources." He points out that "It is a poverty-stricken classroom that does not use open and closed circuit TV, community resource people, films, tapes, and many other resources" (p. 126). Others, however, suggest that in the future, education, in addition to being less book centered (e.g., Bork [1980]), may be less institution centered, with much of the educational process devolving to the home. Rolland (1979), for example, foresees the establishment of an educational "datornet," an electronic network that could become the primary mode of instruction at all levels. Electronic forms of education might include computer-aided instruction, educational television, and even robot teachers (Freeman and Mulkowsky [1978]). Dunn (1979) suggests that two-way interactive television could reach 80–90 percent of the homes in the United States by the year 2000, making degree programs offered outside institutions the norm. In the next 20 years, Dunn believes, one-quarter of the existing liberal arts colleges could disappear because of technological developments, changes in public expectations about higher education, economic factors, and social changes. McHale (1978) also expects that improved communications technology will facilitate an increasing tendency toward the "open university," not tied to a particular location.

Not all writers predict that electronics will replace the human instructor. Indeed, technology could increase the availability of highly skilled teachers. For example, holography could allow an instructor to be present simultaneously in many different classrooms thousands of miles apart (Kotler [1978]).

Although Clarke (1980) accepts the inevitability of electronic tutors, he believes that the teaching profession will survive the electronic revolution just as it survived the advent of printing. Schools will still be needed to teach young children social skills and discipline, and universities will still have to provide facilities such as laboratories.

In the age of electronics, however, the entire substance and content of education may change. It is not even certain that the written word will remain the primary vehicle of human communication (Wagschal [1978]):

We are witnessing the demise of the written word as our primary means of storing and communicating information. By the time my four year old son reaches adulthood, there will be hardly any compelling reason for him to be able to read, write or do arithmetic. He will have more—not less—access to the accumulated wisdom of the peoples of the globe, but the three R's will have succumbed to the influence of inexpensive, fast, reliable computers that call up information instantly in response to the spoken word. (p. 243)

This is not a universally accepted belief. Ong (1979), for example, clings to the need for writing and the printed word: "All this is to say that writing, and to a degree print, are absolutely essential not just for distributing knowledge but for performing the central noetic operations which a high-technology culture takes for granted" (p. 2).

McHale (1978) believes there will be a shift from learning what is known to mastering techniques (i.e., to "learning how to learn"). Similar sentiments have been expressed by Joseph (1979a).

The distinction between education and entertainment and between education and work may blur as identical technologies are applied to all three. Changes in work scheduling and types of work will bring about a cyclic life pattern. Instead of education and leisure followed by years of work and then by more leisure and perhaps education in later life, the new environment will permit one to alternate between work and education throughout life. The worker of the future will tend to change jobs more frequently and will look for employment that provides flexibility, growth, and educational opportunities (Best [1978]):

During single and non offspring years, the appropriate pattern could be longer work weeks of 45–50 hours with annual vacations of 8 to 14 weeks and some sabbaticals. During the early childbearing years, there would be shorter work weeks of 25–40 hours with moderate vacations of 2 to 4 weeks. Late and post childbearing years: 40–45 hours with long annual vacations of 5–8 weeks and extended sabbatical leaves. Old age: short to moderate work weeks of 25 to 40 hours and long vacations and sabbatical leaves. Time income tradeoffs and flexiyear contracts might be an important part of such a scheme. (p. 14)

A cashless, checkless society, achieved by electronic transfer of funds, is a distinct possibility. This will facilitate shopping from the home, where the consumer will select from catalogs and advertisements shown on television on demand.

In commerce, the paperless office is already beginning to emerge. The office of the future will most likely incorporate television, tape recorders, word-processing machines with the capacity to store text, and other electronic devices (Vail [1978]). Computer conferencing and electronic mail will be commonplace. Free-lance secretaries may operate via computer terminals in the home. The paperless office is discussed further in Chapter 3.

Art, culture, and entertainment will also change. As Gordon (1965) has pointed out, "The same machines which free man from the burdens of work and production will also, to a large measure, help him use his newly acquired leisure" (p. 93). Artists will use computers to construct images and compose music.* Television will be three-dimensional, and video disks will permit personal ownership of large quantities of written and visual records for study or entertainment. Electronic games will increase in popularity, and telecommunications links may lead to worldwide groups of game enthusiasts.

There is the possibility of a democracy in which all citizens can use telecommunications facilities to voice opinions and cast votes. The communication gap between constituents in their homes and their government representatives could be reduced to microseconds (Gregory [1979]).

This chapter has presented an idea of the changes that might occur in our society during the next 20 years. The review is by no means complete, and several important areas, such as energy, agriculture, and space colonization, are not discussed. Nevertheless, even this selective overview should indicate the changing environment to which libraries and librarians will need to adapt. A more complete picture of this "wired society" is provided by Martin (1978).

Emphasized here is the fact that the pursuit and processing of information will become increasingly important throughout all segments of society. An information-skilled populace will be needed to implement and exploit new technologies applied in all aspects of human endeavor. But demands for information resources can also be expected to increase through other stimuli, like the need to support "lifelong learning," to enhance the use of leisure time, and to satisfy the public's growing interest in "participation" in the broadest sense (e.g., more direct involvement in their own health care). Because the collection, processing, and dissemination of information has become such an essential element in our lives, librarians, as skilled information providers, may encounter the opportunity to raise their social value and recognition.

This brief glimpse into the future has deliberately excluded certain important elements: technological forecasts relating to computers

---

* In 1981, it was announced that New York University's School of the Arts had received a grant from the National Endowment for the Arts to support the establishment of an "electronic art gallery."

and telecommunications and the application of technology to various aspects of information transfer, including publishing. Since future developments in these areas can be expected to have a major impact on libraries and librarians, these topics are examined in the next two chapters.

2 Technological Capabilities and Prospects

The expression "age of electronics" in the title of this book refers to an era in which all human activity is dominated by computers and telecommunications. It hardly seems an exaggeration to refer to the achievements of the computer industry in the past 30 years as spectacular. These three decades have seen an explosive growth in the number of computers, an increasing diversity of applications, rapidly declining costs of data storage and data processing, and an incredible decrease in the size of the computer needed to perform a particular task. Kubitz (1980), quoting Hogan (1978), has demonstrated size and efficiency factors by comparing the first electronic computer, ENIAC, with a tiny modern microprocessor. The results appear in Table 1.

There is no evidence that the period of rapid advances in compunications technology is coming to a halt. In fact, there is every reason to believe that the rate of progress will accelerate greatly over the next 20 years.

Information Processing Technology

The credibility of a transition to a largely electronic society depends, first and foremost, on the availability of terminal devices. Clayton and Nisenoff (1975, 1976) estimated that there would be approximately 3 million such terminals in the United States in 1979 but pro-

Table 1   A Modern Microprocessor vs. ENIAC, the First Electronic
Computer

Criterion	Microprocessor vs. ENIAC
Size	300,000 times smaller
Power needed	56,000 times less
Memory (RAM)	8 times more
Speed	20 times faster
Number of active elements (tubes or transistors)	About the same
Number of passive elements (resistors and capacitors)	80,000 fewer
Add time	About the same
Failure rate	10,000 times better
Weight	Less than 1 pound vs. 30 tons

SOURCE: From Kubitz (1980), who based his data on Hogan (1978), by permission of the Graduate School of Library and Information Science, University of Illinois.

ject a number approaching 100 million by 1995. They estimate that, by the year 2000, there will be two telephones and two terminals for each inhabitant in the United States. Baker (1979) quotes an AT&T prediction that there will be 1 billion terminals in North America by the year 2000. The exact form these terminals will take is unclear. Some, presumably, will be domestic television receivers, others will be home computers, and a number may be miniterminals installed in homes by businesses for special purposes (e.g., terminals installed by the telephone companies to replace printed directories).

Nisenoff et al. (1977) predict a growth from 55,000 mainframe computers in the United States in 1980 to 90,000 in 1990. In the same time period, they forecast a growth of minicomputers from 300,000 to 1.25 million and a growth in microprocessors from 12 million to 100 million. Kubitz (1980) forecasts that by 1987 half the households in the United States will have some form of intelligent terminal.

Improvements and potential improvements in the power, cost, and size of computers have been presented by Branscomb (1979), who points out that it is increased performance in electronic circuitry, more than anything else, that has contributed to the overall improvements in power, cost, and size. The fact that complete integrated circuits can be etched onto a single silicon chip half the size of a fingernail means that computing power can be distributed cheaply wherever it is needed and that a minute computer — a microprocessor — can fit on a single chip. Silicon technology has already brought switching speeds into the range of picoseconds (trillionths of a second), but it seems limited in terms of its potential for future increases in efficiency. The basic limitation is caused by the fact that an electric signal can travel no faster than the speed of light (little more than one inch in 0.1 nanosecond). To avoid unwanted transmission delays, integrated circuits of silicon semiconductors must be so densely packed that they generate heat that is extremely difficult to draw off without damaging the circuitry. As Branscomb points out, "the power laws of physics make it difficult for us to envision the development of midget supercomputers with silicon semiconductors."

Branscomb suggests that a new technology — Josephson technology — which is based on the cooling of metal alloys to the temperature of liquid helium, may offer the greatest promise for use in future processors of high speed, small size, and low power dissipation. In the laboratory, fragments of circuitry built on this principle have demonstrated switching times that are faster than 20 trillionths of a second.

Clayton and Nisenoff refer to the "throughput" capabilities of mainframe computers in terms of millions of instructions executed per second (MIPS). They forecast that this performance is likely to continue to rise by an order of magnitude every decade, at least to the year 2000. Kubitz (1980) suggests a growth from 50 MIPS to 500 MIPS within the 1980s.

Regarding size, Emery (1978) has pointed out that a single microelectronic chip around ¼-inch square now has the "raw computing power" of a whole roomful of early computer circuitry. According to Kubitz (1980), a chip can currently hold one million components, compared with only 30 in 1965. Clayton and Nisenoff project that computer systems in the year 2000 will use chips with at least 100,000 logic circuits per chip. Conceivably, packing densities as great as 1 million logic circuits per chip will be in production by then. At the research and development stage, however, chips packed with 1 billion logic circuits could be reached before 2000. Sheils et al. (1980) point out that parts of the transistors now crowded onto chips are less than 3 microns wide, in contrast to a human hair, which is 100 microns wide. Yet, very-large-scale integration (VLSI) of circuits will produce submicron components by the mid-1980s.

Regarding cost of storage, Kubitz (1980) reports that 100,000 bits of memory cost \$1.26 per bit in 1954 but less than \$0.01 in 1978. Branscomb claims that the growth of computer storage capacity at a given cost has averaged almost 35 percent per year for the past 20 years. He calculates that the full text of 20 million books (approximately 70 trillion bits) could be stored on less than 20 IBM 3850 Mass Storage Systems. Even if the rate of growth of storage capacity at a given cost slowed to 21 percent per year, the investment needed today to store 20 million books would, 100 years from now, store 15 billion electronic libraries, each containing 20 million books.

Clayton and Nisenoff show that videodisks represent both the highest achievable packing density for mass storage media and the lowest cost per bit. For magnetic bubble technology, these authors project a decline in cost from present levels of around 10^{-2} cents per bit to 10^{-5} cents per bit by 2000.* In contrast, the optical digital disk† only costs 10^{-7} cents per bit, and one disk can hold 10 billion to 100 billion bits. The cost of publishing data on videodisk has been estimated at less than \$2 per disk in quantities of 10,000 (Goldstein [1981]). Savage (1980) notes that videodisks containing 10 billion bits of information (equivalent to a half million typewritten pages) already exist and can be accessed in 250 milliseconds or less. A laser-encoded digital videodisk announced by Philips under the code name Megadoc, but yet to be released, can store 500,000 pages of journal text on a single side. If high-quality illustrations are included, 50,000 pages per side can be stored. The industry is now working toward the development of disks that will accommodate 100 billion bits per side, equivalent to approximately 80 200-megabyte disk packs. At this rate, videodisk technology would be economically competitive with microfiche as a mere storage medium. Its advantages over microfiche, however, are tremendous: The disk can be accessed randomly

---

* Bell Telephone Laboratories already claims to have developed a bubble memory chip capable of storing 11.5 million bits.

† A distinction can be made between optical video disks and optical digital disks. The former are designed to store visual images, such as films, but digital information can also be encoded on the video signal. The latter are designed specifically to store digital data (Goldstein [1982]).

and can incorporate text, high-quality static pictures, and motion pictures. Videodisks, like magnetic disks, can be assembled into "packs." Savage claims that six double-sided disks in a pack, read by 12 optical heads, would now give access to 1 trillion bits of information. He goes on to suggest some possible applications:

Since words and images can be recorded on it and reviewed from it quickly from any location, the videodisc may eventually become the electronic equivalent of paper and microfilm. The range of possible applications is limitless. For example, discs, when integrated into word-processing systems, could become electronic filing cabinets for documents — including images received by facsimile. Hospitals could employ discs to store patient records, complete with x-rays and graphs, as well as written, and even spoken, words. Retailers could use discs to maintain lists of lost or stolen credit cards. Business analysts could review credit information on selected companies stored on discs. Households could maintain home computer data bases and applications software on discs. Local telephone operators could access long-distance directories from discs. The military could keep parts drawings of aircraft or missiles on discs. And mail-order houses could distribute product catalogues and buyer's guides via discs. (p. 24)

Kubitz (1980) has made more specific suggestions on the relevance of videodisks to publishing operations and libraries:

The impact that optical disks could have is obvious. . . . They can be used for books, journals and all manner of educational materials, from fix-it instructions to academic texts. They could also be used for computer programs, quadraphonic records, games and movies with 4-channel sound from the "movie-of-the-month club." They are an almost ideal archival storage medium. At present, the shelf life is at least ten years and probably much more. This is in contrast to magnetic-type memory which must be rewritten every three to four years. The morning newspaper could come on a disk. Subscribers to magazines could get a copy of every magazine published each month. Academicians could receive all journals and simply read those they wished to. Library patrons could check out disks, or perhaps they would simply have one made containing the books they wanted. At $10 per 10,000 books, that's only 0.1 cent per book plus the recording charge. It is assumed, of course, that publishers will supply books in disk form — perhaps an updated disk each year. Of course, they probably won't send a disk but will simply transmit new books, as they are published, to libraries for recording. One book can be "read" in 0.2 seconds and sent to a home recorder. Thus, one could simply browse through the card catalog using the home computer system and, having selected the desired volume, have the book sent over a high-speed link to the home recorder. After storing it, one could curl up next to the fire with the flat panel display and read, referring occasionally to the full-color pictures from the book displayed on the computer's color television screen. (p. 159)

Videodisks and videocassettes are already collected and circulated by some public libraries.

Pursuing the cost picture somewhat further, Nisenoff et al. project a decline in the cost of intelligent terminals from $1,900 in 1980 to $1,300 in 1990, with typewriter-type units declining from $600 to $325 in the same period. In terms of cost/performance rates for mainframe computers, they forecast a decline from $15,000 per MIPS in 1980 to $10 per MIPS by 1990. These forecasts seem somewhat conservative. The Source Telecomputing Corporation has recently announced terminals in the range of $500–$600. Mass production could bring the retail cost of a videoterminal into the $200–$300 range. Branscomb estimates that, if the cost per bit of on-line memory and per circuit of logic declines at 21 percent per year (these declines have been more rapid over the past two decades), the computing power that costs $5 million today could be 15 billion times lower by 2078 — a mere .03 of a cent. He is quick to point out, however, that it is more likely that the largest computers of 2078 will sell for about the same price as they do today, while their power and usefulness will have increased 15 billion times.

Chen (1980) has suggested that the microprocessor may be the third major cultural invention of this century, following the automobile and television. He predicts that a shoebox-size microcomputer in the year 2001 could have the same capabilities as a large mainframe computer of today (e.g., an IBM 370/168) and could cost as little as $1,000. Much of the software needed to exploit the computer will be built in as "firmware," and this will allow the machine to be programmed in a simple problem-solving language (Seligman [1980]).

Tiny microprocessors have already found their way into many households in the United States in the forms of electronic toys and games and in the latest models of various domestic appliances. New automobiles incorporate microprocessors to regulate fuel use, adjust engine performance, and provide early warning of possible malfunctions, among numerous other tasks. Indeed, the General Motors Corporation claims it is the world's largest producer of computers. Microprocessor-controlled devices have even been surgically implanted in the human body.

The microcomputer revolution, according to Joseph (1979b), may cause a temporary decline in the production of large mainframe computers. Lecht (1979) predicts that, sometime in the early 1980s, the cost of an item of hardware will be exceeded by the cost of vendor software at installation. As more and more firmware (including self-correcting features) is built into computers, however, the two cost curves will again approach one another late in the 1990s. Joseph (1979b) believes that the rate of obsolescence of hardware will be retarded as greater standardization is introduced into interfaces, terminals, and protocols. The promises, as well as possible threats, of microelectronics are discussed in detail by Rada (1980).

The home-computer market is still an infant. Sheils et al. (1980) estimate that just 200,000 such machines are now in use in the United States. Nevertheless, home computers are presently being used in a wide variety of applications, from game playing to the management of stock portfolios and domestic finances. A home computer can be connected to a telecommunications network, giving the user access to an incredible range of information resources. For example, for $15 per hour in peak daytime hours and as little as $4.25 per hour in off-peak periods, the owner of a home computer can connect with the data base of the Source Telecomputing Corporation. Among the resources offered are the full text of UPI wire releases, stock market reports, world airline schedules, consumer information, news items from *The New York Times,* and an electronic mail facility. The computer industry is expanding its horizons beyond government, business, and the scientific establishment and is looking toward serving the needs of the ordinary consumer. The home-computer market could well "take off" in the 1980s.

Assessing the potential impact of home computers, Papert (1977) has said,

During the nineteen eighties small but immensely powerful personal computers will become as much a part of everyone's life as the TV, the telephone, the printed paper and the notebook. Indeed computers will integrate and supersede the functions of these and other communicational and recreational home technologies. I emphasize: this will happen independently of any decisions by the education community. The driving force lies in industry. This computer presence has a tremendous potential for psychological impact including improvement of the process of learning. It will affect adults, children and babies in homes as well as in schools and in places of work. Although the coming of the computers is inevitable, the way they will be used can be influenced very profoundly. (p. 258)

For completely electronic communication systems to be viable, however, the cost/performance ratio for telecommunications must continue to improve. Emery (1978) shows that communications costs have been declining steadily but at a slower rate than the declines for electronic circuits and for computers in general: 11 percent, 33 percent, and 25 percent per year, respectively. These costs are expected to decline at rates of 11 percent, 25 percent, and 40 percent per year within the next decade. Clayton and Nisenoff point out that the capacity of communication channels to transmit information (measured in bits per second) has increased six orders of magnitude in the past century, which amounts to an annual increase of 15 percent. They quote AT&T on the percentage of total telecommunications revenue accounted for by data transmission: approximately 30 percent in 1970 and projected to be 80 percent by 1990 and 95 percent by 2000. Clayton and Nisenoff also predict dramatic decreases in the cost of satellite communications, from nearly $100 per year for a two-way voice channel in 1980 to $10 per year sometime between 1990 and 2000. The most optimistic estimates indicate that this channel could cost as little as $1 per year by 2000.

Branscomb expects that enormous improvements in the cost/performance ratio for telecommunications will come from optical-fiber technology. Already, a single glass fiber the diameter of a human hair can transmit 50 million bits per second. At this rate, the full text of 40,000 books could be transmitted from Washington, D.C. to Los Angeles in approximately one hour. According to Branscomb, optical technology will eventually take advantage of the tremendous bandwidth (600 trillion Hz) of the visible light laser, which is 100 million times the capacity of today's optical-fiber techniques. Instead of transmitting books at the rate of 40,000 per hour, a single optical channel could transmit them at the rate of 1 billion per second.

Continued improvements in telecommunications will result in a "shrinking world." Over the next 10–20 years, we can expect to see the establishment of international compunication protocols (Doll [1979]) and viable regulations for transborder data flow (Veith [1980]). Multiple competing networks, together with private corporation networks, will reduce international communication costs and allow communication from any one point on the earth to any other point to be achieved in less than two seconds (Doll [1979]). These networks will tend to incorporate "intelligence" (e.g., the ability to translate the language of any computer into its own internal code and to retranslate it to the language of the receiving terminal or computer), and the distinction between communication and processing of data will become increasingly blurred. Moreover, the international communication networks of the future may be based on tariffs that are largely independent of distance. All these developments will create a milieu conducive to geographically dispersed corporations (Doll [1979]) and to the "work-at-home" phenomenon alluded to in Chapter 1 (Wedemeyer [1980]). They are also expected to boost the information industry into a $500 billion-a-year enterprise, by far the biggest business in existence (Sheils et al. [1980]).

3   Some Applications of Technology

Chapter 2 described some current achievements in computer and telecommunications technologies and summarized forecasts relating to the future of these technologies. In this chapter, the use of computers and telecommunications in ways that are already impacting on the distribution and use of information is examined. In particular, procedures that substitute electronic communication for use of print on paper — procedures that are leading us, in effect, into a paperless society — are considered. The first such application discussed is computer conferencing.

Computer Conferencing

Computer conferencing, which allows individuals to communicate with each other through on-line terminals, is a medium capable of replacing certain types of communication now handled through telephone conversations, correspondence, or face-to-face meetings. The basic capabilities of a computer-conferencing system relate to the composition, transmission, and receipt of messages. Such a system can be used for personal dialogues between individuals or for group dialogues. It is the group dialogues that are referred to as conferences. These may be public (any member of the conferencing network may participate) or private (open only to invited participants).

When a member of a conferencing network logs onto the system, he may first receive a notification of any new messages waiting for him. In addition, he may receive confirmation that messages he sent to other participants have actually been received.

To send a message, a user first composes and edits his message via his electronic notebook or "scratchpad." Once this is done, the writer indicates to whom the message is to be transmitted. It can be sent to a single network member or transmitted to several members simultaneously. The system usually has some means of informing the addressee that a message is waiting should he be using the network at the time the message is transmitted. Otherwise, he will receive this notification the next time he logs on to the system. Hence, the communication tends to be delayed (asynchronous, or "store-and-forward," communication) rather than immediate, although fully interactive (synchronous) communication, terminal to terminal, is certainly possible. The person-to-person communication of a computer-conferencing network is more rapid than mail—several communications can be exchanged within a single day—and allows simultaneous distribution of the same message to several individuals. Its advantage over the telephone is that communications are sent and received at the convenience of network participants; no time is wasted trying to make telephone contact, and the frustration of constantly missing each other is avoided. A computer-conferencing network can also provide for electronic storage of messages and can allow messages to be indexed to facilitate subsequent search and retrieval operations.

A composed message, rather than being transmitted to designated individuals, can be put into a "conference" data base, allowing any member of that conference to read it. Conferences, whether public or private, will normally be restricted to particular topics. Thus, a group of individuals interested in a particular area of research can exchange information very effectively and on a continuous basis. In fact, the communications exchanged within such a conference constitute a kind of informal journal dealing with a specialized subject field. Communications can be as long as research papers submitted to printed journals. In fact, formal electronic journals will likely emerge from some of these informal conferences.

Public conferences can be used for the exchange of all kinds of information, such as notices of forthcoming events, broadcast appeals for information of a particular type, and general opinion pieces (electronic "letters to the editor"). Private conferences can be used for collaboration in writing research proposals and reports. Electronic invisible colleges, comprised of workers continuously exchanging information in some specialized subject field, tend to emerge in the computer-conferencing environment. Such groups have been referred to as "on-line intellectual communities" (e.g., by Kochen [1977]).

Computer-conferencing networks may offer other facilities to users, including indexed directories of members and conferences; the ability to index authored items; and the ability to search conference data bases by keywords, names, or other characteristics. They are also likely to have a "news" feature, a way of keeping participants informed of new developments in the system itself.

A brief history of computer conferencing has been given by Hiltz and Turoff (1978). Work began in the 1960s but the first operating system seems to have been EMISARI (Emergency Management Information System and Reference Index), which was implemented within the Office of Emergency Preparedness in 1970 (Turoff [1972] and Kupperman and Wilcox [1972]). The FORUM system, developed by the Institute for the Future, was subsequently made widely accessible through the Tymshare network under the name of PLANET (Lipinski and Miller [1974] and Vallee et al. [1974–1978]).

Conferencing features have also been introduced into systems for computer-aided instruction, including the PLATO system, and the Oracle system at Northwestern University (Schuyler and Johansen [1972]).

At present, one of the most active conferencing systems is the Electronic Information Exchange System (EIES) operated at the New Jersey Institute of Technology. Supported initially by the National Science Foundation, EIES is based on the use of minicomputers and is accessible through the Telenet communications network. It is covered in detail by Hiltz and Turoff (1978).

Electronic Mail and the Paperless Office

Closely related to the concept of computer conferencing are electronic mail and the paperless office. Both concepts have emerged from recent developments in the field of word processing. The history of word-processing capabilities can be traced from the typewriter to the electric typewriter, to the magnetic-tape typewriter, to more sophisticated "stand-alone" devices (capable of automatic generation of repetitive letters and having extended capabilities for the editing and reorganization of text), to terminals connected to on-line networks.

Except for the last of these, the technological improvements were all designed for the more efficient production of paper copy, which is still distributed through conventional mail services. Even facsimile transmission, which has become economically attractive for high-priority communications since the emergence of inexpensive "fax" units (e.g., the Qwip system of Exxon Corporation), generates paper copy at the point of receipt. Existing data-processing and communications facilities, however, allow correspondence in a completely electronic mode; that is, they allow the paperless office.

Developments have occurred with great rapidity in the electronic mail/automated office arena. A number of organizations (e.g., Combustion Engineering, Inc., the Dow Chemical Company, and Citibank) have developed their own systems, and electronic mail systems (e.g., the Computer Corporation of America's COMET system) can now be purchased for use within an organization's own data-processing environment. In one application of the COMET system at the Digital Equipment Corporation, 350 users in three different locations were linked by the system in 1979, with additional users and locations to be added at a later time. COMET operates through a network of minicomputers. The Citibank system was expected to reach 1,000 of its offices by the end of 1979 and to eventually serve 6,000 offices. The United States Electronic Mail Association has recently been formed, its membership consisting of administrators and consultants having responsibilities for electronic mail systems; and the U.S. Postal Service is investigating alternatives for the implementation of an electronic distribution system of its own to counteract the competition expected from private enterprise in the very near future. The Mailgram service of Western Union, offered jointly with the U.S. Postal Service, already combines electronic intercity transmission with conventional local-delivery methods. The more recent Intelpost is a facsimile system using satellites to transmit text and nontext material internationally. A $1.7 billion program to permit the U.S. Postal Service to implement electronic mail by 1985 is in effect. Some forecasts suggest that, within the next decade, it is possible that as much as 80 percent of business mail in the United States can be converted to electronic distribution and that mail of a nonbusiness nature will begin to be handled electronically during this period. It has also been estimated that as many as 350 of the Fortune 500 companies could be using electronic mail by 1982 (Bolger [1979]).

Costs of electronic distribution can certainly be expected to decline relative to the costs of conventional distribution, and evidence exists that electronic distribution is already less expensive. Rogoff (1974), for example, has claimed,

If allowance is made for the cost of delivery [of] mail to the recipient's desk, the transmission cost of the hand-delivered letter is probably higher than that of all forms of desk-to-desk transmission and delivery via the right form of electronic terminal. (p. 34)

Burns (1977) has also produced data, derived from the U.S. Postal Service, to show that business communication costs are already "heavily in favor of digital data transmission" (see Figure 2).

The Yankee Group, a leader in this field, has projected the growth of electronic mail from 1978 to 1983, when 2 billion messages per year will be sent (Figure 3). It also forecasts the rapidly declining cost of electronic messages in this same time period (Figure 4). Costs might be as low as $0.25 or even $0.15 per message by 1985.

According to Panko and Panko (1977), the Hewlett-Packard HP–2026 system (commercially available) can transmit messages for $0.05 each within the United States and $0.25 internationally. This includes all hardware and transmission costs but excludes labor.

In a completely paperless office environment, one can type a memorandum at a terminal or dictate a longer communication for subsequent input by a secretary.* To the message, which is input with the aid of text-editing and formatting features, codes are added, representing those individuals to whom the message is to be sent. Keywords or other descriptors, needed for future retrieval activities, can also be added. Once entered and transmitted, the message is available to a recipient as soon as that person logs on to a terminal and enters a "mail scan" mode. If the recipient is already on-line at the time a new message is transmitted, the system can alert him to the existence of this message before he logs off the system.

In the electronic office, terminals are used to transmit and receive

---

* In the longer term, direct voice input could presumably circumvent keyboarding.

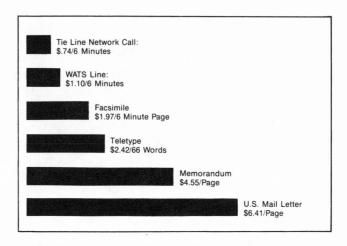

Figure 2 Communications costs, 1976. (From Burns [1977]. Reprinted with permission of *Datamation Magazine,* © Technical Publishing Co., a Dun & Bradstreet company. 1977. All rights reserved.)

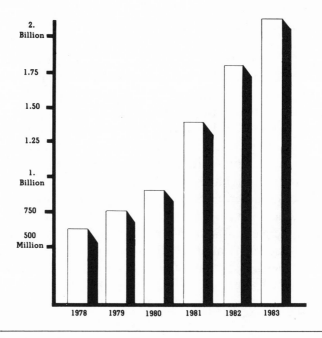

Figure 3 Electronic message traffic, 1978–1983. (Reprinted by permission of the Yankee Group.)

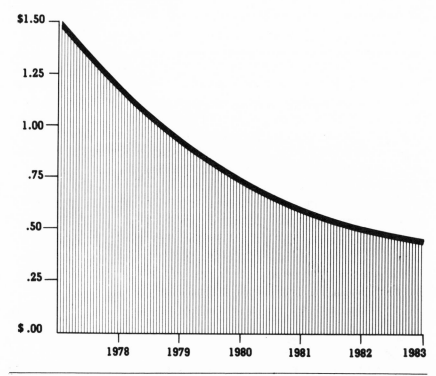

Figure 4 Cost of one item of electronic mail, 1978–1983. (Reprinted by permission of the Yankee Group.)

mail and to retrieve it from electronic files. All mail transmitted electronically within a particular organization can be searched for and retrieved on the basis of codes added by the transmitter or the recipient. In addition, it is possible to permit the searching of the most recent mail in a full-text scan mode. In the automated office, the entire correspondence file of the organization can be stored in electronic form. Moreover, the system is able to confirm that a message transmitted was actually received. The productivity of the electronic office is discussed by Bair (1980).

Although an organization can now adopt an electronic mail system for all internal communication, it cannot communicate electronically with other organizations unless they have compatible systems and can be reached through some existing communications network. The true potential of electronic mail systems will be reached only when, through system compatibility and network linkage, both inter- and intraorganizational correspondence can be handled. National communications systems such as AT&T's Advanced Communications Service (ACS) (see Rinder [1978]) and the Xerox Telecommunications Network (XTEN) could make electronic mail, and many other capabilities, available to small and large businesses within the near future.

ACS and XTEN are elaborate data communications networks, the former operating via cable and packet-switching computers and the latter via radio frequencies transmitted by satellites. Both systems are designed to accept many different types of terminals and computer hookups. They can store data and computer programs and can be used for electronic mail and conferencing. XTEN also allows voice and facsimile transmission. Although intended primarily for business applications, these systems could eventually be extended to home use.

It is already possible to integrate the handling of incoming paper copy mail with the processing of electronic internal mail, as White (1977) has pointed out in his discussion of electronic processing at Citibank:

To take full advantage of electronic mail and file capabilities, however, we must convert to the system all documents that originate outside the network. We are planning to develop that capability, using high speed facsimile devices and digital display techniques so that the MWS (Management Work Station) can accept and display not only external correspondence and reports, but photographs and charts as well. We are also looking at optical reading technology as a means of transmitting standard typed documents over the electronic mail system. (p.86)

The ability to put typed and printed pages into machine-readable form has been greatly enhanced by the appearance of the Kurzweil Data Entry Machine, which can "learn" the characteristics of any typeface using the Roman alphabet. Related Kurzweil devices can produce output capable of electronic transmission and can also generate Braille and voice output.

Other valuable capabilities can be realized within automated office systems. For example, an individual may use the system as an electronic notebook, memo pad, or calendar. When he arrives at his office in the morning, he can log on to the system to check his appointments and to identify other tasks that must be completed that day. The electronic system can also save time in scheduling meetings among key personnel in an organization. The person requesting the meeting can use the system to obtain rapid feedback on dates and times convenient to all participants. Alternatively, assuming that the appointment calendars of these individuals are stored electronically, the system itself could identify uncommitted date/time slots on which the meeting might be held. A convenient "pend" capability is another advantage: An incoming message, designated for later action, will automatically reappear in the incoming mail on the date specified.

In the long run, the major advantage of electronic mail systems may be their portability. Working from the home becomes increasingly feasible, since an employee can gain access to all needed files through a home terminal. Similarly, portable terminals can allow employees to keep in close touch with current developments in the office while traveling on company business. The terminal used to access electronic mail files can also be used for other processing activities, including computation and the searching of external information resources. Home-computer users or small businesses already have an electronic mail facility from the Source Telecomputing Corporation, which also gives them access to a wide range of data bases.

A conceptualization of the paperless office environment has been prepared by the Yankee Group (Figure 5). Here, electronic mail can be exchanged by two offices directly (i.e., terminal to terminal) or messages can be dictated into a telephone for input to word-processing equipment. Typed or printed material can be sent via facsimile transmission, or optical character readers can be used to put such material in digital form. Some material (perhaps archival) may be stored on computer output microfilm, but much will be held in main digital storage. Presumably all material will be indexed for efficient retrieval. This is by no means futuristic, since all these technologies now exist.

A glimpse at a few existing capabilities, as implemented in an electronic office at the Continental Illinois National Bank and Trust Company, is given by Rout (1980). Referring to a company executive, Rout describes these capabilities as follows:

Sitting at his desk in Chicago, he can push some buttons on the keyboard of a computer terminal and staff memos will appear on a television-like screen. He can respond with his own memos, which will instantly materialize on the screens of colleagues overseas, or be stored for them to retrieve later if their terminals are busy or turned off. And by pressing a few other buttons, he can view bank financial data stored in a computer down the street. (p. 17)

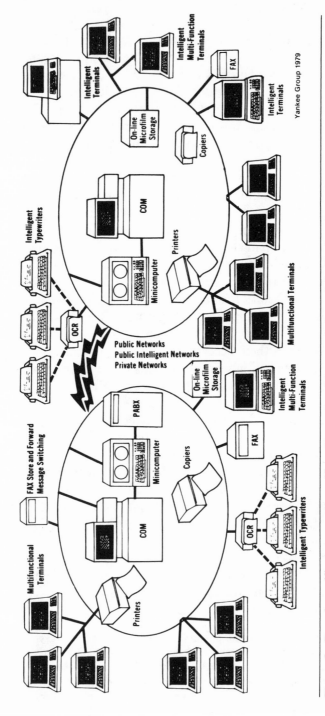

Figure 5 Paperless office to paperless office. (Reproduced by permission of the Yankee Group.)

Electronic mail and computer conferencing are by no means restricted to the business community. Several years ago, ARPANET, a Department of Defense network linking some 180 computers in military and civilian centers, offered a computer mail capability to academic and other researchers. The capability also exists within several computer-aided instruction networks. An electronic mail system, linking all senior administrative officers, has been installed at Stanford University, and other academic institutions can be expected to follow suit (Magarrell [1980]). Moreover, home computers linked to telecommunications networks could put electronic mailbox capabilities into a majority of homes in the not-too-distant future, as could two-way television, discussed on pp. 36–50.

Even though several companies have already adopted electronic mail systems, and many others are experimenting, the process of converting to a paperless environment may not be free from trauma. Larson (1980), for example, reports on a recent experience at the Reliance Insurance Company. Reliance has estimated that 25 percent of its workers' time is spent in creating, storing, and distributing paper records and that 80 percent of such records, once stored, are never referred to again. Taking their employees by surprise, the company ordered a "paperless day." The experiment was not universally popular. Nevertheless, Reliance hopes to cut its storage of paper 75 percent by 1983.

Several writers (e.g., Rout [1980]) have reported on the great reluctance of some executives to move to a paperless mode of operation, especially if this means typing at a keyboard, which many view as a menial task. Additional animosity arises from the fear of electronics or of being unable to perform effectively in an electronic environment with "infallible computers that remind bosses when reports are due, the pressure of being always reachable through a portable computer terminal and the danger of overcommunication." The dehumanizing effect and possible unemployment consequences of automation have also been mentioned as potential pitfalls (e.g., Stewart [1979]).

Continued movement toward the paperless office seems inevitable, however, as Dordick et al. (1979) have suggested:

Labour costs are rising rapidly. There is a need to increase productivity in executive board rooms, offices and factories and the changing composition of the labour force is pressuring for more creative jobs. Candidates are emerging for executive posts who are familiar and comfortable with terminals, computers, and their languages. These factors will probably lead to a network marketplace for business systems in the $15 to $25 billion range by the mid 1980s. However, organizational and personal resistance to change will slow the adoption process so that the full potential for this market is not likely to develop until the mid 1990s. (p. 221)

Many librarians are now using electronic mail in one form or another, and its use by the profession seems to be moving toward a more official status. For example, a recent press release (March 30, 1981) from the Special Libraries Association (SLA) has announced the experimental use by SLA of Tymnet's On-Tyme Electronic Mail Service, which allows members to communicate electronically with SLA headquarters.

Facsimile Transmission

"Facsimile transmission" (Costigan [1978]) refers to the ability to "read" a print-on-paper document on one facsimile machine and to transfer it, via telecommunications lines, to a second machine, where it is reproduced once more as print on paper. Significant advances in "fax" have occurred during the last few years, and costs have been dropping. According to Josephine (1980), the cost of transmissions sent at lower nightly rates is already competitive with first-class postal rates, and, of course, facsimile transmission is much faster and more reliable.

Network communication among owners of facsimile equipment now offers a store-and-forward capability (i.e., if the transmission is not received the first time, the system continues to try until it is received), as well as the ability to send the same document to several locations in a single transmission. In newer equipment, resolution is considerably improved and transmission time reduced. Facsimile devices are beginning to be used to link libraries and information centers and to replace interlibrary loan for items needed immediately (Saffady [1978] and McKean [1981]).

Two-Way Television

Television has become a pervasive element in the lives of virtually all citizens of the developed world and is rapidly penetrating the less-developed countries. But the television we take for granted as a source of entertainment has obvious limitations. First, although the number of available channels tends to be increasing (especially through the spread of cable television), the viewer is still restricted to the programming offered by a limited number of networks. No possibility exists for tailoring the transmission to the needs or wants of a particular individual. Second, and perhaps more important, television has been an entirely passive medium. The owner of a television set can receive entertainment or information but cannot use the medium to transmit information himself.

Work on two-way or "interactive" television, however, has been proceeding for some years. For example, Stetten (1971 a, b) and Volk (1971) have described attempts by the MITRE Corporation to combine its TICCIT (Time-shared, Interactive, Computer-Controlled, Information Television) system with a low-cost home-terminal unit to demonstrate the feasibility of using standard TV sets as "home-computer–driven displays." The MITRE group used signal transmission by microwave link to cable TV (CATV) in homes in Reston, Virginia. TICCIT provided computer-generated or controlled information that could be selectively received and displayed by individual television sets using one channel on a wide-band cable. Six hundred sets could receive separate pieces of information provided by the computer at a typical rate of once every 10 seconds.

TICCIT provided both broadcast and selected information on demand. Broadcast information included reports on skiing and local fishing conditions, baseball scores, racing form, and stock exchange reports. On-demand information included a personalized telephone directory, weekly calendars, television guides, and what Volk calls "interactive yellow pages." Information about food stamps, veterans' benefits, and social security could be requested via the user's television set. TICCIT also permitted interaction with an off-track betting system that Stetten claimed would subsidize educational services provided by the system.

One of MITRE's major concerns in developing TICCIT was to "broaden the consideration of CATV content to a large new range of interactive services having high potential social impact." MITRE attempted to achieve "democratization" through a service whereby two-way TV would allow any group or individual the "economic and physical ability to express . . . thoughts to anyone who wished to tune in on them." TICCIT was also intended to provide a complete curriculum of five semesters of junior-college courses.

Achievements in this field during the past few years have been dramatic, and many have come from outside the United States. In particular, the United Kingdom has been a leader in this specific application of technology. Unfortunately, developments have occurred so quickly that it is difficult to keep pace with them.

Basically there are two different methods by which predominantly textual material can be delivered to a domestic television receiver. The two methods were originally known as "teletext" and as "viewdata." Collectively the techniques are sometimes referred to as "videotext" or "videotex" (Fedida and Malik [1979], Sigel et al. [1980], Criner and Johnson-Hall [1980], and Cherry [1980]). Regrettably, the terminology relating to this technology is becoming very confusing, especially since some systems now incorporate both methods (Veith [1981]).*

Teletext, which has been implemented in the United Kingdom as Ceefax† by the British Broadcasting Corporation (BBC) and as Oracle by the Independent Television Authority (ITA), is more limited in its capabilities than is viewdata. Text to be transmitted is broadcast with the TV picture signal and fills unused lines of the signal. To accept this text, the normal domestic receiver must be equipped with a special converter. Customers can communicate with the system by use of a keypad. They can receive news flashes transmitted during a regular television program or can select various types of information (e.g., news, financial, food prices) from a displayed contents page. Because the system uses the regular TV signal and only those lines not used for regular broadcasting, it is very limited in its capacity for holding pages of text. Moreover, the user has access only to informa-

---

* The International Consultative Committee on Telephones and Telegraphs (CCITT) has adopted the term *videotex* as a generic name for all systems that transmit text to a television screen by means of a telephone network. Clearly, this excludes teletext systems, which transmit via television broadcast signals, and thus there is no satisfactory generic term embracing both technologies. The term *two-way television* is used here as the *summum genus*, although some object to considering teletext systems as either "two way" or "interactive." This seems hairsplitting, since any service in which a user can select a certain category of information at a time he wants to see it can be regarded as both two way and interactive, at least at some minimal level.

† Later, the BBC introduced a further system, Orbit, on a second channel.

tion made available by the BBC and ITA. Other organizations cannot make information available through these systems.

The viewdata system, offered by the British Post Office as Prestel, uses a completely different technology. Information is transmitted to television sets by telephone lines rather than by TV signals. Special-purpose television receivers are needed, although regular receivers can be converted to this purpose. Communication, again, is by some form of keypad.

As with Ceefax and Oracle, the user can select information from a contents page. The Prestel data base, however, is much richer and is unlimited in size. The present scope is well summarized by Carr (1981):

Company news and reports are available for the local businessman, economic forecasts for the student, road, rail and air information for the traveller, restaurant and entertainment guides for the visitor, *Which* reports for the consumer, food price tips for the housewife, car reports for the motorist, legal comments for the solicitor, commodity prices for the industrialist, career guidance for the unemployed, and so the list goes on. (p. 15)

In addition, users can view the full text of 10,000 articles from a 20-volume encyclopedia, consult the journal *Euronews* (news from the Commission of the European Communities), and apply the system to such problems as the calculation of mortgage payments. This information is provided for a fee by "information providers" who use Prestel as a vehicle for reaching a potential audience.

The current British situation has been described in more detail by Martyn (1979):

There are at present two types of systems which display textual information to users on the screen of a television receiver. The systems are called teletext and viewdata; there are two teletext services, Ceefax and Oracle, supplied by the British Broadcasting Corporation and the Independent Television Authority, respectively, and one viewdata service, called Prestel, supplied through the Post Office.
The basic difference between the two systems is that teletext is broadcast with the television picture signal filling the space assigned to some of the lines which build up the picture on your screen but which do not appear in the picture you see, whereas the viewdata signal is carried over the normal telephone lines. Both systems use color television sets, but monochrome sets can in principle also be used. Sets are now available in the shops which will receive teletext only, and sets are now becoming available, initially through the rental companies, which will receive both teletext and viewdata. It is possible to buy plug-in modules — they plug in the aerial socket — which will convert ordinary color TV receivers to teletext receivers, at a cost usually

around £200, and it seems likely that at some future date, similar devices will be available to convert to viewdata receivers too, although none are commercially available yet.

To use Ceefax, a viewer presses a button or a switch, usually on a handheld keyboard quite similar to those now supplied for remote operation of a normal TV set. This switches out his normal picture and presents him with a contents page or pages, each page title bearing a number. The viewer then presses the number of the page he wants to see on his keypad. As the pages are transmitted one after the other, at a rate of four a second, his decoder then picks out the selected page when it is transmitted, and holds it on the screen for as long as required. Ceefax is deliberately limited to 100 pages on each channel (BBC1 and BBC2) at the moment, which means that the average waiting time for a selected page to be presented is 12½ seconds; because of the way it transmits the pages one after the other, much more than 100 pages in the system would mean unacceptably long delays in accessing a particular page. The sorts of information carried are basically current awareness, news items, covering several pages of world news, financial news, sports, current food prices, weather news, radio and TV programmes, jokes and puzzles, and so on; there is also a newsflash facility, which allows one to watch a television programme, and when a newsflash is issued it will appear over the picture. BBC journalists continually update the pages, so that the information content is continually up to date. At present, Ceefax and Oracle are free services, inasmuch as the user pays nothing for their use other than the initial outlay on buying the decoder, either already installed in his new set or to plug in the back of his existing one.

Viewdata systems, or at least the only one we know about, Prestel, are quite different. Because they are accessed over the telephone lines, the first operation in using the system has to be establishing the telephone connection, which at present is done by dialing a number (or on the latest receiver, by pressing a button) and, on receipt of the appropriate tone, putting a signal into the TV set via a modem. That is to say, access to the system is slightly more complicated. Prestel has to be paid for by the user whereas teletext is free at present (although it's possible that users may have to pay in some way, perhaps by an increase in license fee, in the future). Teletext offers a small number of pages of information, whereas Prestel is potentially virtually unlimited.

Probably the most important difference is that Ceefax is a service wholly compiled, controlled and distributed by the BBC, in that the Corporation decides what information shall be put into the service, compiles it, maintains it and can change it whenever it wishes (and correspondingly for Oracle). In the case of Prestel, the Post Office operates the system, in the sense of providing and operating the computers, maintaining the telephone network, and doing the accounting, including revenue collection, but apart from some information which it puts up on its own account, telling users about the system and so on, it does not commission or generate or update any of the information content itself, but instead, rather like the advertising manager of a newspaper, it sells space to Information Providers, who are then free to put up whatever they like, providing it's not actually obscene. In effect, the BBC has a moral responsibility directly to its users, but the Post Office responsibility is to the Information Providers. (pp. 217–218)

In Prestel's London test market, four of the heaviest-used terminals are coin-operated. They are located in a hotel, a department store, the British Tourist Authority office, and a pub. Apparently, many inquiries have been received from libraries on the installation and cost of the system. The producers claim that the microprocessor can be programmed so that the library may be charged for only a subset of the data base. Libraries could then provide certain services free of charge while requiring patrons to pay for services such as videogames. In fact, Prestel is already being used experimentally in public libraries in London, Norwich, and Birmingham (see Martyn [1979]), as an additional general reference source and as a medium for making available local information of interest to a library's community. In the latter case, the library itself becomes the information provider. More recently, the Department of Industry has made available £10,000 to install Prestel receivers in 36 British public libraries. Prestel has also been used in academic libraries.

The U.K. system was chosen over other competitors by the European Broadcaster's Union to be used with a closed-circuit television system to inform all European TV studios of the results of European parliamentary elections. International competition to Prestel includes the French system, Antiope, which is currently undergoing trials in New Orleans, Montreal, Toronto, Buenos Aires, and Peru, with the expectation of full public service by 1982–1983. Prestel and Antiope are vying for sales in the world market. An important boost to Prestel was the decision by General Telephone and Electronics (GTE) to market a U.S. version (GTE Viewdata) compatible with U.S. computers, terminals, and telecommunications systems. However, the Columbia Broadcasting System has recommended to the Federal Communications Commission that it adopt a modified version of Antiope as a national U.S. broadcast teletext system standard. The Canadian system, Telidon, is now offering strong competition to all other systems.

LINK, a New York–based company that publishes the monthly *Viewdata/Videotex Report*, has given five reasons why viewdata can be considered "the most important innovation in personal communications since television":

1. Viewdata uses existing "friendly" technology — the telephone and the TV set — to bring consumers and businessmen thousands of pages of textual information and

simple graphics in seven colors. Inexpensive and easy to operate, viewdata may be the first computerized information distribution system with mass appeal.

2. Viewdata's information storage capacity is practically limitless. In addition, viewdata "pages" can be updated as often as three times per day. Thus business people whose product is timely information (news, stock market reports, reservations, etc.) can make use of this new medium.

3. The Prestel viewdata system currently being tested in the U.K. supplies 1,000 customers with almost 200,000 pages of information on the stock market, news, weather, restaurants, travel reservations, road conditions and much more. Advertising, direct marketing, shop-at-home, encyclopedia publishing and newscast applications are all being tried right now!

4. Hardware and software research is constantly improving viewdata technology. For example, Canadian researchers are testing a viewdata system with refined graphics capabilities. With improved graphics, viewdata will offer retailers better display advertising capabilities. Other viewdata systems are experimenting with downloading software to intelligent terminals—making for a faster and more economical means of updating the software.

5. Viewdata is a mass communications medium at the same time it is a personalized communications medium. As a mass medium, it has the ability to distribute an enormous quantity of information to a great many people, all the while tabulating exactly how many consumer accesses there are to a single page. As a personal medium, viewers can choose from a multitude of pages exactly which ones they choose to access. And viewers can have a response button with which they can send messages to other viewdata users, order goods from retailers, subscribe to a magazine, etc.

Developments in this field are occurring so rapidly that it is virtually impossible to keep abreast of them. Nevertheless, some major current activities must be described.

Qube is a two-way interactive cable system installed by Warner Cable Corporation in Columbus, Ohio in 1977. It offers 30 channels, controlled by the user through touch buttons on a keypad console. Of these 30 channels, 10 provide both public and commercial television stations, a public-access channel, and a program guide. Other channels offer first-run movies, soft-core pornography by request, and self-help courses such as shorthand. The Qube system (Wicklein [1979]) offers nonviolent children's shows, automatic police and ambulance calls, and a motion-sensing burglar alarm. Users may interact directly with Qube by evaluating products, stating opinions on social and political issues, and participating in a "Gong Show"–type amateur presentation. Qube regularly schedules town meetings and government hearings, during which users may respond from their homes and participate in an electronic referendum. "Columbus

Alive" is a talk show with its own polling computer that scans all subscriber homes at six-second intervals and collects billing and audience response data. It compiles answers to such questions as "Is the TV set on?", "Which channels?", and "What was the last response button pressed?" Response buttons allow for "yes," "no," or multiple-choice responses.

The computer bills subscribers for their selections automatically. For example, the shorthand course may cost $0.75, whereas an Ohio State University football game may cost $9.00. Wicklein is enthusiastic about Qube and the response it has received in Columbus but is concerned about privacy issues: "Two-way cable is fun, but it might be a method of invading the user's privacy if we are not careful." Warner Communications is presently building a second Qube system which is intended to reach 200,000 homes in Houston.

Teletext systems have been offered in several U.S. cities. Salt Lake City's KSL broadcasts on the unused scan lines on the television so that the user may select normal television reception, teletext, or both concurrently. Among KSL's offerings (Loveless [1978]) are multiple-page listings of supermarket prices, boxed captions for the deaf, and store and display features for later viewing. There is also a message paging system capable of storing 2 million different addresses. KSL uses the British Ceefax system.

The use of interactive TV systems has been introduced in Dayton, Ohio by VIACOM. This system was brought in "through the back door" by linking it with a TOCOM III home security system that includes fire, intrusion, and medical alarms. At that time, Dayton already had a CATV system that offered pay-TV movies. This situation was notable in that it was the first installation of a two-way system over an existing cable system.

A development using a different strategy is being tested on a professional market by Reuters news service in New York City. The Reuters data base consists of financial and stock market information, general news, sports news, and racing results. Information is distributed to cable systems via the SATCOM I communications satellite. Each user has a video monitor, keypad, or full typewriter keyboard. Outman (1978) notes that, unlike most two-way systems, the Reuters system places no limit on the number of queries that may be answered simultaneously. This is achieved by having the entire data base circulating through the cable at nearly 5 million words per minute. The user is able to scan headlines and then go to any segment for which more information is desired. The Reuters service offers a continuous update of news events. One interesting feature involves a user's selection of a stock portfolio. An investor selects stocks and inserts his own prices. When the security or commodity reaches the preset price, an alert or alarm signals the user that it is time to buy or sell.

In Chicago, Field Electronic Publishing has announced plans to set up 110 information kiosks in areas of high pedestrian traffic. The kiosks will provide access to hundreds of pages of constantly updated video information, piggybacking on the WFLD television broadcast signal.

Another two-way interactive (although specialized) system has been reported by Lorenzi (1976). This University of Cincinnati system provides medical and drug information to patient-care areas via closed-circuit and cable TV. A high-resolution camera is used that is capable of transmitting all types of images including microfiche and detailed tables and graphs. The use of two-way television for specialized information is being demonstrated in local and rural areas:

Television makes it technically feasible to offer people in many different locations ready access to visual impact materials and can obviate the need to leave a patient care area in order to obtain important information. Further, it can be employed to allow useful interactive discussions in spite of great distances between the information source and the user of information. (p. 362)

It is planned that this system ultimately will use both television and telephone nodes two-way from a centralized resource area (the library) to medical facilities such as hospital emergency rooms, patient-care areas, outpatient clinics, doctors' offices in rural areas, and doctors in patients' homes.

Television broadcasting tests of the Coaxial Cable Information System using CATV have been conducted in Japan at Tama New Town. This system offers two-way, interactive connections with computers. Tests included automatic repetition telecasting, flash information, a facsimile newspaper, memo copy, broadcasting and response, still picture request, and auxiliary TV. The system has successfully used Japanese ideographic images for transmission. Also in Japan, the CAPTAIN (Character and Pattern Telephone Access Information Network) system allows calls by telephone and permits information to be requested with a keypad containing buttons for 16 categories, including household medical information; a physician and hospital guide; comparative information about shopping, cooking, and department stores; real estate information; and information about ceremonial occasions and traditional culture. Listings also include tours, movies, plays, sports, gambling results, news, jobs, and government proceedings.

In 1978, Canada's Department of Communications introduced a viewdata system called Telidon. Phillips (1980) refers to this as second-generation videotex technology:

First generation videotex systems are basically textual displays with graphics added by coding parts of the screen as colours. In contrast, this second generation system is based on graphics coding which can also transmit text. The computer graphics techniques were designed for very efficient transmission of graphics over long distance telecommunications lines. (p. 169)

Narrow-band telephone lines will transmit Telidon graphics and text at the rate of 120 characters per second. Telidon terminals are being produced by four Canadian manufacturers, and several field trials are underway. Telidon is being tested in Washington, D.C. by WETA and in Los Angeles by the Times Mirror Company. Time, Inc., has announced that it will mount a national Telidon test in 1981. One innovative feature to be tested with Telidon is "interest matching." Hirsch (1980) quotes L. G. Wilson, Bell Canada's project manager for Vista (a test of Telidon with 1,000 residential and business users), as follows:

Interest matching . . . is . . . a kind of "personals column" that will locate a specific product or match users who wish to share common interests and chat, deal or barter. (p. 64)

Viewdata Corporation of America, a subsidiary of the Knight-Ridder newspaper chain, in cooperation with AT&T, began trials of its Viewtron in Coral Gables, Florida in 1980. These trials are particularly noteworthy in that Macmillan is making the full text of a baseball encyclopedia accessible through the home television terminals, and a second publisher, Addison-Wesley, is providing the text of a home health guide. In this and similar experiments, then, reference books are beginning to reach the home in electronic form. Dalton & Co. Booksellers is supplying bestseller lists and brief book reviews via Viewtron, allowing home viewers to order books by entering a credit-card number through the keypad. The latest news from the Associated Press and from the *Miami Herald,* as well as a full range of consumer services, also appear in Viewtron. A viewer can select an item and order it from a Sears catalog, can access airline schedules, and can order meals for home delivery (not electronically!). Weather and stock information, educational programs, and electronic mail are also available (Radolf [1980]).

Other joint ventures of this kind are presently emerging. For example, the Warner Qube system will allow Columbus, Ohio subscribers to access the CompuServe information service, which will make available a wide variety of consumer-oriented data bases, including stock market information and personal financial information programs; it will also allow access to electronic games and an electronic mail facility.

The Online Computer Library Center (OCLC), Inc., in cooperation with Bank One Corporation, also of Columbus, Ohio, has conducted experiments with Channel 2000 in the Columbus area. Via a simple adapter attached to the VHF antenna terminals, an ordinary television set was converted into "a home bank service, an encyclopedia, a library catalog, and a community information service." Consumers could use their television sets to pay bills or check the status of their bank accounts, to access any article in the *Academic American Encyclopedia,* or to reach a data base of public information for the Columbus area and to access the catalog of the Public Library of Columbus and Franklin County. The Channel 2000 trials (described in more detail in Chapter 10) were part of the OCLC "home delivery of library service" program. Through this program, OCLC is cooperating with the Source Telecomputing Corporation to make The Source accessible to libraries that are members of the OCLC on-line cataloging network. The Source, which claims to be the first home-terminal consumer-information network in America, offers access to news, stock market information, electronic mail, games, and almost 2,000 computer programs. Some 90 libraries or other library-related agencies were reported to be using the service in March 1981.

A new development known as Gateway promises to greatly enhance videotex systems. Gateway permits subscribers to use their terminals to access information resources stored in a variety of computers. In fact, by simply selecting the Gateway page of an external computer, the user connects with it, thereby avoiding the "unfriendly preliminaries required to establish network user identity, password and network address of the host computer" (Urrows [1981]).

The telephone companies are working on another development. In France, telephone authorities are already experimenting with small video display units in homes. These units will eventually allow a user to find a telephone number for any subscriber in any city in France, thus avoiding the costly printing and distribution of telephone directories and permitting great reduction of directory-assistance staff (Nora [1980] and Maury [1980]). AT&T has already used Albany, New York as a site for testing its own plans in this area: 83 participants were given video terminals on which listings in the white and yellow pages of the telephone book could be called up. A more extensive trial was planned for Austin, Texas, but the trial was dropped as a result of legal action brought by the Texas Daily Newspapers Association.

The future of interactive television can be considered to be partly tied to the growth of cable television. It has been estimated that approximately 15 million homes in the United States were reached by cable in 1979 and that this number could climb to between 28 and 50 million during the next decade. If 50 million homes were reached, approximately two-thirds of the households in this country would be served. With the rapid development of these interactive television systems, we are getting closer to what Sackman and Nie (1970) described as "information utilities," which bring picture, voice, and text material to the home at the individual subscriber's request.

Baran (1972) has described a Delphi study sent to futurists and "company philosophers." The participants were asked to respond about the nature and size of the likely market for two-way, interactive television systems in the home. Baran's study estimated that this new industry would begin to gain its greatest momentum by 1980 and shortly thereafter become a $20 billion per year industry. The experts polled suggested that education would be the largest single market category in terms of expected revenue for the system operators. The educational services described in this report include computer-aided school instruction, computerized tutors with voice feedback, interactive self-help programs, and correspondence schools. The last service would be conducted through video transmission with paper text support through hard copy facsimile.

The Baran study also suggested that business uses would comprise a large portion of the services provided. These might include the use of two-way services by employees while working at home and caring for young children, remote access to company files with appropriate security measures built in, and banking services such as money-order transactions and financial advice. Recent estimates have forecast widespread acceptance of viewdata-type services, with more than $2 billion in service revenues generated by over 8 million households in 1985, reaching $10 billion in revenues by 1990.

Two-way television offers the possibility of a completely different approach to the distribution of news. It makes possible the "dedicated newspaper." The subscriber to such a service may predetermine the newspaper's organization by submitting a user profile, may request more information on any selected subject, or may reject unwanted detail by a signal to truncate. Baran (1972) predicted the likely occurrence of other general information access services such as a general daily newspaper for all readers, personal daily calendars and appointment or occasion reminders, legal information for the layperson, library access for interactive browsing or slow-scan video transmission of text, shopping with cashless transactions, comparative shopping with store catalogs, and consumer advisory services complete with product ratings. Most of these capabilities have already been implemented, in one form or another, since Baran's report.

Whether teletext or viewdata types of systems will actually replace the printed newspaper as Bagdikian [1971] predicted remains to be seen. A comprehensive Arthur D. Little, Inc. report, *Impact of Electronic Systems on News Publishing through 1992,* suggests that electronic information systems will not be a threat to conventional news publishing for the next decade but that such systems could have a substantial impact on the news industry by the 1990s. The implication is that news publishers need to look beyond print on paper and consider alternative channels for their news and information services.

The matter of social acceptance has been addressed by Marvin (1980):

The question, however, is whether such novelty can displace the comfortable routines of newspaper reading. Not all newspaper aficionados will want to give up browsing the generalist newspaper for the specialist and narrow efficiency of a dial-up newsscreen, and the modest price and great portability of the newspaper that gets on the subway with its reader will be hard to beat in any electronic form. If, in an increasingly energy-conservative world, more and more people give up private driving, for example, reading the newspaper aboard public transportation might be an option of increasing preference. It is a mistake, however, to imagine that consumers will suddenly be asked to choose between newsscreens and newspapers. People who use computerized information services on [video display terminals] at work soon begin to imagine ways they could be put to use at home. Houses and apartments with built-in microwave ovens can have built-in cable and information service connections as well, especially when these are linked to temperature control and home security functions. When such facilities are available as a matter of course, people will learn to use them. A shift in the kinds of information consumers want is less likely to be initiated directly by electronic news than by other kinds of information services which, in achieving acceptance, absorb or reshape those of the traditional newspaper. Consumer preferences, in other words, will be shaped by the entire range of available information options as well as by the features of any single one. (pp. 40–41)

Despite Marvin's hesitation, the electronic newspaper seems to be arriving rather quickly. Viewtron provides news from the *Miami Herald,* the *Wall Street Journal,* and other titles, and the *Columbus Dispatch* is now transmitting its news content to terminals in subscriber homes. Eleven other newspapers, including the *Los Angeles Times,* the *Chicago Sun-Times,* and the *Washington Post* are said to be planning to join the *Columbus Dispatch* in a joint venture of the Associated Press and CompuServe, Inc. (Ris [1980]). Owners of home computers can also access electronic editions of the *Atlanta Constitution* and the *Atlanta Journal* through the facilities of CompuServe. Moreover, electronic publishing of newspapers by no means precludes advertising. In fact, Ris suggests that electronic newspapers are a "natural" for classified advertising:

For one thing, computer ads could easily be updated. And a computer could search all the classifieds for a particular region—or someday the whole country—for a specific item . . . . [W]hile no electronic newspaper has devised a way to transmit display ads as graphically as they appear in newspapers, the viewdata experiment in Florida is coming close. It carries information on movie-theater offerings and restaurants, including complete menus and prices. The system also allows subscribers to shop at home by pushing a few buttons on their computer terminals. (p. 15)

Powell (1980) provides a more detailed discussion of the possibilities for advertising via interactive television.

As an interim measure, news might be delivered by a combination of printed paper plus television display, the reader going to the television set for expanded news on demand. This possibility has been mentioned by Haiman (1980):

The most likely first option would be those things which are simply tabular. We might deliver you the core paper; but instead of delivering the sporting statistics of hits, runs, forward passes, and percentages, we might deliver you in the core paper an "electronic guide" to finding such tabular data on your home television set. In the main paper, we would report the winner of the Boston marathon and the basic details of the race. But suppose you are a real jogging freak, and you want to know the names in order of the top 1,000 finishers. The electronic guide in the newspaper would tell you to dial your cathode ray tube to Channel 16, Index 45, Paragraphs 14 through 240, and you would have the complete list. We would hope to be a participant in the function which put that information there. People would pay extra for this information, for the right to have access to it. (p. 7)

This is not the place to discuss the myriad of social and political issues that accompany installation of two-way TV, but it is clear that there are several major policy issues that will need to be solved. These include (1) the development of technical standards (Baer [1971] and Clark [1978]), (2) the protection of the individual's privacy (Baer [1971] and Wicklein [1979]), and (3) definition of the role of the cable operator as common carrier or direct provider of two-way services (Baer [1971]).

Summary

The best way to summarize Chapters 2 and 3 is to quote from the imaginative forecast of Kubitz (1980) on the probable developments of the next 20 years:

The ever increasing complexity and lower cost of integrated circuit and computer technology will radically change our lives in the next twenty years. The availability of low cost computing and low cost storage will make computers available and economical for everyone whether in business, industry, or the home. What we now call "microcomputers" will become as powerful as present day large computers, but will sell for under $1,000. Large central data banks will be formed as central repositories of information. High-speed digital communications links will be readily available by way of satellite transmission in space and optical fibers on the ground. Digital communications will be brought into the home via the telephone system or cable TV or both. This will allow the user to call the central data banks using the home computer system. The home computer system will have color TV, voice output, limited voice input, possibly a facsimile printer, and an associated flat panel character (book) display. Libraries will evolve toward becoming just one of many data banks. Optical disk storage will provide a solution to the document storage problem. Users will be able to browse through the library or shop from the home computer center. Books can be selected, transmitted to the user and stored locally, and then read using the book display. Banking and financial transactions will also be handled this way. Almost every device in the home that does anything will be electronically controlled. Newspapers and bulk mail will come over the computer system. Magazines will arrive on disk or be transmitted and recorded on the home disk under control of the computer system. (pp. 159–160)

4 Computers and Publishing

Who knows that a day may not come when the dissemination of knowledge, which is the vital function of libraries, will be realised even by means other than those of the printed book?
                    —S. R. Ranganathan, *The Five Laws of Library Science* (1963)

In Chapter 3, various applications of computer technology in the improvement of communication and the distribution of information were mentioned. In this chapter, attention will focus on a topic discussed only tangentially in Chapter 3 — the application of computers to publishing.

The library of the future cannot be examined in isolation. It can only be considered within the context of social change in general and, more particularly, of change within those segments of society with which the library most closely interacts. Hence, the future of the library is inextricably entwined with the future of the publishing industry.

The methods used to communicate in written form have changed frequently over time. The clay tablet, for example, gave way to papyrus which, in turn, was replaced by the vellum codex. The vellum codex itself was superseded by print on paper. There is thus no precedent to support the belief that print on paper will forever remain the preferred means of formal communication. In fact, it seems entirely possible that the age of print on paper will be substantially shorter than the eras dominated by the earlier forms, being measured in hundreds rather than thousands of years. At present, society finds itself in the early stages of a natural evolution from print-on-paper communication to electronic communication. Whether we like it or not, print on paper will eventually give way, more or less completely, to electronics.

It is not difficult to find signs of this evolution. Computer terminals can be seen in airports, travel agencies, car rental companies, banks, and even supermarkets. They can also be found in libraries. In fact, their applications in libraries are considerably more diverse than in most other segments of society.

For approximately the past 20 years, computer-controlled photocomposition, sometimes referred to as computer typesetting, has been applied to produce an increasingly diverse array of publications: indexing and abstracting services, popular magazines, newspapers, technical reports, books, patents, conference proceedings, and scholarly journals, among others. Photocomposition has not yet completely replaced the human typesetter, but each year more and more publications are produced under computer control. Perhaps somewhat unexpectedly, it was a library—the National Library of Medicine (NLM)—that pioneered the use of photocomposition on a full production basis. *Index Medicus* has been photocomposed by NLM since 1964.

Photocomposition has put us in a "transitional phase" in the evolution from print on paper to electronics. Even now, it is possible to identify the remaining steps needed to complete the evolution to a fully electronic publishing environment. These steps are outlined in Table 2.

Phases of Publishing

Table 2 shows the transition from print on paper to electronics as an evolutionary process having three parallel lines of development: publishing phases, forms of publication, and publishing capabilities.

Examination of the publishing phases reveals that the types of publications with which modern libraries are most concerned begin their life in the print-on-paper form. This phase has existed for approximately 500 years, and we have not yet completely emerged from it (although we are already well into the second and third phases of this evolutionary process).

The second, or dual-mode, phase of publishing refers to the production and distribution of a publication in two parallel forms: machine readable and print on paper. This phase began in the early 1960s, and many such publications now exist. *Index Medicus,* for in-

Table 2   Transition from Paper to Electronics

Publishing Phases	Forms of Publications	Publishing Capabilities

1. Paper only
2. Dual mode
3. New electronic only
4. Conversion from
   paper
	1. Indexing/abstracting
	   services
	2. Newspapers/popular
	   magazines
	3. Reference books
	4. Journals
	5. Reports/patents/
	   standards
		1. Static analog
		2. New narrative
		   presentation
		3. Dynamics
		4. Sound

stance, is available in printed and machine-readable forms, as are *Engineering Index, Chemical Abstracts,* and a host of other secondary publications.

One barrier to the more widespread application of photocomposition in the smaller publishing companies is the expensive initial investment needed in hardware and software. This fact, coupled with increasing economic pressures on the publishing industry in general, led to the concept of the "editorial processing center" (Bamford [1972]), a mechanism for combining in a single center the production activities of a number of small publishers. Thus, small publishers could achieve the scale of operation needed to apply computers efficiently and economically without loss of individual autonomy or editorial control. Feasibility and cost-benefit analyses of the editorial processing center have been prepared by Aspen Systems Corporation and Westat Research, Inc. (1975), and by Woodward (1976).

Heldref Publications, a nonprofit organization established by the Helen Dwight Reid Educational Foundation, has been mentioned by the National Enquiry into Scholarly Communication (1979) as one organization that fulfills some of the functions of an editorial processing center. Heldref buys journals and assumes responsibility for their production and distribution. In fact, it took over the operation of 23 journals that were in financial difficulty within the period 1971–1977. Control of editorial policy, however, is frequently left to the originating organization.

The National Enquiry also reports on the activities of the American Anthropological Association, which provides billing, accounting, composition, and production services for eight other scholarly societies in the field of anthropology, and on the new Cooperative Editorial Facility, established under a grant from the Carnegie Corporation, which will use computers and photocomposition technology for editing material and for preparing camera-ready copy for several journals.

The third phase, which has proceeded more or less in parallel with the second, is that in which completely new publications emerge *ab initio* in machine-readable form. These publications never have and never will be issued in print-on-paper form. Among the countless examples of these electronic-only publications now in existence are such data bases as INFORM and the Information Bank of the *The New York Times,* as well as a wide variety of data banks containing economic, chemical, physical, and other types of numerical or statistical data. These data bases can be regarded as "reference books" that emerged in the electronic era rather than in the print-on-paper era. In at least some cases, they represent resources that, for one reason or another, are unlikely to have been published as print on paper: Perhaps they are too highly specialized (the market for a printed product is too limited); maybe they require constant updating; perhaps they are not readily "searchable" in print-on-paper form; or perhaps they are too extensive in their scope and coverage (and therefore very expensive to print and distribute by conventional means).

Until very recently, electronic publications were issued only in the form of magnetic tapes or disks, many directly accessible on-line. Since 1978, however, some new electronic forms have emerged. For example, *CLOAD Magazine,* published in Goleta, California, is a "journal" issued as a tape cassette for use on a home computer. *CLOAD,* which is directed at programmers and home-computer enthusiasts, provides computer programs, games, and other recreational materials. The annual subscription cost is only $36. Clearly, many audiences could be reached by similar journals if the expected boom in the home-computer market actually materializes. One can easily visualize popular mechanics and popular electronics journals being issued in this form, as well as journals directed at other hobby enthusiasts and journals designed to be primarily educational. A great potential advantage of this form is that it permits the inclusion of "dynamic" features — for example, electronic analog models of mechanisms, experiments, and so on — and, in the long run, publication costs are likely to be considerably lower than those of comparable publications in the print-on-paper form.

I have coined the term *electrobook* to refer to a type of "electronic reference book" issued in the form of a hand-held microprocessor. A number of manufacturers have already issued bilingual dictionaries in this form (see Figure 6). Closely resembling a pocket calculator, electrobooks include a keyboard and small readout device. Plug-in modules are available for various pairs of languages (e.g., English/Portuguese). When an English (or Portuguese) word is entered at the keyboard, its Portuguese (or English) equivalent is displayed. Although these electrobooks are now very expensive (a basic unit, without plug-in modules, is likely to cost around $200), it seems entirely possible that costs will drop dramatically, just as they did for pocket calculators. As the "memory capsules" become smaller and less expensive, a whole range of reference books might be issued in this form. Texas Instruments has introduced an electrobook dictionary having a voice output, and the Craig Corporation (Heckel [1980]) is already referring to the possibility of capsules storing "complete dictionaries, recipes, calorie equivalents, useful statistics, and other learning programs." Thus, it is perfectly possible that the entire *Oxford English Dictionary* might someday be issued as a single capsule that could be plugged into a hand-held device of this type. (At present, however, the Craig electrobook can handle only 7,000 words or 256,000 bits, so there is still a long way to go before the pocket *OED* is reached.)

Clarke (1980) sees the electrobook as an "electronic tutor" capable of changing "the very nature of education." He predicts

. . . the portable electronic library—a library not only of books, but of films and music. It will be about the size of an average book and will probably open in the same way. One half will be the screen, with high-definition, full-color display. The other will be a keyboard, much like one of today's computer consoles, with the full alphabet, digits, basic mathematical functions, and a large number of special keys—perhaps 100 keys in all. . . . Whole additional libraries stored in small, plug-in memory modules, could be inserted into the portable library when necessary. . . . Reading material may be displayed as a fixed page or else "scrolled" so that it rolls upward at a comfortable reading rate. Pictures could appear as in an ordinary book, but they may eventually be displayed as three-dimensional holographic images. Text and imagery, of course, will be accompanied by sound. (pp. 77–78)

Grayson (1980) has conceptualized a future electrobook, about the size of a printed textbook, with a greatly expanded display capability.

Figure 6 Example of an electrobook. (Reproduced by permission of Nixdorf Computer Personal Systems, Inc.)

The electrobook and some specifications are illustrated in Figure 7.

Completely new means for electronic distribution of publications will most likely be implemented during the next few years, including, perhaps, the distribution of various types of publications on video-disks. These various forms of electronic publications, some already existing and others yet to come, can be considered the "books" of the electronic era.

The fourth phase of the evolution of electronics, as identified in Table 2, has not yet reached a significant level. This step will occur when existing publications are moved out of the dual-mode phase and issued only in machine-readable forms. Although it is difficult to predict how rapidly this conversion process will occur, the step seems inevitable for many types of publications, for economic reasons if nothing else. There seems little doubt that the cost of producing and distributing publications in electronic form will continue to decline rapidly relative to the costs of publishing and distributing them in print-on-paper form. Already, some print-on-paper publications find themselves competing in the marketplace with rival publications available only through electronic access.

Moreover, for many of the dual-mode publishers, on-line royalty income is increasing rapidly as the market continues to grow. Conversely, the number of subscribers to the equivalent printed products is declining, although income from sales of print on paper may show modest annual increases as a result of substantial increments in subscription costs. As discussed in Chapter 7, significant numbers of libraries have recently canceled one or more subscriptions to printed indexing or abstracting services. These decisions have been influenced by escalating subscription costs, declining library budgets, and the availability of the equivalent data bases on-line. Furthermore, there are "hidden" effects of electronic publishing on income from print on paper because new academic and special libraries are emerging in the electronic age, and several of these are tending to move directly to on-line access without ever subscribing to indexing/ abstracting services in print-on-paper form. These various trends — already clearly discernible — coupled with the fact that the on-line access market is potentially vast and relatively untapped (whereas the print-on-paper market is saturated and actually declining for certain publications), suggest unambiguously that the future lies with electronic publication and not with the distribution of print-on-paper

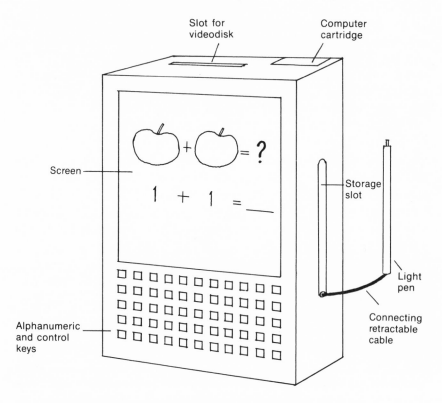

Size: 6½″ × 9″ × 1½″ (about the size of a textbook)

Weight: 3–4 lbs.

Output: Flat screen display on front cover; measures 6″ × 6″. Full-color images in freeze frame for full motion. Capable of displaying alphanumerics and constructed graphics. Computer-synthesized voice response.

Input: Touch-sensitive panel. Alphanumeric keyboard, with special control keys. Light pen. Book contents (the images, narrative, and logic for interacting and displaying the contents) can be changed by replacing laser-read videodisk.

Computer
Capability: Similar to a personal computer, with 1 million bits of random-access memory. High-level language, with English-like commands. Computer programs can be changed with a small, replaceable cartridge.

Figure 7   A future electronic book. (From Grayson [1980].)

publications. It appears inevitable, then, that many types of publications will disappear in their paper form and will only be accessible electronically. The more forward-looking publishers have already seen the writing on the wall. For example, J. William Baker (1979), president of Macmillan of Canada, has said,

First to disappear will be scientific journals and certain types of reference works. Books which consist largely of data, especially data subject to change, will become obsolete. The Macmillan *Dictionary of Canadian Biography,* recently released in its fourth edition, is unlikely to appear in book form in its fifth edition. (p. 265)

The question, then, is no longer "Will the complete evolution to electronic communication occur?" but, rather, "When will it occur?" Put another way, to what extent will print on paper have disappeared by, say, the year 2000? A Delphi study on the future of electronic publishing, involving librarians, publishers, and technologists, has been undertaken and reported by Lancaster et al. (1980). The following are among the specific forecasts made by the participants in the study:

1. Fifty percent of existing indexing/abstracting services will be available only in electronic form by the year 2000. The 90 percent level of conversion will not be reached until after that time.

2. Existing periodicals (in science and technology, social sciences, and the humanities) will not reach even the 25 percent level of conversion until after 2000.

3. By 1990, 25 percent of existing reference books will be available only in electronic form. The 50 percent level of conversion will occur after 2000.

4. By 1995, 50 percent of newly issued technical reports will be available only in electronic form. The 90 percent level will be reached after 2000.

It must be noted, however, that these forecasts relate to the worldwide production of publications. Had the study been restricted to the United States, a greatly accelerated forecast would probably have emerged.

As might be expected, the Delphi participants predicted that actual conversion to electronic publishing will lag behind economic feasibility, which, in turn, will lag behind technological feasibility. Most participants agreed that the stage of technological feasibility has already been reached and that the economic feasibility stage, if not here, is close at hand. Technologists participating in this study predicted that developments in this area will occur more rapidly than did participating librarians. Predictions made by publishers lagged behind both groups.

Returning to Table 2, the evolution from print on paper to electronics proceeds through three fairly distinct stages: print on paper only, dual-mode publication, and electronic publication only. Looking at it another way, the computer is first used as a device to facilitate printing on paper. Later, as the need to print and distribute paper declines or disappears, computers and telecommunications combine to produce publications and make them accessible, obviating the need for paper completely. These stages can also be identified in the application of computers to libraries. For example, computers are used for many years to print catalog cards and microfiche. Later, the need to print cards or fiche disappears and the on-line catalog replaces the card and microfiche catalogs.

Intellectual Forms

Table 2 also illustrates the evolution of publications in terms of "intellectual forms." The list seems to represent the sequence in which these forms are affected by electronics. Indexing/abstracting services were the first to move into the dual-mode phase. The reasons for this are logical: They tend to be the largest and costliest publications, they require the most in the way of sorting and record-manipulation operations, and their machine-readable versions have more obvious applicability and marketability—in literature-searching activities—than the machine-readable versions of other types of publications. By the same token, these secondary publications will likely lead the way into the final step of the evolution.

Photocomposition was applied at a relatively early time to the production of certain newspapers and popular magazines, but little if any use was made of the machine-readable text once the tapes had been used to print on paper. Only very recently has it become possible to access the full text of such publications through on-line facilities. Mead Data Central, for example, is now producing a data base, NEXIS, which includes more or less the complete text of the *Washington Post, Newsweek, Duns Review, The Economist,* other magazines, and technical journals (e.g., *Chemical Engineering*), as well as releases from Reuters, the Associated Press, UPI, and other services and several newsletters. CompuServe is now making the *Columbus Dispatch* accessible through home terminals. The user can "call up" for video display the full text of selected items from the newspaper; news can also be stored for future home reference.

A similar situation has occurred in book publishing. Photocomposition has been used extensively in book publishing, but, until recently, no real use has been made of the machine-readable byproduct after the generation of print on paper. Now, however, reference books are becoming accessible through on-line networks of one kind or another. *The Foundations Directory,* the *Federal Register,* and the *Encyclopedia of Associations* are already accessible online, and Bowker has recently made *Books in Print, Ulrich's Periodicals Directory,* and *American Men and Women of Science* accessible through the facilities of Bibliographic Retrieval Services, Inc. (BRS). BRS now offers a publicly available file, Booksinfo, which contains 700,000 entries from *Books in Print.* OCLC, Inc., made the full text of the *Academic American Encyclopedia* accessible, via domestic television receivers, in its Home Delivery of Library Services Program. Macmillan makes available a baseball encyclopedia, and Addison-Wesley a consumer guide to medical care through the home delivery program, Viewtron, operated experimentally by the Viewdata Corporation of America in Coral Gables, Florida. In 1980, the on-line availability of *Encyclopedia Britannica* through Mead Data Central was announced. With these developments, newspapers, popular magazines, and reference books have moved squarely into the dual-mode phase.

Books have already reached the "electronic-only" phase. The electrobook was discussed on pp. 57–59. *The Computer Cookbook* (Holt [1980]), which was written, published, and delivered to customers in electronic form, is another example. It was written at home on a terminal and transmitted to the publisher, CompuServe, through satellite links and land lines. It can be "browsed" on-line by customers at $5 per hour. Alternatively, they can purchase it outright by having it transmitted onto their own floppy disks or printout machines for $30. A detailed analysis of the feasibility and impact of electronic delivery of handbook-type information has been made by Krall Management, Inc. (1977).

The Electronic Journal

The scholarly journal has been influenced less than other forms of publications. Although several such journals are photocomposed, none has been accessible on-line in full-text form until very recently. Now, however, the American Chemical Society is making the full text of 16 of its journals accessible on-line. Other publishers can be expected to follow rapidly.

It is probably fair to say that on-line journals are still in an embryonic stage of development. Some on-line systems or networks do contain features that can be regarded as types of "journals." The simplest is merely a "news" feature designed to inform users of recent developments and capabilities of the system/network itself—a type of on-line newsletter. Turoff and Hiltz (in press) have recognized the existence of several types of journals within the Electronic Information Exchange System (EIES) operated by the New Jersey Institute of Technology. The most basic is the EIES newsletter, CHIMO, produced weekly. Each "issue" contains an average of three to five pages. Some of the news items are complete and self-contained. Others are similar to abstracts, referring the reader to more complete items in public conferences or notebooks.

Another EIES feature, Paper Fair, is essentially an unrefereed journal. Any EIES user can place a paper in this journal. Frequently the contribution will be a draft of a paper intended for presentation at a future meeting or for submission to a more formal journal. In its Paper Fair form, the item may be available to other EIES users six months to one year before it is accessible in any other form. An author can write an article in his own EIES notebook, using the system's text-editing facilities, and then transfer the article into Paper Fair as a means of soliciting feedback. He may then revise the text before submitting it elsewhere. At any time, he can generate hard copy. Obtaining a copy of a paper within Paper Fair or any other EIES conference is a simple, rapid, efficient, and inexpensive procedure. EIES thus provides a document-delivery capability within the framework of a computer-conferencing system. By putting a paper into this public conference, an author is, in effect, soliciting review and reaction from EIES users. Thus, it is a convenient way of obtaining informal peer review before a paper is submitted to the more formal procedures of a conventional journal.

The closest thing to a "conventional" journal in electronic form was the basis of an experiment within EIES in 1979. It dealt with "mental workload"—considerations of human factors in the man-machine interface in such stressful environments as an airplane cockpit or an air traffic control tower. Like conventional print-on-paper journals, it was to have a defined scope, editorial standards, and formal refereeing procedures. Refereeing would be anonymous and all communication among authors, editors, and referees would be achieved by on-line interaction. Any interested person could subscribe to membership in this journal. An article would be published when it was accepted. Thus, the data base would expand continuously, but markers could be used to tell any particular member where he left off in reading the journal. A user could read abstracts or full text, search authors or titles, print text, and enter comments (anonymous or signed) on any article in the journal. These comments, along with author responses, would be stored for use by all journal readers. Thus, a type of "public refereeing" would be achieved. More rapid dissemination of research results and lower costs—a reader prints out only those articles of immediate interest—would be primary advantages of such a journal.

This prototype was not as successful as its organizers had hoped. The problems encountered are discussed by Guillaume (1980), Senders (1980), and Moray and Stocklosa (1980). According to Senders, the major problems encountered were primarily those of the man-machine interface. Despite the failure, however, all these authors seem optimistic about the long-term future of electronic journals.

In 1980, the British Library awarded a grant to Loughborough University to establish an experimental on-line journal on "computer human factors." The grant covers the analysis of costs, effectiveness, and impact of the proposed journal (Shackel [in press] and Singleton [1981]). Lea (1979) mentions an informal electronic journal, *Online Education News,* developed in England at the Department of Library and Information Studies, Manchester Polytechnic. It is a newsletter whereby lecturers at library schools can exchange information on teaching methods relating to on-line systems. In 1981, Online, Inc.

announced a new data base, The Online Chronicle, which is intended to be the electronic equivalent of the news pages in the printed journals *Online* and *Data Base.*

Other informal electronic journals exist within various networks or computing environments. Engelbart (1975), for example, refers to extensive experience with such a journal within NLS, an on-line system at Stanford Research Institute:

> The Journal is an NLS subsystem with basic methods for handling full-text computerized items that parallel those of open-literature professional journals and associated library services—i.e., a permanent record of any published item, citation conventions by which later readers can retrieve and access references to other items, and catalogs and indices for retrieval aid. Each of these processes is done much faster in our computer environment, and other computerized services may be added. Altogether this provides a very powerful foundation for a new level of collaboration via recorded dialogue. (p. 173)

> The NLS Journal serves its users in a manner similar to professional journals, with these significant quantitative differences: fast, flexible computer aids serve an author in creating a dialogue item, and help multiple authors to collaborate toward that end; publication time is very much shorter; significant "articles" may be as short as one sentence; cross-reference citations may easily be much more specific (i.e., pointing directly to a specific passage); catalogs and indexes can be accessed and searched online as well as in hard copy; and full-text retrieval with short delays is the basic operating mode. The end effect of these changes is a form of recorded dialogue whose impact and value has a dramatic qualitative difference over the traditional, hard-copy journal system. (p. 175)

Economics of Electronic Publishing

Cost data relating to electronic journals have been published by Senders (1977), Senders et al. (1975), Roistacher (1978a), and Folk (1977).

Drawing on experience with on-line composition at the Center for Advanced Computation, University of Illinois, Roistacher has concluded that a paper of 15 pages could be written in about 22.5 hours of connect time. At computer costs of $2 per hour and communication costs of $3 per hour, the paper could be composed for a total cost of around $110–$120 or approximately $7.50 per published page. At off-line night rates, however, these costs could be even lower: $1.60 per hour for computer services and $2 per hour for communication, for a total cost of $81 or $5.40 per published page.

Roistacher contrasts this with the present composition costs for technical journals, which he claims are around $25–$28 per page and which will obviously go much higher.

Roistacher's estimates for the number of hours needed to compose a paper are well below those of King et al. (1976). King's figure of around 80 hours per paper, however, must include a considerable amount of "think" time, which would not necessarily involve the use of on-line resources. Even if we multiply Roistacher's figures by four, we have a situation in which the electronic composition is at least economically competitive with the conventional composition. The costs of the latter can only get worse; the costs of the former are quite likely to improve. Roistacher goes on to point out that, for a journal publishing 300 papers a year, with an average length of 15 pages (i.e., 4,500 printed pages), storage in direct-access files could cost as little as $2,200 per year. He estimates computer support for editorial processing of this journal to be no more than $5,000 per year.

Folk (1977) contrasts central storage costs for maintenance of an electronic journal with the distributed storage costs associated with maintaining printed journals on library shelves:

Suppose one printed volume of a journal costs $25 and is purchased and shelved by 100 libraries at a total cost of $2,500. Storing 100 volumes requires about ten square feet of library floor space or, at current construction costs, about $400. Thus, the capital cost of the volume to the library system is $2,900. A volume is about 5 megabytes (MB), or 1,000 pages of 5,000 bytes (or characters) each. An AED controller and disc system would hold 100 different journals for a cost of $750 per journal. Mass storage devices with much cheaper costs (less than $1/MB) are commercially available, but for a distributed system using minicomputers, a single system will not exceed a few hundred megabytes. (p. 81)*

This cost analysis is very modest, both in terms of subscription costs and in the number of libraries considered. It is clear that the economics of storage greatly favor the electronic journal as either subscription cost or the number of libraries providing access to a particular title increases.

For transmission costs, Roistacher estimates that a user could ac-

---

* In a private communication, Roistacher indicated that one year of a journal could probably be stored on-line for $500 per year and that costs are dropping at approximately 26 percent per year. If an access time to text of one minute is tolerable, the journal could be stored on tape for around $10 per year.

cess any part of an electronic journal (contents page, abstracts, or full text) at approximately $1.80 per hour plus $3 per hour in network costs. In non-prime time, these costs could be reduced to as little as $3 per hour for computation and communication. An article of 15 pages could be printed out on a 30-character-per-second (cps) terminal at a total prime-time cost of around $1.90 or non-prime-time cost of $1.40. It could be printed off-line on a line printer for about $0.20. In this case, costs of handling and mailing must be added.*

Folk (1977) quotes a value of $1–$5 — depending on the location of the user in relation to the data base and on the time of day — for printing a 10-page, 50,000-byte article on a 30-cps terminal. He points out that this is inexpensive compared with the cost of an interlibrary loan, which he estimates to be around $7–$8.

In a realistic cost-benefit comparison, the electronic system might already outperform present operations. A number of years ago, Senders et al. (1975) undertook a more complete economic analysis of the "electronic journal." They calculated that the full text of 25,000 science journals (i.e., about half of the present world output according to the best available estimates) would require 4×10^{12} bits of on-line storage each year. If laser memories were used, this would cost some $1.2 million per year, which is a very small amount considering the quantity of text involved. Taking only journal production costs into account, Senders et al. estimated the cost of the electronic journal to be equal to that of the paper journal by 1978. When all "hidden costs" were considered, however, including the costs of disseminating to terminals and use by scientists on-line, they predicted that the cost of the electronic journal would equal the cost of the paper journal by 1996 and would be cheaper thereafter.

Senders (1977) has discussed capital and other costs in the following terms:

> For an initial investment of approximately £100,000,000 this year, we could effectively substitute an electronic system which would be almost identical in cost to the present paper publishing systems. The capital costs would be spread over 5 years. The actual cost in the first year would be close to £700,000,000 or £800,000,000, which is a very small figure in comparison to the overall actual cost of distributing the world's scientific literature. If we try to make electronic a small journal of about

---

* In a later paper, Roistacher (1980) estimated that storing an "average size" paper for one year on-line could cost $5.29 but that transmitting it through Telenet would actually cost $3.55.

900 pages per year with no more than 2,500 subscribers, both private and institutional, the economics of the situation indicate a crossover point in the middle or late 1990s. However, if we set up a system to handle the entire body of English language scientific publications at once, the crossover point has already been passed. This is true even though we assume an enormous initial investment for the supplying of terminals to scientists in sufficient numbers to ensure that access can be had by all.

None of the above cost figures take into account the value of saving time. The delay in publication implicit in the electronic system is the editorial processing time, which runs about six weeks for most of the North American journals. The average lag in publication for the North American journals is about one year, and in certain of the social sciences and humanities, as much as two years. No one seems to be able to equate dollar savings with time savings, but there seems to be some correspondence. This would suggest that the crossover points actually occurred some time ago. My original estimate of the crossover for the North American corpus of scientific information, based on a comprehensive model of costs, was around 1971. (pp. 6-7)

This cost analysis appears somewhat pessimistic in a number of respects. First, it assumes that the journal will bear the full cost of the telecommunications network, including terminal costs. This is unrealistic because the overall network is likely to exist for other reasons, since the scientists will use terminals for many different purposes. Moreover, all the potential savings — in writing and recording time; in communication among authors, publishers, and referees; and in dissemination and use costs — are not taken into account. If the present science communication system is realistically costed, it represents very considerable expenditures indeed. King et al. (1976), for example, have estimated that the total annual cost of disseminating scientific and technical information in the United States by the present procedures is more than $12 billion; the electronic system has the potential for offering considerable savings in a number of the total functions involved.

The fact remains, however, that while the dual-mode phase of publishing has recently reached the scholarly journal, no formal journals have yet emerged in electronic form only; that is, there now exist no electronic journals having all the social trappings of the scholarly journal in paper form — a board of editors, referees, imprimatur, and so on. Nevertheless, some such journals are now in the planning stages. Moreover, the great current interest in electronic publishing is attested to by the recent establishment of new journals specifically devoted to this subject.

As for the other publication forms identified in Table 2, some reports, standards, and patents are already photocomposed, but the full text of such publications is not normally distributed in machine-readable form or made accessible on-line.

New Capabilities

The third dimension of Table 2 is capabilities for presentation of information. In general, computers first change how things are done and later change what is done. Thus, in publishing too, electronics can be expected to lead to completely new capabilities for the presentation of information. Publications now accessible on-line look much the same as their print-on-paper equivalents. Essentially they are printed pages displayed on a screen. It seems likely that the first electronic journals will also be more or less static analogs of the printed page. In the future, however, electronic publications will likely free themselves from the entirely static limitations of narrative text printed on paper, and will thereby have a very profound effect on the way information is presented. First, perhaps, "hypertext" types of capabilities will be used to present narrative data in a somewhat different form (Nelson [1972, 1974, 1978]). For example, an electronic textbook could look much different from a textbook printed on paper. It need not be designed to be read in one particular sequence; it may be designed to allow many alternative reading pathways or to permit reorganization into various sequences to meet the needs of different instructors, courses, or students. At any point in such a text, a student could enter an annotation, a comment, or a question to an instructor. Instructor responses could also be incorporated and, in fact, for any portion of the text, a student could gain access to the questions and comments of other students and/or the responses of several instructors. Even the bibliography for such a text need not be static. Indeed, the text could be interfaced with an on-line retrieval system in such a way that the reader could get virtually immediate access to citations representing the latest literature on any topic discussed in the text. Furthermore, the text itself could be constantly updated by computer conferencing among the authors.

Many of these features already exist, at least experimentally (e.g., within the "living text" system incorporated into PLATO at the University of Illinois), and plans have been made to experiment with other aspects. At the University of Illinois, a "living textbook" of pathology is being developed and used in instructional programs (Thursh and Mabry [1980]). The Hepatitis Knowledge Base, developed by the National Library of Medicine (Bernstein et al. [1980]), is an example of a state-of-knowledge compilation that is kept current through the development of group consensus achieved via computer conferencing (Siegel [1979]).

A sophisticated computer-aided instruction (CAI) system, such as PLATO, can incorporate very effective analog models. It is possible to build an analog model of a scientific experiment in, say, chemistry or genetics, as well as analog working models of various types of equipment (Chabay and Smith [1977], Kane and Sherwood [1980], and Smith and Sherwood [1976]). Clearly, electronic publications need not be restricted to the static properties of the printed page.

The true capabilities of electronics in publishing will be reached when completely new and dynamic publications emerge. If a picture is worth a thousand words, then a dynamic analog model should be worth at least ten thousand. Visualize, for example, an on-line encyclopedia that incorporates dynamic analog models of equipment and experiments. Even the tactics/strategy of a historical battle could come to life on the terminal. Such a presentation would, in fact, closely resemble the current electronic games. Or think of the capabilities of future journals in scientific/technological fields. Rather than describing what happens when loads of a specific intensity are applied to a particular type of structure, a journal in applied mechanics could demonstrate these effects. Moreover, since computer programs could be incorporated into a contribution to an electronic journal, the reader could actually perform new experiments of his own. The possibilities are limited only by the imagination.

Sound output is also possible with an electronic encyclopedia. In certain subject areas (e.g., music, poetry, ornithology), encyclopedia articles could be greatly enhanced through this feature. The *Wall Street Journal* has reported Kenneth Kister, author of the *Encyclopedia Buying Guide*, as saying that through such new capabilities, "Encyclopedias will be released from the bondage of the printed word."

Martino (1979) has predicted that videodisks may someday replace printed books completely. A videodisk playback device could locate and display any recorded image and hold it on the screen for as long as needed. Such compilations as encyclopedias could combine passages of text with animation, film footage, still photos, diagrams, or actual demonstrations and recorded experiments.

Negroponte (1979) has described a multimedia "book without pages." The reader, seated in a chair whose arms are equipped with a joystick and touch-sensitive pad, can view whole-wall displays, enjoy octaphonic sound, and have access to a "continuous speech recognizer." Negroponte claims that his facility can be likened to a universal encyclopedia "that takes you to Patagonia, sings Cosi Fan Tutti, animates the preparation of Coulibiac, or monitors the progress of herpes zoster" (p. 56.1.8).

Oettinger (1968) has referred to the possibility of using holography to enhance future publishing capabilities:

By using computers to manipulate pictorial information in two or more dimensions, we gain an important quality lacking in the printed page . . . . Not only can we present a sequence of images, as in books or movies, but a single image as well can be grown, viewed from varying standpoints, superimposed on or merged with another, or changed in form right before one's eyes at the command of either man or machine. (p.77)

In other words, the application of the computer to publishing will do much more than simply display the printed page on a screen. As Brown (1977) has stated,

. . . the revolutionary transformation of learning in our society that we see as possible for the 1980's is not simply a consequence of the incredible computer technology that will be available then. It would not revolutionize education, for example, to place the *Encyclopedia Britannica* within the memory banks of every home computer. While this is worthwhile, it would not be qualitatively different from placing the books themselves in the home, only cheaper.

The unique quality of the computer that does make possible a revolution is that it can serve as a *cognitive tool*. It can be an active agent — a servant, assistant, consultant or coach — in a way that books and television cannot. With vision, with planning, with dedicated research, our citizens can be employing this tool to open a new frontier of the mind within a decade. (p. 300)

Although we tend to take the printed book for granted, linear text printed on paper has many limitations. Von Foerster (1972), for example, sees the printed book as the "bottleneck in man's communication channels." De Grazia (1962), discussing information systems of the future, also notes problems associated with this form:

It is doubtful that basic library materials would be bound; the bound book is, after all, an incident of the history of the human mind, an instrument that should not be allowed to outlive its usefulness; it is functional in certain parts of the social intelligence system at certain times and for limited purposes; it should not be permitted for minor technical reasons to become a fetish of the communications sphere; its main advantage is that it cannot easily be torn apart, which is also its main disadvantage. (p. 40)

The evolution depicted in Table 2 applies most clearly to publications distributed primarily to convey information rather than those intended to entertain or "inspire." Perhaps it is unlikely that novels or popular magazines will be read at on-line terminals. It is highly probable, then, that novels, "bestsellers," and popular magazines will last much longer in print-on-paper form than other types of publications. When they finally are replaced, however, it will be by something other than "conventional" on-line systems. Perhaps the novel as an art form may eventually give way to original dramatic presentations issued on audiotape, videotape, or videodisk. It has also been suggested that electronic technology could produce completely new approaches to traditional literary forms. For example, Bolch (1980), writing on the use of home computers, has said, "We even started writing an electronic interactive epic novel, in which the outcome depends on the choices made along the way by the "reader," with the result that the novel never ends the same way twice" (p. 28).

Such developments, if they occur, are likely to happen much later than the developments shown in Table 2. For this reason, public and school libraries may be affected somewhat less by publishing developments in the next 20 years than those libraries—academic, governmental, industrial—that deal more with research materials.

Within the past two decades, and particularly within the 1970s, computers and telecommunications have been used in many innovative ways in information-handling applications. A number of these were discussed in preceding chapters. Technological applications relevant to future information systems include computer conferencing, text editing and word processing in general, electronic mail and the "paperless office," computer-aided instruction, satellite communication, "interactive" television, and on-line searching of data bases. So far, these applications—while closely related in many ways—have existed as entirely separate activities. It is not unreasonable to expect, however, that they will someday be brought together into a completely paperless communication network. In other words, they will form the communications infrastructure of a paperless society.

Summary

Even within the past four years (1979–1982), some notable break-throughs have occurred. On-line searching of data bases and data banks has certainly taken hold in academic and special libraries, but, so far, public libraries have hardly been affected. One reason is that few data bases of interest to public libraries have been made accessible. This situation is rapidly changing. Indexes to newspapers and popular magazines are now on-line, and, as mentioned earlier, the full text of certain newspapers can be accessed. Moreover, several conventional "reference books" are already usable in on-line form, and many more sources of this type will become accessible in the near future. It seems reasonable that on-line technology will make possible some form of cooperation in "reference service" in the same way it made possible OCLC and other cooperative cataloging ventures. For example, an on-line reference file of "difficult questions answered," maintained cooperatively by a large group of libraries, could become a kind of "growing encyclopedia," the single most important source for question-answering activities in libraries of all types. Another significant development in this area is the ongoing experimentation with Prestel (Martyn [1979]) in public and academic libraries in the United Kingdom. Here the Prestel facilities are used to provide an alternative to printed reference books as a source of information, as well as to make available important community data bases compiled by the libraries themselves.

An important development in the electronic delivery of the full text of journal articles has recently been announced in Europe. Elsevier Science Publishers, Pergamon Press, Blackwell Scientific Publications, Academic Press, John Wiley & Sons, and Springer-Verlag have announced plans to launch the ADONIS (Article Delivery over Network Information Systems) project early in 1984. The full text of journals published by these entities (collectively they publish around 1,500 journals in science and technology) will be stored on a laser-encoded digital videodisk. For purely textual material, 500,000 pages can be stored on a single side of such a disk. If high-quality illustrations are included, about 50,000 pages can be stored on each side. Libraries will be able to access this text through an on-line network in lieu of requesting photocopies from other libraries. The expected advantage for libraries is that access will be cheaper and more rapid. Publishers will benefit because royalty payments will be included in the price of access. Development of ADONIS has been stimulated by the finding that photocopy requests made to the British Library Lending Division are dominated by requests for articles issued by commercial publishers and that 80 percent of all requests are for articles five years old or less.

Other significant advances made during 1979–1982 include plans for making the full text of certain reference books accessible through domestic television receivers (the experiments of OCLC and Viewtron mentioned on p. 63) and plans for implementing "formal" journals within computer-conferencing networks (Turoff and Hiltz [1980]). There is evidence, then, that various technologies are beginning to coalesce. Most importantly, computer-conferencing systems, home computers, and domestic television are all being used, at least in a preliminary way, to make publications available. The widespread adoption of on-line technology by the public library to make important information resources available to library users, together with probable rapid growth in the home-computer and interactive-television markets, will put terminals within the grasp of the general public. Moreover, it seems likely that terminals will creep into the homes in other ways (e.g., distributed by the telephone company). As these various developments greatly increase access to on-line terminals, society will take a quantum jump into the paperless communication age. Furthermore, the move away from paper and toward electronics could be very positive in the long run in improving access to information. As Haug (1975) has stated,

The invention of the printing press revolutionized knowledge dissemination in the Middle Ages by making duplication, preservation and accessibility of books enormously simpler than was the case with the old hand-written manuscripts. The electronic computer can again revolutionize knowledge availability and utilization by the geometric advances in the scale of its storage and the speed of its retrieval. No longer need knowledge be packed only in the professional's head or in a specialized library, where it is relatively inaccessible. It can be available not just to those who *know*, but also to those who *know how to get it*. (p. 205)

5   A Paperless Communication System

I first became interested in the possibility of information transfer in a completely paperless mode in the early 1970s while working as a consultant for the Central Intelligence Agency. The intelligence community in the United States is in a unique position regarding completely electronic systems because the volume of messages handled is so large that it makes efficient manual dissemination extremely difficult, rapid distribution of information is critical, and many messages are transmitted to the intelligence agencies over wire communications lines and are thus easily captured in machine-readable form. The intelligence community, then, has both the need for electronic distribution and exploitation of information and the ability to implement electronic systems.

In the mid-1970s, the Central Intelligence Agency conceptualized a paperless system having the following capabilities:

1. Incoming "electric" messages would be disseminated directly to the terminals of intelligence analysts without the need to generate intermediate paper copy. The dissemination would be automatic for some messages, based on analyst interest profiles, and machine aided for others.

2. Analysts would read an incoming message on-line and would then (a) dispose of it, (b) store it for future action, (c) reroute it to another analyst, (d) store it in a personal electronic file, (e) index it in any way desired or (f) annotate it.

3. Analysts could communicate with other analysts on-line.

4. Personal electronic files would replace personal paper-copy files.

5. On-line terminals would give analysts access to their own information files, those of their parent branches, agency-wide files, and a wide variety of external data bases.

6. Files of documents would be accessible for searching in a full-text mode.

7. A document-delivery system would allow the full text of any item to be presented at a user terminal via digital or microform transmission.

8. Document files would be interfaced with "computation" programs so that data could be extracted from text and manipulated in various ways.

9. An analyst would compose intelligence reports on-line with the aid of text-editing facilities and could disseminate these reports over the on-line network.

A small prototype system, demonstrating most of these capabilities, was designed, implemented, and evaluated (Lancaster [1978]). It was received with great enthusiasm, and a full-scale, agency-wide implementation is now underway (Hooper and Henderson [1980]).

The apparent success of these activities within the intelligence community, together with the various technological developments reviewed within the previous three chapters, raises the possibility that, at some future date, completely paperless communication systems could emerge in the sciences and in other fields. The scenario that follows suggests the capabilities that such a system could provide.

A Scenario

A completely electronic approach to the dissemination, storage, and exploitation of information is illustrated in Figure 8. The system user illustrated could be any professional; assume here that he is a scientist with a terminal in his office. Very likely he has a second terminal in his home. In addition to the video terminal illustrated, he will certainly have a completely portable terminal that he can take home and carry when traveling.

It is difficult to predict what these terminals will look like in, say, 1990 or 2000. Certainly they will be much more sophisticated than

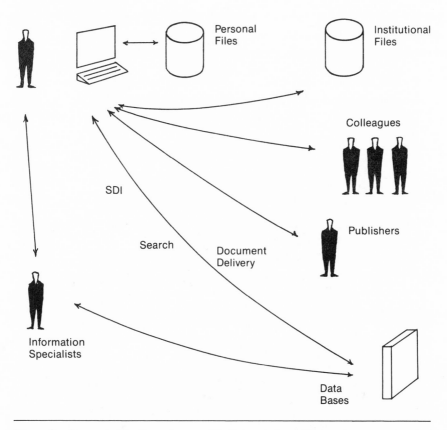

Figure 8 Conceptualization of a possible future information system.

those currently available. Cawkell (1978) has presented one vision of the typical office terminal of the future. His "consumersole" (Figure 9) includes a "continuous plasma screen" with graphic display capabilities; a keyboard; a videophone display; and facilities for voice input, handwritten input, and printout on paper. A somewhat similar, although less futuristic, terminal has been conceptualized by the Yankee Group (Figure 10). Kubitz (1980) has this to say about the possibilities for terminals:

Color displays, speech output and expanded character sets are certainly possible in home terminals. In addition, it has been predicted that a book-size display will be available in the 1980s. Such a display will allow all written material to be stored in

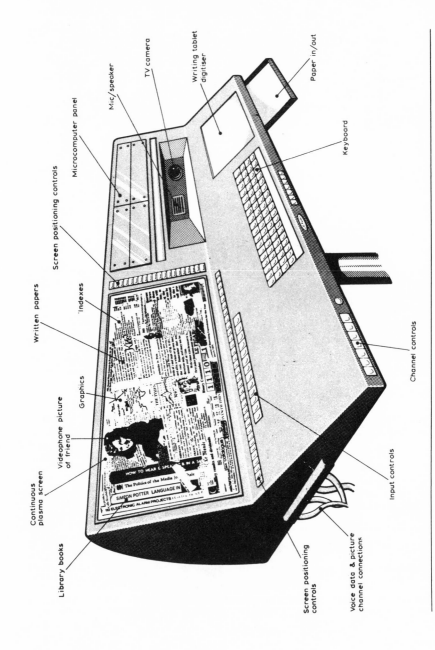

Figure 9 "Consumersole" as conceptualized by Cawkell (1978). (Reprinted by permission of *Wireless World*.)

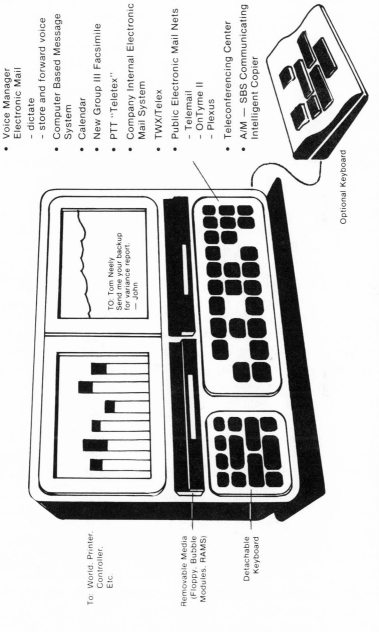

ACCESS TO:

- Voice Manager
  Electronic Mail
  - dictate
  - store and forward voice
- Computer Based Message
  System
- Calendar
- New Group III Facsimile
- PTT "Teletex"
- Company Internal Electronic
  Mail System
- TWX/Telex
- Public Electronic Mail Nets
  - Telemail
  - OnTyme II
  - Plexus
- Teleconferencing Center
- A/M — SBS Communicating
  Intelligent Copier

TO: Tom Neely
Send me your backup
for variance report.
— John

To: World. Printer.
Controller.
Etc.

Removable Media
(Floppy. Bubble
Modules. RAMS)

Detachable
Keyboard

Optional Keyboard

Figure 10 Future terminal as conceptualized by the Yankee Group. (Reprinted by permission of the Yankee Group.)

digitally encoded form. One would simply play the book through the home computer center and read it off the display. One need not go to the library to browse, of course, since that will be done by interrogating the library computer system or by perusing the latest acquisitions on TV. (p. 146)

The portable terminal might be a lightweight typewriter device, closely resembling those now available, or it might incorporate a compact, flat video display, perhaps some form of plasma panel. The home terminal could stand alone or, more likely, be a terminal component in a complete home computer. Conceivably, the home computer will be part of a much larger entertainment/educational center, including television, tape deck, and some form of video recorder.

The exact configuration of the user terminal is not important here. Of much greater interest is what it can do. First, it will be used for record keeping and composition. The scientist maintains an electronic notebook or several types of notebooks, which serve as memo files where he can record thoughts, descriptions, and results of experiments, draft reports, calendar and diary information, quotations and further material extracted from other electronic files, and any other information that he would normally record on paper. Notebooks can be indexed and thus can be searched on index terms or, possibly, words in text. His electronic calendar, perhaps the first thing he consults when he logs on the system in the morning, will provide an efficient reminder of what he hopes to achieve that day.

The scientist will receive much, if not all, of his professional mail in electronic form. Some items will be disposed of immediately, while others will be stored in personal electronic files. These files, like the notebooks, can be indexed in any way and will thus be easy to search.

The scientist will communicate with many colleagues through his terminal. Such communication will include private messages (mail) and messages to groups (conferences) and can be synchronous (immediate and interactive) or asynchronous (delayed).

He will also want to write more formal reports to reach a wider audience. In other words, he will wish to publish electronically — to become better known; to establish priority for his work; to have his work recorded in a more formal and permanent form; and to secure the recognition he may need for purposes of promotion, tenure, or increased financial reward.

The scientist will write his report at his terminal, using sophisticated text-editing and formatting facilities and drawing freely from materials he has been accumulating for his report in his notebooks and other electronic files. His terminal is likely to have dual screens. On one he can call up material he has stored. On the other, he composes his report. Text can be transferred from one screen to another by simple commands. Writing the report will be greatly facilitated, not only by the text-editing capabilities, but by the ease with which he can incorporate quotations, illustrations, and bibliographic citations drawn from his own files and from other electronic resources.

The report, in draft form, can be circulated to colleagues for review by merely transferring the text from a private workspace to some semipublic file and sending, to those he wants to read it, a message indicating how it can be accessed. The same message can be sent to several addresses through a single command.

Based on the comments of his colleagues, the scientist may wish to revise his report. When he is ready to publish it, he can have the characteristics of his contribution (e.g., keywords in the abstract) matched against an on-line data base of journal characteristics. This referral data base will tell him the names and addresses of those journals most likely to accept his contribution and, at his request, will provide to him their statements of scope and policy.

The report is submitted to the journal editor in much the same way that it was submitted informally to the author's colleagues. Since the report is already in machine-readable form, the publication process will be very rapid. The editor of the journal, after a preliminary review, can match the characteristics of the report against an electronic index of available referees to find not only those referees that are best-suited to review the work, but those that are likely to have the time to allow the review process to be completed rapidly. All communication among editor, author, and referees will be handled through electronic mail, and the whole process of acceptance, modification, or rejection can be expedited.

It can be seen that the formal electronic publication may closely resemble formal publication in print on paper. For example, electronic journals may very well be issued by professional societies and commercial publishers and have editors, editorial boards, policies and standards for acceptance of contributions, and some form of refereeing. Acceptance of a contribution by an electronic journal, however, means that the contribution will be added to a particular data base rather than collected with other contributions and put out as a regular issue of a paper journal. Electronic journals need not be published at regular intervals, since contributions can be added to the data base as soon as accepted.

The refereeing will also resemble present procedures in that a paper will either be accepted by a particular journal or it will not, but certain aspects of the process may differ, as Roistacher (1978a) has suggested. At present, the acceptance or rejection of a paper is a binary decision, and not all papers are rejected only on the basis of quality. In Roistacher's view, acceptance criteria for the electronic journal could be less stringent, and there would be much less reason to reject a paper because of space restrictions. Each paper submitted to an electronic journal could carry a numerical score reflecting the referees' judgment of its quality. If an author wishes a low-score paper to be accepted, it could be. It might, however, go into a second-level data base, so it would have some stigma associated with it. In any event, it would carry the score assigned by the referees. Roistacher points out that a form of "public refereeing" would also be possible. Readers of a report could put their own assessments of its quality into an on-line comments file that would be linked to the file of journal text so that future readers could read report and comments together. Readers might give the report their own numerical score (on the same scale used by the referees), which would also be carried by the journal. Thus, the electronic journal would provide a mechanism through which an author, slighted by his referees, could be vindicated by his peers.

Whatever form the refereeing takes, the author's report will be considered published when it has been accepted into a data base. It seems reasonable to suppose that an electronic journal data base will resemble a print-on-paper journal data base, inasmuch as it will have a title, editor, and defined scope. Thus, one can visualize a *Journal of Applied Physics* data base, a *Transplantation* data base, and so on.

Other aspects of the electronic journal are less clear at this point, including the form in which the journal is made accessible and the way in which it is paid for. Presumably the text of each electronic journal will be accessible on-line. Each contribution will carry a unique identifying number so that a specific item can be requested in order to be viewed at the user's terminal. This is a simple document-delivery service that would presumably replace many user visits to libraries, as well as much of the present interlibrary loan/photocopying traffic. Users could also browse the contents pages of stored journals and, possibly, files of author-supplied abstracts. They could search journal files by subject terms (assigned by authors or editors) and/or keywords in titles or abstracts. In this on-line mode, the user would pay according to the volume and type of his use; browsing of contents pages, for example, may be charged at a lower rate than a request for delivery of full text.

There is no reason to suppose that the journal publisher will provide on-line access and associated services. Indeed, it is much more likely that the pattern of distribution and use of electronic journals will be similar to the present pattern of distribution and use of secondary data bases: The publisher creates the data base and then makes it available for exploitation by on-line service centers, with these service centers returning royalty income to the publisher.

The publication of journals in electronic form should allow much more efficient access to information than is currently the case. Now the typical scientist may subscribe to one or two journals and perhaps regularly scan a handful of others provided by his colleagues or by a library. This is inefficient because, while many of the articles in the journals he subscribes to and in the additional ones he scans may not be directly relevant to his interests, many other articles of direct relevance may be published in journals he never sees. If he uses *Current Contents* (published by the Institute for Scientific Information), he will be able to keep up with the contents of a wide selection of additional journals. Otherwise, he will have to rely on the scanning of printed indexes or abstracting publications or, better, on some form of Selective Dissemination of Information (SDI) service based on one of these secondary data bases. The disadvantage of this is that the secondary publications tend to lag many months behind the primary literature.

With electronic publication, the possibility exists for some form of SDI service provided directly from the primary literature, without the delays associated with SDI based on secondary data bases. Instead of subscribing to two or three journals, the scientist would subscribe to an SDI service whereby his interest profile is matched against keywords in titles and abstracts of communications recently added to a large selection of journal data bases in electronic form. After logging on to some system, and asking for the SDI mode, the scientist would view titles of all communications identified as matching his profile since the last time he used the SDI facilities. Having selected a relevant title, he could ask for an abstract and/or the full text to be displayed. He would also be able to record his reactions to the article in a public comments file, thus giving subsequent readers the benefit of his own assessment.

Although the distribution of journal data bases for electronic access on demand, coupled with some form of SDI service, seems to be the most attractive solution to the information dissemination problem, it is not the only method. Alternative or complementary methods include the distribution of journals as tape cassettes, for use with home computers, as videodisks, or in some other electronic form that has not yet been invented. It is quite possible that some electronic journals not only will be *accessible* on-line, but will be *distributed* as well.

The scenario presented here raises a very important question: "Will secondary publications—indexing and abstracting services—be needed in the electronic publication era?" If on-line services can provide efficient SDI and retrospective access to primary literature directly, the secondary services, at least in their present form, could eventually become redundant. If this does happen, the present publishers of secondary services might instead provide SDI and retrospective search facilities based on the primary literature in those subject areas that they now index and abstract. In this case, these organizations would become the on-line service centers of the electronic publication age. This is dealt with further in Chapter 11.

There is another possibility. The "control" of the primary literature in any subject field could be handled through an on-line "cooperative" network of information centers in much the same way that OCLC provides a cooperative approach to on-line cataloging. Some professional organization might provide a "core" data base (indexing and abstracting the primary literature) in some subject area, in the way that the Library of Congress Machine Readable Cataloging (MARC) tapes form the core of the activities of OCLC. Various participating information centers would add to this core those additional publications within the scope of the data base that come to their attention. Perhaps this type of activity will be needed even in the electronic age, because there seem to be definite advantages in forming a data base that is comprehensive in its coverage of relevant publications in all forms — journal articles, technical reports, patents, standards, laws and regulations, and so on.

Returning to Figure 8, it is easy to see that the hypothetical scientist in this scenario will use his on-line terminal for many purposes. He will use it as an electronic notebook, diary, and calendar; compose his reports on it; transmit and receive reports and personal mail; confer with his peers; receive SDI notices; build personal electronic information files (replacing his present paper-copy files); search his own files and those of his employer; search a wide range of external data bases and data banks; request and receive the full text of publications (not only journal articles, but patents, technical reports, standards, specifications, laws, and other text items); and communicate with information specialists.

In this electronic environment, it is assumed that the scientist will do most of his own searching for information. On-line referral data bases will be available to help him decide on the most appropriate data bases or data banks. On some occasions, however (e.g., if he were faced with the need to search an unfamiliar data base or to conduct a search in a subject area tangential to his own field of specialization), he may prefer to delegate a search to an information specialist. The information specialist he contacts (there will be on-line directories to help him in this choice, too) will probably provide some form of information analysis service. The specialist will interact on-line with the scientist to discover his true needs and will then select and search the appropriate sources, evaluate and edit the results, and finally submit the evaluated results for on-line access by his customer.

The paperless communication system described is more than just technologically feasible — virtually everything alluded to is already happening in one form or another. True, these activities have not been blended into a single processing system, but already there are signs that some of the technologies are merging. This could lead to the eventual realization of a paperless system resembling the form described.

There is no question in my mind that the next few years will see a rapid and inevitable move away from print on paper toward paperless human communication. It is my belief that the paperless system described could materialize by the year 2000, less than 20 years from now.

6 Libraries and Technology

The information presented in the preceding chapters, and especially the scenario in Chapter 5, could have profound implications for the library profession. Before focusing on the impact of electronic communication on libraries and librarians, it is necessary to consider the role of libraries in the communication process and the effects of technology as it has been applied to libraries in the past 20 years.

The principal means by which information is transferred within social structures are shown as a "cycle" in Figure 11. The "user community" is composed of individuals working in a particular subject area. Some of these persons will be involved in research and development activities and some in a variety of other activities that are loosely referred to as "application" activities. All are users of information, and some will also be creators of information products. This means that certain people, whose activities are presumed to be of interest to others in the community, will describe their work in reports of some kind. This is the role of the author in the communication cycle. There tends to be a fairly strong correlation between authorship and the type of activity in which an individual is engaged. Those involved in research and development are expected to report the results of their work and, in general, are more likely to have something of interest to report than those engaged in other pursuits. But not all authorship is born of research. Some writings, for example, record the opinions of the authors. Others record the results of practical experience. Yet others simply entertain.

Authorship in itself is not a form of communication. The work of an author has little or no impact on the professional community until it has been reproduced in multiple copies and distributed in a formal

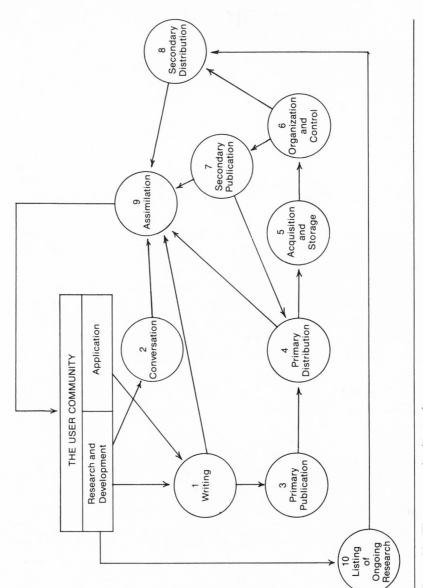

Figure 11 The communication cycle.

manner (i.e., published). This is the role of the primary publisher. The primary publication in this communication cycle reports original work or thought. In science, the journal is usually considered to be the major mechanism of formal communication. Primary publications are distributed either directly to the user community through subscription and purchase by individuals or indirectly to the user community through subscription and purchase by libraries and other types of information centers.

Information centers (this term is used generically to include libraries) play an important role in the information transfer cycle. Through their acquisition and storage policies, libraries provide a permanent archive of professional achievement and a guaranteed source of access to this record. In addition, they organize and control the literature by cataloging, classifying, and indexing it. Indexing and abstracting services and the publishers of national bibliographies also play important roles in organization and control of information. They are responsible for the publication and distribution of *secondary publications*, services that provide a guide to and synopsis of the primary literature. A major publication of this kind is *Chemical Abstracts*, which indexes and abstracts the world's literature of interest to chemists. *Psychological Abstracts, Resources in Education,* and *Library and Information Science Abstracts*, to name only three of several thousand, fulfill similar functions for their respective fields. Some secondary publications may go directly to the user community; most, however, go to institutional subscribers (e.g., information centers).

Information centers also have "presentation and dissemination" functions in the communication cycle. These constitute a form of secondary distribution of publications and information on publications and include circulation of materials as well as various types of current-awareness, reference, and literature-searching services.

The final stage in the cycle is assimilation. This, the least tangible, is the stage at which information is absorbed by the user community. Here a distinction is made between *document* transfer and *information* transfer. The latter occurs only if a document is studied by a user and its contents are assimilated to the point that the reader is informed by it (i.e., his state of knowledge on its subject matter is altered). Assimilation of information by the professional community may occur through primary or secondary distribution. Different documents will have different levels and speeds of assimilation associated with them, and some may never be assimilated at all because they are never used. One measure of assimilation is the extent to which a publication is cited by later writers.

The processes of formal communication are presented as a cycle because they are continuous and regenerative. Through the process of assimilation, readers may gain information that they can use in their own research and development activities. These activities, in turn, generate new writing and publication, and so the cycle continues.

The importance of this communication cycle cannot be overemphasized. Economic, social, and industrial progress all depend on discovery and invention. These, in turn, rely heavily on the ability of the research community to assimilate the results of previous research, since in modern research, progress is made through group endeavor and gradual accretion, with one group building on the work of another. But the results and interpretation of completed research can only be assimilated if they are properly reported and efficiently disseminated. Authors, publishers, librarians, information scientists, indexers, abstractors, and many other individuals play important roles in this communication cycle. A breakdown in the cycle could have very serious consequences, because science would stagnate if achievements were no longer reported, disseminated, and assimilated.

Figure 11 is oversimplified in one important respect: It gives some detail on the dissemination of information through formal channels but little on the processes of informal communication. Much informal communication occurs through the conversation channel. Generally the informal and formal channels disseminate similar information (i.e., the results of the same research and experience). The informal channels, however, disseminate information in a different format than the formal channels, and do so much more rapidly. Also, they disseminate information to those individuals who, for one reason or another, choose not to use the formal channels.

Clearly, libraries play a very important role in the process of formal communication. Their major responsibilities are the collection, organization, and control of information sources, and the provision of various types of services based on these sources. These services are the secondary distribution functions of the information transfer cycle (versus the primary distribution functions, which are mostly performed by the primary and secondary publishers). To begin with, libraries perform an important archival function. They acquire and maintain a permanent record of human achievement as reflected in books, periodicals, and other types of documents. In the United States, this role is primarily assumed by a group of research libraries comprising three national libraries, university libraries, and research libraries maintained by government agencies and private institutions. The other types of libraries—public, college, school, and industrial—are much less concerned with the archival function, except that all may accept some type of archival responsibility regarding materials of local interest. Thus, a public library may collect and preserve local history and biography, and an industrial library may collect and preserve important corporate records.

Of course, modern libraries are no longer purely archival. Indeed, librarians expend much effort trying to dispel the idea that preservation is their major responsibility. Instead, they emphasize their role in providing various types of services to a designated community. Most libraries today are more concerned with information services, in the broadest sense of the term, than with the physical artifacts they collect per se.

The Library as an Interface

The library can be viewed as an interface between a particular community of individuals and the universe of available information sources. The community served is usually defined geographically (as in the case of public libraries) or by institutional affiliation (all employees of a company or the students/staff/faculty of a college). In a few cases (e.g., the national libraries), the community is essentially open-ended. Also open-ended is the universe of information sources, since a modern library will exploit and make available information sources beyond those it owns. As a matter of fact, it is becoming less and less meaningful to distinguish between sources owned and sources not owned, a point that will be covered on pp. 140–150.

A conventional model of the interface role of the library is

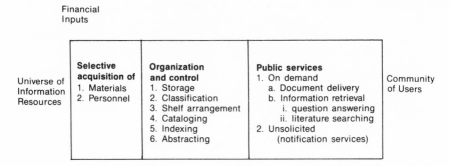

Figure 12   Conventional model of the interface role of the library.

depicted in Figure 12. The library exists to bring together (i.e., interface) the community of users and the universe of information
resources. It is supported through financial inputs, which are used to
acquire materials (mostly printed resources) and the personnel
needed to exploit these resources effectively. Library services represent a marriage of materials and personnel.

Selective acquisition of materials is one of the critical operations
performed by libraries. No library, however large, acquires everything published. In fact, a library will generally acquire only a very
small fraction of the output of the publishing industry. Therefore, it
is very important that each library allocate its limited resources so as
to acquire those materials that have the greatest probability of satis-
fying the needs of its users. This implies the existence of appropriate
selection criteria embedded within a collection development policy.
This, in turn, implies that the librarian must have a good working
knowledge of the characteristics and needs of the people to be served,
as well as of material published.

The problems of selecting material and optimizing allocation of
funds in the acquisition process are becoming increasingly complex
as information resources are issued in a growing variety of forms.
The librarian can no longer restrict attention to print on paper but
must also acquire and make available microforms, phonograph
records, tape cassettes, films, slides, videotapes, and videodisks.
Resources in machine-readable form that, although they are accessible through computer terminals located in the library, may be

physically housed in facilities hundreds or thousands of miles away must also be contended with.

Diversity of format is not the only problem associated with the selection and acquisition of materials in the 1980s. Indeed, libraries now find themselves in a precarious position as the literature store continues to grow, the costs escalate, and library budgets decline in relative purchasing power. For example, the expenditures of an academic library may more than double in a seven-year period. During the same period, the materials expenditures may increase 75 percent (the difference between these increases being largely accounted for by increasing personnel costs), whereas actual growth in items acquired may be as little as 35 percent (the discrepancy between 35 percent and 75 percent being due to the rapidly increasing costs of publications). This situation of burgeoning operating costs, coupled with rapid growth of the literature and a relative decline in purchasing power, had led some to declare that the library as an institution is in a state of crisis.

After selection and acquisition, the next major activity depicted in Figure 12 is the organization and control of materials. A library must make the resources it collects physically and intellectually accessible to the user community. This is accomplished in a number of ways. Books and other materials are classified according to their subject matter and are arranged on library shelves such that resources on the same subject are brought together. Pamphlets and similar materials may also be organized within vertical files in an analogous subject arrangement. The organization of materials according to subject matter provides a measure of intellectual access at the same time that it allows for physical access. Intellectual access also is provided by the library's catalog, which most likely is arranged by author and title as well as by subject. In some libraries, particularly those devoted to restricted subject areas, the staff may go beyond the cataloging of books, periodicals, and other resources as complete entities and prepare detailed indexes of the contents of such materials. In some libraries, too, abstracts summarizing the contents of these resources may be prepared.

Most libraries, however, do not index in detail the materials they acquire. Instead, they purchase printed indexing and abstracting services, or use the on-line equivalents of these, to provide this detailed level of intellectual access. In a sense, the libraries fulfill their organization and control activities in two separate but complementary ways:

1. By purchasing secondary literature (indexing/abstracting services) that provides guides to and synopses of the primary literature
2. By building in-house tools to facilitate access

The organization and control activities of libraries are certainly important, but they are only a means to an end. That end is the provision of various types of services to the community of library users. The organization and control activities of libraries, more specifically, produce various tools to facilitate the offering of public services.* One such tool is shelf organization. Another is the catalog.

Public Services

Services offered to the public may be categorized in a number of different ways. The categorization shown in Figure 12 and expanded upon in Figure 13 is as useful as any. In Figure 13 user services are treated in two alternative ways: In general, libraries provide either documents or information; usually the information provided is also drawn from documents. Thus, library services can be divided broadly into document delivery services and information retrieval services.

The document delivery services provide users with books, periodicals, films, phonograph records, and other materials. Various levels of document delivery can be identified. At one level, a user is provided with the particular item (a "known item") that alone can satisfy his need (i.e., there is no substitute). On other occasions, the library may be called on to supply items of a particular type, such as gothic novels, books on Scandinavian cooking, or reports on the design of earthquake-resistant structures. Some users, particularly those patronizing public libraries, have more general document delivery requirements. They come to the library to find something interesting to

---

* In traditional library terminology, services offered directly to the community are referred to as public services or user services, whereas the behind-the-scenes services of the library are known as technical services.

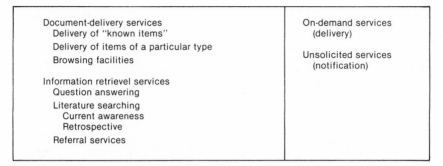

Document-delivery services Delivery of "known items" Delivery of items of a particular type Browsing facilities Information retrievel services Question answering Literature searching Current awareness Retrospective Referral services	On-demand services (delivery) Unsolicited services (notification)

Figure 13 Two alternative categorizations of user services in a library.

read but have very little idea what this something might be. They are browsers, and the library must provide a good selection of materials—possibly with an emphasis on recently published items—for them to browse among.

The information retrieval services of libraries can also be subdivided. There are question-answering services, which provide answers (usually factual) to users' questions. The user is not referred to a book or other document but is given a direct answer to a question. In the public library, much of this question-answering activity is done over the telephone ("telephone reference service"). Since many questions can be answered promptly, the question-answering function of libraries is sometimes referred to as "quick reference."

Literature searching is the other major component of "reference service" in libraries. Here, the end result of a literature search is the delivery of a group of documents (or, more usually, references to or abstracts of these documents) to a user in response to a subject-related request. Although special libraries, especially those in industry, have traditionally provided a high level of literature-searching service to their users, extensive literature searching on behalf of users has been much less common in public and academic libraries. In general, these libraries have not had sufficient personnel to offer such literature-searching activities. Instead, they have made available to users a range of literature-searching tools (i.e., bibliographies and indexing/abstracting services) to help users undertake their own searches, possibly with assistance or instruction from the library staff. When literature searches were undertaken by the libraries themselves, it was usually to produce some form of selective bibliography aimed at a group of potential users. In other words, literature-searching activities in many public and academic libraries were for many years restricted to limited services to groups rather than personalized service to individuals.

This situation has changed rather dramatically in the past decade, since many libraries have adopted services that give them on-line access to a wide range of machine-readable data bases. The rapid growth of these machine-readable files and of on-line access to these resources has greatly expanded and refined the literature-searching capabilities of libraries and allowed even small libraries of very limited resources (e.g., the one-person hospital library) to offer a high level of literature-searching support to their users. This topic will be discussed further on pp. 105–108.

Literature-searching services can be divided into the two categories of "retrospective search" and "current awareness." A retrospective search, as its name implies, is a search of the past literature to identify items that deal with a particular subject. It is performed on demand and frequently deals with a quite specific topic. Most often the person requesting such a search is trying to find information that will assist in some problem-solving or decision-making situation.

Literature searching can also be performed for purposes of "current awareness"; that is, a search can be conducted at regular intervals to identify newly published material useful to particular individuals in keeping them informed of developments in a selected subject area. In its most sophisticated form, a current-awareness service will use a computer to match a statement of a person's interests (user interest profile) against characteristics of items newly added to one or more machine-readable data bases. The output of such a Selective Dissemination of Information (SDI) service is likely to be a printout of citations or abstracts delivered to the participants at regular intervals.

In terms of computer processing, retrospective searching and SDI are identical operations. SDI differs from retrospective searching in two ways. First, it is unsolicited (i.e., once a participant has contracted for service, he can receive regular outputs without making further requests). Second, because it is designed to give "background" information rather than to produce information needed for a specific problem-solving/decision-making situation, it deals more in generalities than in specifics. Thus, for purposes of current awareness, a user may wish to know what is being published on a wide range of family-planning topics. To solve a particular problem, however, that person may request a retrospective search on a very specific topic (e.g., experience with injectable contraceptives in Southeast Asia). In the current-awareness situation, the user may be quite lax in judging relevance; more or less anything on family planning is of interest. In the restrospective search situation, however, the standards are quite different — only items dealing squarely with the use of injectable contraceptives in Southeast Asia are acceptable.

SDI is not the only type of current-awareness service. A library that subscribes to a good selection of periodicals and displays current issues on open-access shelves is providing a current-awareness facility. That same library may issue a "new book list" — another type of current awareness service. Use of a computer to match user interests with documents is the most sophisticated form of such service, for it allows a level of personalization that is difficult to achieve efficiently or economically in any other way.

The other major service identified in Figure 13 is "referral," a term that embraces a wide array of activities. The staff of many public libraries will assist users in choosing a good book to read. This service, sometimes referred to as a "reader's advisory service," is a type of referral; in this case, the user is being referred to a book owned by the library. A more conventional view of referral, however, is an activity that refers a user to an outside source of information. A referral activity answers the question "Where can I go to get information or advice or service on . . .?" Most libraries offer referral services, and many public libraries have established elaborate procedures for identifying sources of information (legal, health care, hobbies, recreation, and so on) in their communities and for referring users to those sources.

Not all the public services offered by libraries are specifically identified in Figure 13. Nevertheless, document delivery and information retrieval activities, using these terms in the broadest possible sense, are the major services provided by libraries. Many "special" services offered by libraries are merely forms of document delivery or information retrieval (e.g., document delivery services to particular categories of users, such as the blind, the socially disadvantaged, or the hospitalized) or public relations/promotional services designed to encourage use of the basic services of document delivery and information retrieval. Thus, activities like storytelling for children and "great books" discussion groups can be viewed as subtle mechanisms for encouraging certain segments of the community to visit the library and make some use of its basic services.

As represented in Figure 13, and implied in the earlier discussion, some of the services offered by libraries are performed only when a user expresses a need. They are "on demand" services. An obvious example is question answering. A library does not normally answer a question until it has been asked. Other services, however, are unsolicited. Unsolicited services are mostly notification services — telling people things whether they specifically ask or not. All current-awareness services, in a sense, can be regarded as unsolicited. A list of new books on gardening, distributed to local gardening clubs, is an unsolicited service that may be provided by a public library. This distinction between on-demand services and unsolicited services leads us naturally into a further discussion on the basic functions performed by libraries. These functions can be related to the ideas of accessibility and exposure.

Accessibility and Exposure

Considering once more the interface role of the library, as depicted in Figure 12, one can identify two major objectives that the library, whatever its type, carries out for the community it serves. On the one hand, its objective is to make the universe of information resources as accessible as possible to the user community. On the other hand, its objective is to expose the user community to those information resources of greatest relevance and utility. These two objectives are not incompatible; they are two sides of the same coin. Making resources accessible implies a relatively passive role. When a user needs a particular document, documents of a certain type, or information on a selected topic, the role of the library is to make this material/information available to the user, whether from its own resources or from external sources. Exposure, on the other hand, implies a service that is more dynamic: The role of the library is to inform users of potentially relevant information without waiting for those users to levy demand on its resources. Providing accessibility and providing exposure are interfacing activities since both bring users and resources together. The only difference is that, for the former, the library waits for the user to take the initiative, whereas, for the latter, the initiative is taken by the library itself.

The idea that the major function of the library is to make accessible those resources of greatest potential value to the user population suggests an alternative and less conventional model of the interface role of the library. In effect, one can consider that the major function of the library is organizing the universe of information resources according to various levels of accessibility, as illustrated in Figure 14. In this model, the complete universe of information resources is accessible to the community served by a particular library. But different elements in this universe are accessible at different levels. In an ideal situation, the materials most likely to be needed are most accessible (physically, intellectually, and psychologically) to the library users. Figure 14 might represent, for example, the differential accessibility provided by an academic library. The most accessible resources are those purchased by the library and placed on open shelves. Slightly less accessible are resources stored in closed-access bookstacks. Less accessible still are resources owned by the library but stored in some off-site storage location. Finally, all resources not owned by the library represent a further level of accessibility. They too are accessible to library users (through photocopy, interlibrary loan, and referral activities), but not as conveniently or rapidly as the resources owned by the library. Note, however, that Figure 14 does not distinguish between things owned and things not owned. It merely depicts things owned as more accessible than things not owned. Accessibility is represented in the diagram as a kind of spectrum of values.

Interestingly enough, the further we move into the electronic age, the less important is the distinction between what is owned and what is not owned (this point will be taken up again in Chapter 9). On the one hand, procedures for referral to external information resources and for acquiring documents not owned have become much more efficient through the use of resource directories and union lists, improved photocopying procedures, and on-line networks as means of identifying who has what and of requesting the supply of documents or information. On the other hand, computer terminals give a library

Other Published Sources

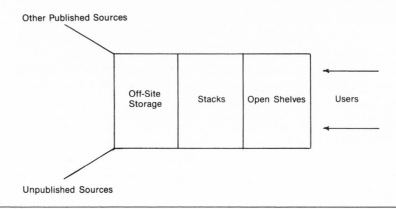

Unpublished Sources

Figure 14 Levels of accessibility of information sources provided by an academic library.

ready access to information resources not located on-site. If an information resource is readily accessible to library users through the medium of on-line technology, it matters little whether it is owned by the library or not.

Interinstitutional Relationships

The information transfer cycle shows that libraries cannot and do not exist in isolation; they interact with other components within the cycle, especially with other libraries. Since no library can afford complete self-sufficiency, great emphasis is placed on cooperation or "resource sharing" among libraries. The most common form of this is interlibrary lending and supply of photocopies. Libraries also cooperate in cataloging, in coordination of acquisitions, and, perhaps, in physical processing of materials.

Publisher-library interactions are also important, since libraries form the largest market for many types of publications and are virtually the only buyers of the major indexing and abstracting services and many of the more expensive science journals. In addition, libraries themselves may be publishers or compilers of publications. In the United States, the three national libraries have extensive publishing programs and are responsible for the production of major bibliographic services, including the *National Union Catalog, Index Medicus,* and the *Bibliography of Agriculture.*

The interactions of the various components of the information transfer cycle can be quite complex, and, unfortunately, conflicts of interest may occur. A notable example is the area of copyright. To provide effective document-delivery services, libraries and other information centers would like a fairly free hand in producing photocopies of selected portions of books, journals, and other publications. The publishers, on the other hand, have their own commercial interests to protect. In their view, library photocopying should be drastically curtailed or, if allowed to continue, should lead to reimbursement at a fair rate to compensate the publisher for possible loss of sales.

A particularly complex interaction now exists between publishers and libraries in the area of costs/pricing. To combat escalating costs of publications, particularly periodicals, libraries are relying more and more on resource sharing. But this creates a vicious circle. Through cooperative acquisition policies, libraries collectively reduce their subscriptions to periodical publications. This, in turn, prompts further price increases as publishers attempt to recover the income lost through declining numbers of subscribers. Moreover, rapid increases in costs of subscriptions to journals have caused drastic reduction in the amount of money available for purchase of monographs and other types of materials, thus putting more pressure on the publishers of these materials and causing further price increases in this sector also.

The rapid growth of machine-readable data bases and of on-line access to these has caused further difficulties in publisher/library interactions. Publishers of indexing/abstracting services in dual mode (print on paper and electronic) are now faced with difficult pricing strategies. How much of the cost of data base production should be charged to print-on-paper subscribers and how much, by way of royalty payments, to the on-line users? There is already evidence that libraries are beginning to cancel some subscriptions to print on paper in favor of on-line access on demand (see Chapter 7). Many of the dual-mode publishers are finding that subscriptions to the printed version are declining and that income from on-line royalties is increasing rapidly relative to income from print-on-paper products. This point, too will be dealt with in more detail in Chapter 11.

The Application of Computers

To date, libraries have been affected by computers and telecommunications in two ways. First, and by far the less important, has been the application of computers to the internal record-keeping activities of libraries (acquisitions, receipt of serials, circulation, and cataloging). The end results of this application are the disappearance of paper records, including card catalogs, and the formation of networks to permit libraries to share and exchange records (cooperative cataloging, interlibrary loan, shared cataloging and circulation records, and so on). In addition to the immediate impacts of computers on libraries—increased productivity, reduced costs, shorter delays, and improved service capabilities—there have been many secondary benefits. The ability to link libraries through telecommunications and to link libraries to computer facilities has greatly increased the opportunities for library cooperation and "networking" and has made possible the use of a single computer for storing and manipulating the records of several institutions. Library automation procedures, because they pave the way for increased levels of cooperation, have also led to greater standardization within the library profession. Finally, automated facilities, if properly designed, can give the library manager evaluation and monitoring data more extensive and refined than ever before.

Despite these advantages, I regard the use of computers for record keeping as the less important application because, while it has undoubtedly improved efficiency, reduced cost, and increased cooperation, it has had no significant impact on the structure of the library or the services it provides. In library automation of this type, the computer merely improves efficiency in handling records for bibliographic materials in print-on-paper form. Handling of the materials themselves is virtually unchanged; there is no fundamental metamorphosis of the library. The effect is cosmetic. To the visitor, an automated library looks only marginally different from the library without automation.

The use of computers and telecommunications to allow libraries to access outside data bases is a much more important and far-reaching application because it not only increases a library's capabilities for literature searching and question answering, but completely changes the economics of access to information. It also completely changes all previous notions of "collections," "libraries," and "librarians."

In Chapter 4, the emergence of machine-readable data bases and data banks was noted. The growth in publicly accessible files of this kind has been nothing less than spectacular, from just one in 1965 (MEDLARS) to several hundred today. The ability to access these resources on-line, a development of only the last decade, has given a highly sophisticated literature-searching capability to libraries of all types and sizes. Small libraries, in particular, have been able to enhance their information services greatly through investing in a terminal and training staff in the techniques of on-line searching. Libraries have not been slow to accept this innovation, as the growth in on-line searches (Figure 15) will confirm. A single on-line terminal can now provide entry to several hundred data bases and data banks, allowing access to several million bibliographic records, and to files rich in numerical and other types of data. New data bases and data banks seem to appear almost daily. This development has not been limited to North America. Western Europe is close behind, and on-line searching is now penetrating rapidly within Central and South America and other parts of the globe.

Lewis (1980) has produced data on the growth of machine-readable information sources. He estimates the existence of 1,400 data bases (bibliographic) and data banks (numerical) in 1980:

	1976	1977	1978	1979	(1980)
Bibliographic files	337	422	533	565	(600)
Numeric data banks	149	368	568	715	(800)
Total	486	790	1101	1280	(1400)

It seems that approximately 600 of these data bases are now accessible on line. Lewis also estimates that around 1.25 million on-line searches were performed in Europe in 1980. By 1985, he projects 15.6

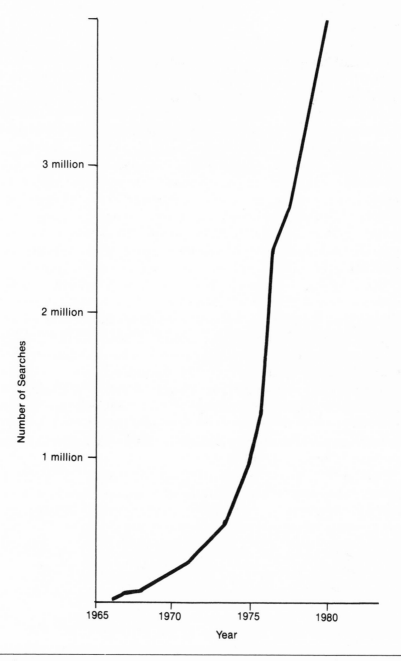

Figure 15 Number of computer-based bibliographic searches performed in the United States, excluding searches in "shared cataloging" data bases. (From data supplied by Martha Williams, Coordinated Sciences Laboratory, University of Illinois.)

million such searches in the United States and 3.9 million in Europe, for a total of almost 20 million searches.

International Data Corporation has predicted that data base access will account for some $1.6 billion in remote service revenues in 1983. The total remote services market is expected to generate $7.6 billion in revenues in 1983.

On-line services have done more than vastly improve the quality of information services. They have had a very profound impact on the economic aspects of these services. Before computers, the only way to make an information source accessible was to buy it. When a library purchases a book or periodical, it does so for one reason only: to make it accessible to library users. This accessibility is achieved through a capital investment in the physical availability of materials on library shelves. Through its acquisitions policy, a library divides the universe of bibliographic resources into those things it adds to its collection and those it does not. In effect, the universe of bibliographic resources has been divided into two levels of accessibility: things immediately accessible and things less accessible. A subscription buys only access. The cost is incurred whether or not the item is ever used. Because of the difficulties of determining need and predicting demand, many items added to large library collections are never used at all. They are in the collection as a kind of insurance; buying them is the only way of making them readily available should they be needed by a library user.

The ability to access a data base on-line changes this. A library need not make a capital investment in an electronic publication to make it accessible. It can be accessed *when needed;* the library pays only for the amount of access used at the time it is used. This has a number of important implications. First, in the print-on-paper world a library can afford access only to those publications whose cost will be offset by a certain level of expected use. But this is untrue of the electronic environment, where all publications are equally accessible. A source needed once every five years is just as accessible as one needed daily and may cost no more to use. In other words, the distinction between what a library owns (i.e., has within its four walls) and does not own begins to break down.

This can be carried further. A library of, say, an industrial organization can provide question-answering and literature-searching services from sources physically present in its collection and from sources that can be remotely accessed. Probably the remote sources are already more important than those physically present. What, then, is the collection of the library? Does it make any sense to say that it includes the physically present sources but excludes those remotely accessed, even though the latter are used more and are more important to the operations of the library? Obviously it does not.

The fact is that, through the capabilities of electronic access, libraries are becoming "disembodied." This process will continue at a greatly accelerated pace as the developments forecast take place (i.e., as print-on-paper publications give way and are eventually completely replaced by electronic publications). A research "library" of the future, then, need not contain any printed materials at all. It could be a room containing only terminals. Apart from archival repositories of printed records of the past and institutions designed primarily to lend inspirational/recreational reading materials, the libraries of today could well disappear.

In the next chapter, evidence is presented of a migration from print-on-paper subscriptions to electronic access on demand. A discussion of the probable long-term impact of this phenomenon on libraries and on librarianship as a profession follows.

7 The Migration from Print on Paper

The impact of on-line searching on subscriptions to printed publications has recently been considered in the professional literature. Barwise (1979), in the most complete analysis conducted to date on the interaction between printed products and on-line data bases and the effect of this interaction on pricing policies, concludes that on-line services have so far had a negligible effect on sales of printed products. On the other hand, he points out that there is great uncertainty about the possible impact during the period 1978–1985. In a survey of the use of five data bases peripheral to medicine, Timour (1979) discovered little evidence of a decline in the use of printed products since on-line access had become available to major biomedical libraries. Indeed, for some data bases, use of the printed product is said to have increased. Timour himself seems to favor cancellation of at least the more expensive printed services:

> But considering subscription prices of $2,565 for *Biological Abstracts* and $3,700 for *Chemical Abstracts,* plus binding costs for each, one can conjecture that a reallocation of these subscription fees would go far in making more on-line searches available and would save a substantial amount of shelf space in the process. (p. 333)*

Pfaffenberger and Echt (1980) analyzed the use of the printed *Science Citation Index* and its machine-readable equivalent, SCISEARCH, in one academic library. They concluded that even with recent royalty increases and the fact that reduced royalty rates apply

---

* Neither price given in this quotation is correct as of 1982. For *Chemical Abstracts*, the price is now substantially higher.

to subscribers to the printed product, the volume of use favored cancellation of the subscription and complete reliance on on-line access for current searches.

Stanley (1979) has reported the results of a questionnaire survey completed by directors of information services in 55 chemical, petroleum, pharmaceutical, and manufacturing companies. Large, medium, and small corporations were all represented. Fifty-two percent of these organizations reported the cancellation of at least one hard copy subscription as a result of the availability of the equivalent* data base on-line. It is noteworthy that virtually no information service that has failed to cancel a subscription is at present giving serious consideration to the cancellation possibility. On the other hand, several of those organizations that have discontinued some printed subscriptions are now considering cancellation of further titles. This suggests the existence of two camps within the information services/library field: those directors who seem quite happy to substitute electronic access for print on paper and those who still look at on-line services as complementing print on paper rather than replacing it. There is also evidence in Stanley's study that the availability of a data base on-line has prevented some organizations from entering a new subscription to the printed equivalent.

The Enoch Pratt Free Library in Baltimore, Maryland, referring to the benefits of on-line searching, notes the money it has saved by no longer subscribing to expensive journals and indexes (such as *Chemical Abstracts*). Andrew and Horsnell (1980) make this related comment about one of the potential benefits of Prestel in the public library:

An indication of the cost of a public library acting as a Prestel user is that, in 1979/80, the London Borough of Waltham Forest's use cost was about £300. However, one vital aspect of libraries' participation in Prestel is that the information on the Prestel database is invariably more up-to-date than that in reference books and even periodicals and newspapers. Having Prestel can therefore enable a number of reference book and periodical orders to be cancelled to make compensatory savings. (p. 424)

---

* Although I have used the term *equivalent*, the machine-readable data base is not always exactly equivalent to its printed counterpart (e.g., it may exclude abstracts or have a slightly different scope).

Other evidence of a migration from print to on-line use has been presented by Trubkin (1980).

Some further evidence of the migration from print to on-line use has been presented by data base producers. Creps (1979), for example, in discussing the *Engineering Index* situation, has reported that revenue from the sale of printed products is still growing, but very slowly, whereas revenue from sales of magnetic tapes is growing "erratically." On-line royalty income, however, is described as "growing rapidly." Use of the on-line data base is now increasing at the rate of 23 percent per year. A similar situation exists with *Chemical Abstracts*. Here, subscriptions to print on paper still account for 80 percent of the revenue. The number of subscribers to the printed service is declining, but revenue from sales is actually increasing approximately 10 percent per year, due to ever-increasing subscription prices (now set at $5,000 per year). Nevertheless, while revenue from print on paper is increasing at 10 percent per year, that from on-line use is growing at 25 percent per year. As of 1979, these on-line revenues amounted to approximately $1.8 million annually.

There is some obvious concern among secondary publishers about declining subscriptions to print on paper. Some are countering by forcing the nonsubscriber to print on paper to pay substantially more for on-line access.

In an effort to cast further light on the impact of on-line services on sales of print on paper, a study was performed by the Library Research Center, Graduate School of Library and Information Science, University of Illinois, during October 1979 to February 1980. Two hundred libraries—50 large university libraries, 50 smaller university libraries, 50 U.S. Government special libraries in science and technology, and 50 private industrial special libraries—selected through random sampling, received a mailed questionnaire that included only four items. It asked each library to indicate which of 36 printed data bases were subscribed to and which of 27 machine-readable data bases (the equivalents of the 36 printed tools), were made use of. It asked which, if any, of the 36 printed tools had been discontinued within the past five years, and whether or not the decision to discontinue had been influenced by the availability of on-line access. It also inquired which printed services other than the 36 listed had been discontinued in the past five years as a result of the availability of the equivalent data base on-line. Finally, it asked each library to indicate if it was considering cancellation of any subscriptions to indexing/abstracting services due to the availability of the data base on-line. Libraries were also invited to comment on the probable transition from print-on-paper to on-line access.

As shown in Table 3, a high rate of return (73 percent) of fully usable questionnaires was achieved. ("Fully usable" here refers to questionnaires from libraries giving all the data requested.) For some of the analyses, however, the base for the data extracted is 164 (all returns) rather than 146 (fully usable). The returns from academic libraries were greater than those from the nonacademic community.

Table 4 shows the percentage of responding libraries in each category claiming to make some use of on-line search services. These figures should be treated with caution in terms of further extrapolation. It would be tempting to conclude that 77 percent of all special libraries in science and technology in the United States are now using on-line services. This may or may not be true. One suspects that the group of nonrespondents may include a higher proportion of libraries that make no use of on-line services. Thus, a value of 77 percent may be somewhat inflated.

Table 3   Response Rates

| | | Returns | | | |
| | | Total | | Usable | |
Type of Library	Number	Number	Percent	Number	Percent
Special libraries in science and technology in the Federal Government	50	41	82	33	66
Nongovernmental special libraries in science and technology	50	34	68	30	60
Research libraries that are members of the Association of Research Libraries (ARL)	50	41	82	39	78
University libraries that are not members of ARL	50	48	96	44	88
Total	200	164	82	146	73

Table 4 Percent of Responding Libraries Making Use of On-line Services

Type of Library	Percent
Special libraries in science and technology in the Federal Government	76
Nongovernmental special libraries in science and technology	77
ARL member libraries	100
University libraries not members of ARL	88
Total	85

A comparison of Table 5 with Table 6 shows some similarity between the data bases most held in printed form and the data bases used on-line by most libraries in this group. It is important to note, however, that the tables do not in any way reflect *volume* of use of the various sources. The ranking merely reflects the number of libraries owning each printed source (Table 5) and claiming to make some on-line use of each data base (Table 6). The discrepancy between the 36 items of Table 5 and the 27 of Table 6 is accounted for by the fact that some of the machine-readable data bases are equivalent to two or more of the printed sources. It is also important to recognize that this study was restricted to major data bases for which the machine-readable versions have more or less direct printed equivalents. Data bases existing in machine-readable form but not in printed form, or vice versa, were excluded from the investigation.

Although the tables show definite similarities, there are some differences. In particular, it is possible to identify certain data bases held by many libraries in printed form but used by few libraries online (the *Congressional Record* is a notable example), as well as some data bases used by many libraries on-line but held in printed form by comparatively few. The Management data base, for example, is used by 81 of the libraries, whereas *Management Contents* is held in printed form by only 20. This phenomenon is shown more clearly in Table 7. Here, each data base included in the study (*A*) is listed with its printed equivalent (*B*). The remaining columns list the number of libraries using the tool on-line only (*C*), the number subscribing to

Table 5   Data Bases Held in Printed Form by Responding Libraries, Ranked by Number of Libraries Holding

Rank	Data Base	Number of Libraries
1	*Chemical Abstracts*	107
2	*Dissertation Abstracts International*	97
3	*Biological Abstracts*	96
4	*Congressional Record*	93
5	*Engineering Index*	86
6	*Pollution Abstracts*	83
7	*Physics Abstracts*	82
8	*Psychological Abstracts*	82
9	*Government Reports Announcements*	81
10	*P.A.I.S. Bulletin*	81
11	*Resources in Education*	77
12	*Science Citation Index*	76
13	*Historical Abstracts*	75
14	*Electrical and Electronics Abstracts*	73
15	*Current Index to Journals in Education*	71
16	*Social Sciences Citation Index*	68
17	*Weekly Government Abstracts*	67
18	*Bio Research Index**	67
19	*Computer and Control Abstracts*	65
20	*Library and Information Science Abstracts*	65
21	*Bibliography and Index of Geology*	63
22	*American Doctoral Dissertations*	60
23	*Bibliography of Agriculture*	55
24	*Environment Abstracts*	53
25	*Metals Abstracts*	53
26	*Foundation Grants Index*	51
27	*Food Science and Technology Abstracts*	45
28	*P.A.I.S. Foreign Language Index*	36
29	*Energy Information Abstracts*	35
30	*World Textile Abstracts*	28
31	*Federal Register Abstracts*	28
32	*Petroleum Abstracts*	21
33	*Alloys Index*	21
34	*Management Contents*	20
35	*World Patent Index*	4
36	*Central Patents Index*	3

*Now *Biological Abstracts/RRM.*

Table 6 Data Bases Used On-line by Responding Libraries,
Ranked by Number of Libraries Using

Rank	Data Base	Number of Libraries
1	National Technical Information Service	112
2	CA Condensates or CA Condensates/CASIA*	102
3	SCISEARCH	97
4	Comprehensive Dissertation Index	96
5	COMPENDEX	95
6	BIOSIS Previews	92
7	ERIC	88
8	INSPEC	87
9	Psychological Abstracts	84
10	Management	81
11	AGRICOLA	80
12	Social SciSearch	76
13	Enviroiine	71
14	P.A.I.S. International	69
15	Pollution	69
16	Energyline	67
17	LISA	67
18	Historical Abstracts	57
19	Foundations Grants Index	56
20	Geo Ref	56
21	METADEX	53
22	FSTA	49
23	FEDREG	40
24	C Record	37
25	World Textiles	34
26	TULSA	25
27	WPI	18

*Now CA Search.

print only (*D*), the number both subscribing to print and using the tool on-line (*E*), and the number doing neither (*F*). *C* plus *E* equals the number of libraries using the data base on-line, whereas *D* plus *E* equals the number subscribing to the print form. The discrepancy between *C* and *D* represents the difference between libraries using a data base in on-line form only and those using it in print form only.

The major purpose of the Library Research Center's study was to determine the extent to which the libraries surveyed have canceled

Table 7 Comparison of On-line Use and Subscriptions to Printed Tools

A Data Base	B Printed Equivalent	C On-line	D Print	E Both	F Neither
AGRICOLA	Bibliography of Agriculture	28	3	52	81
BIOSIS Previews	Biological Abstracts* Bio Research Index†	10	14	82	58
CA Condensates (CHEMCON) or CA Condensates/CASIA‡	Chemical Abstracts	12	17	90	45
Comprehensive Dissertation Index	Dissertation Abstracts International* American Doctoral Dissertations	12	14	84	54
COMPENDEX	Engineering Index	26	17	69	52
C Record	Congressional Record	5	61	32	66
Energyline	Energy Information Abstracts	39	7	28	90
Enviroline	Environment Abstracts	27	9	44	84
ERIC	Resources in Education* Current Index to Journals in Education	15	5	73	71
FEDREG	Federal Register Abstracts	30	18	10	106
Foundation Grants Index	Foundation Grants Index	17	12	39	96
FSTA	Food Science and Technology Abstracts	19	15	30	100
Geo Ref	Bibliography and Index of Geology	8	15	48	93
Historical Abstracts	Historical Abstracts	5	23	52	84

	Electrical and Electronics Abstracts				
	Computer and Control Abstracts				
LISA	Library and Information Science Abstracts	24	22	43	75
Management	Management Contents	64	3	17	80
METADEX	Metals Abstracts*	19	19	34	92
	Alloys Index				
NTIS	Weekly Government Abstracts*	18	18	94	34
	Government Reports Announcements				
P.A.I.s. International	P.A.I.S. Bulletin*	11	23	58	72
	P.A.I.S. Foreign Language Index				
Pollution	Pollution Abstracts	9	23	60	72
Psychological Abstracts	Psychological Abstracts	11	9	73	71
SCISEARCH	Science Citation Index	32	11	65	56
Social SciSearch	Social Sciences Citation Index	16	8	60	80
TULSA	Petroleum Abstracts	15	11	10	128
WPI	Central Patents Index*	14	1	4	145
	World Patent Index				
World Textiles	World Textile Abstracts	15	9	19	121

* In the case of data bases for which there are two or more printed equivalents, columns D and E do not add up to the totals for the printed equivalents given in Table 3. This is because, in this table, columns D and E add up to the number of libraries subscribing to *at least one* of the printed equivalents. In Table 3, on the other hand, subscribers to each printed tool are separately identified.

† Now *Biological Abstracts/RRM*.

‡ Now CA Search.

subscriptions to printed tools within the past five years. These data appear in Table 8. The values should be viewed with caution. First, they reflect cancellations of subscriptions but not necessarily cancellations of all subscriptions in a particular library. Thus, a large academic library may have canceled one subscription to *Chemical Abstracts* but may still hold additional subscriptions. Second, as the footnotes to the table indicate, some cancellations may not be complete. For example, the monthly issues to *Engineering Index* may have been canceled but the annual volume retained (or vice versa). Likewise, certain libraries reported the cancellation of a particular section of *Chemical Abstracts,* but it was not always clear if this was the only section subscribed to. The best that can be said for the data is that, on the surface at least, they indicate a loss of income to the publishers from sales of printed tools, a loss that the publishers themselves recognize and report. Unfortunately, it is not known how many of the responding libraries entered new subscriptions to these titles during the same period. This factor is probably insignificant, but one cannot be absolutely sure.

Another defect of the study is that it did not determine how many subscriptions to each service are held by the responding libraries. Consequently, it is not possible to estimate with certainty the extent to which the cancellations have contributed to loss of income to publishers from this group of libraries. Consider, for example, the *Bio Research Index* (now *Biological Abstracts/RRM*). Table 5 shows that this is currently held by 67 libraries, and Table 8 shows seven cancellations in the past five years. If each of the 67 libraries holds only one subscription to this tool, and if no new subscriptions have been entered by the responding libraries in the past five years, it would be possible to say that, within the group of respondents, subscriptions to *Bio Research Index* have declined almost 10 percent (7/74) in the past five years. Unfortunately, this assumption cannot be made with certainty, but a loss of subscriptions in the range of 5–10 percent is probably realistic for perhaps the first five titles of Table 8. Moreover, this trend is likely to continue, as shown in Table 9, which indicates titles "under consideration" for cancellation among the responding libraries, where this consideration is influenced by the availability of equivalent data bases on-line.

There is another restriction on the data in Table 8. The cancellations reported are cancellations for all types of reasons, not just

Table 8 Titles Discontinued Within Past Five Years by Responding Libraries, Ranked by Number of Cancellations

Rank	Data Base	Number of Cancellations
1	*Engineering Index**	11
2	*Chemical Abstracts* †	9
3	*Bio Research Index* ‡	7
4	*Physics Abstracts*	7
5	*Science Citation Index*	7
6	*Pollution Abstracts*	6
7	*Bibliography of Agriculture*	6
8	*Dissertation Abstracts International* †	5
9	*Metals Abstracts*	5
10	*Biological Abstracts*	4
11	*Weekly Government Abstracts*	4
12	*World Textile Abstracts*	4
13	*Environment Abstracts*	3
14	*Bibliography and Index of Geology*	3
15	*Electrical and Electronics Abstracts*	3
16	*Social Sciences Citation Index*§	3
17	*P.A.I.S. Foreign Language Bulletin*	3
18	*Computer and Control Abstracts*	2
19	*Government Reports Announcements*	2
20	*P.A.I.S. Bulletin*	2
21	*Congressional Record*	1
22	*Resources in Education*	1
23	*Current Index to Journals in Education*	1
24	*Foundation Grants Index*	1
25	*Library and Information Science Abstracts*	1
26	*Alloy Index*	1
	Total	102

* Monthly issues or complete subscription.

† One or more sections canceled.

‡ Now *Biological Abstracts/RRM.*

§ In one case only, a cumulation was canceled.

because of the availability of equivalent data bases on-line. As Table 10 illustrates, less than 10 percent of the 102 cancellations are due solely to availability of on-line access, although more than 40 percent of the cancellations (8.8 percent + 32.4 percent) have been influenced somewhat by the availability of equivalent data bases on-line.

Table 9   Titles Under Consideration for Cancellation by Responding
Libraries Due to Availability On-line

Rank	Data Base	Number of Libraries
1	*Chemical Abstracts*	7
2	*Government Reports Announcements*	4
3	*Engineering Index*	3
4	*Science Citation Index*	3
5	*Electrical and Electronics Abstracts*	2
6	The following titles were each mentioned by a single library: *Biological Abstracts, Dissertation Abstracts International, Environment Abstracts, Index Medicus, Encyclopedia of Associations, Monthly Catalog of U.S. Government Publications, Economics Abstracts International, Commonwealth Agricultural Bureaux Abstracting Services, Excerpta Medica, Food Science and Technology Abstracts, Psychological Abstracts, Physics Abstracts, National Union Catalog, Surface Coatings Abstracts, U.S. Patent Gazette, Pharmaceutical News Index, P.A.I.S. Bulletin, Social Sciences Citation Index,* and *Pollution Abstracts.*	

Of the 102 cancellations reported, approximately 60 percent were canceled by academic libraries. Cancellations by groups of libraries are as follows: 23 in special libraries within the Federal Government, 18 within nongovernment special libraries, 31 among Association of Research Libraries (ARL) members, and 30 in university libraries that are not members of ARL.

Libraries were also asked to identify printed data bases, other than those listed, that have been discontinued in the past five years, where the decision to discontinue was at least influenced by accessibility online. Twelve further titles were mentioned. Of these, only *Excerpta Medica* was mentioned by more than a single library. *Excerpta Medica* subscriptions have been canceled by three of the responding libraries in the past five years.

What do these data mean? Clearly, subscriptions to many secondary services in printed form are declining. But the reason for this

Table 10 Reasons for Cancellation of 102 Subscriptions

	Number	*Percent*
Solely influenced by availability on-line	9	8.8
Partially influenced by availability on-line	33	32.4
Not influenced by availability on-line	60	58.8

phenomenon is only partly attributable to the availability of these tools on-line. More important is the fact that subscription costs are increasing while the relative purchasing power of many library budgets is declining. The data do, in fact, suggest that on-line services have so far had rather little direct effect on subscriptions to printed services. Whether or not this effect can be termed "negligible," however, is a matter of personal interpretation.

The comments of the respondents suggest that there is a "hidden" effect of on-line services on sales of printed products, an effect that is not clearly demonstrated in the data: Although some libraries are reluctant to discontinue a printed tool that may have been subscribed to for many years, on-line services are to some degree preventing certain institutions from entering *new* subscriptions to services in print-on-paper form. This is particularly true of libraries that have emerged in the "on-line age." As one government respondent points out, "Because our library is relatively new and specialized, it is not a matter of discontinuing subscriptions, but rather of not subscribing initially." Another respondent, the librarian of a small special library in an academic environment, was even stronger on this point: "We simply never ordered them in the first place. Our library is only 4 years old and the availability of on-line services has made us want *all* of them! For us, print subscriptions are obsolete." This particular library holds only 1 of the 36 print services listed on the questionnaire and is considering discontinuing it. An almost identical situation was reported by another library subscribing to only one of the printed tools: "Our library is three years old. On-line indexes have been utilized from the very beginning." Another pertinent comment from an industrial library suggests that some libraries are just now beginning to question their policies regarding the printed tools: "We went on-line in 1974. It took us until 1979 to begin to question our rationale for continuing the published editions. This may be the last year we buy them (1980)."

Within the academic environment, it seems that there are two major barriers to the substitution of on-line access for printed forms. The first is the fact that libraries are unable or unwilling to absorb the full cost of on-line searching. The second is that present on-line services seem generally to be regarded as unsuitable for unmediated use. The following quotations echo the views of several of the academic respondents:

We expect to continue our subscriptions to the printed versions until on-line access is possible without a librarian as intermediary.

We would cancel printed versions of some files only if the library could absorb the cost of all needed computer searches, which we cannot afford at this time.

I don't think that's likely to happen in a university environment until on-line access is demonstrably cost effective compared to subscription in "real dollar" terms and on-line searching systems become simple enough for end users to conduct their own searches.

Since we currently must charge for computerized searches, the cancellation of a printed index in favor of an on-line data base would work a hardship for those unwilling or unable to pay. We would take this step only if the library found it economically feasible to absorb all costs.

Should our users ever become proficient at searching on-line bases themselves — perhaps it will happen more quickly than we imagine after experience with an on-line catalog — we would cease subscribing to a variety of A/I services.

It is clear that the future attitude of librarians on this important matter is also going to be affected by the rising costs of printed subscriptions relative to the rising costs of on-line services.

If the publishers of the paper indexes keep raising prices 20%–25% per year, it's a cinch we will start dropping the lesser used paper subscriptions and absorb the costs of connect and staff time to search on-line free for users on demand.

From all this, it seems reasonable to conclude that the availability of on-line access has so far had a minor effect on the cancellation by libraries of print-on-paper subscriptions. Nevertheless, there is evidence to suggest that increasing numbers of libraries are now beginning to question their policies concerning subscription to print versus on-line access and that cancellations may occur at an accelerated pace in the future. Moreover, loss of subscription income to publishers as a direct result of on-line access exceeds loss due to cancellations alone, since the availability of a data base on-line may prevent the initiation of new subscriptions by certain information services.

The transition from print-on-paper to electronic access in information services may proceed through three recognizable, though overlapping, phases:

1. Existing libraries adopting on-line use of data bases not held in printed form, or not available in printed form
2. New libraries/information centers adopting on-line access in lieu of subscribing to print versions of well-established publications; some existing libraries preferring on-line access to *new* publications where such publications are also issued as print on paper
3. Existing libraries discontinuing printed subscriptions in favor of on-line access

The first two phases have already been reached. The third phase is just beginning, but it is entirely possible that a substantial move into this phase will occur within the next decade. The process of conversion from print to electronics will be accelerated by the simplification of search procedures to reduce the need for intermediaries, the increasing availability of terminals to provide ready access to on-line services, and the changing attitudes among librarians regarding the proportion of their budgets to be allocated to print-on-paper access versus the proportion to be allocated to on-line access.

8 The Future of the Library: Some Forecasts

Since the beginning of the century, numerous predictions have been made about the future of the library. Many of these have been reviewed by Lancaster et al. (1980), so little detail is given here. Nevertheless, some indication of the scope of the literature may be a useful background for the forecast and discussion to follow in Chapter 9.

The task of categorizing earlier studies is not an easy one, particularly since forecasts relating to the library cannot be completely divorced from those concerning broader aspects of human communication. The forecasts range from the conservative (the library of the future looks only cosmetically different from that of today) to the revolutionary (libraries as we now know them essentially disappear), along the following scale:

1. Libraries provide much the same type of service that they do today. Their internal functioning, however, is greatly improved through technology, such as microform storage and the application of computers, and they deal with an ever-increasing diversity of materials.

2. Networking activities, facilitated by computers and telecommunications, improve the effectiveness and cost-effectiveness of library service in general and make every library a point of efficient access to a vast national library resource.

3. Libraries reduce or even eliminate dependence on print on paper and deal primarily with resources in machine-readable form.

4. The need to visit libraries declines as technology permits libraries to deliver services directly to offices and homes.

5. Local libraries decline substantially in importance, or even disappear, as individuals can access information resources directly through telecommunications, regardless of where these resources happen to be. Individuals can build and store their own personal information files in electronic form.

6. Individuals become members of on-line "intellectual communities." The distinction between formal and informal communication tends to blur, since on-line networks provide access to individuals (electronic mail, computer conferencing), as well as to a wide variety of information sources in textual and other forms.

7. New information service capabilities emerge, including the ability to query data banks that will answer questions directly (rather than referring the user to another source) or even deduce answers to questions.

Automation of Technical Processing

Although the above list is merely a categorization of the major thrusts of many earlier forecasts, it could actually represent an evolutionary sequence of developments. We are already squarely into the first two phases, and it is not necessary to elaborate further on these except to point out that current automation activities still seem to be constrained by what has been done in the past. Take, for example, the on-line catalog. Conceptually, present on-line catalogs are little more than card catalogs made accessible electronically. In fact, they are usually derived from the conversion of an existing card catalog. True, they may offer more flexible searching capabilities, but they generally store no more information about an item than does the card catalog (and maybe even less) and are still seen as providing access in essentially linear form, necessitating the continuance of cataloging codes that may be quite obsolete in an electronic environment. A true on-line catalog could be quite different. In the case of monographs, for example, what might be stored is a machine-readable representation of the title page (front and back) and table of contents. Cataloging, in this case, would consist of recording these data in machine-readable form via an optical character reader.

Perhaps the most sophisticated view of phases one and two of this evolution, in which computers are merely used to process records representing documents that remain as print on paper or microform, belongs to Salton (1977). An essential feature of Salton's "dynamic library" is a type of automatic classification that is adaptable to changing interests and patterns of use among the community to be served. The dynamic library would allow users to query on-line catalogs in plain English; the machine-readable records could, over time, be reclassified to accommodate new associations implicit in uses actually made of these files; and automatic retirement procedures, based on usage factors, could be implemented.

Migration to Electronic Access

As discussed previously, an early stage of the third phase has already been reached. For many libraries, electronic access to machine-readable resources is currently more important than subscriptions to printed tools in literature-searching activities, although such resources have so far had much less impact on question-answering and document-delivery services. A greater impact has been predicted, however. For example, Overhage and Harmon (1967) have said that "libraries will consist of millions of computer words, not millions of documents," and Bolt, Beranek and Newman, Inc. (1964), have suggested that

The library will promote an active partnership between its documents and the user. In place of the passive printed page, remote stations will enable its user to call forth, examine, and intercompare many small pieces of text, no matter where originally they may have resided in any of millions of documents. (p. 10)

Overhage and Harmon also predict that print-on-paper information from the past will be translated on demand into machine-readable form. Saunderson (1977) envisions the complete disappearance of print on paper. The text of any document will be stored in a form suitable for transmission over some telecommunications network:

New knowledge will be recorded only in machine-readable form. If such are still in existence, word processors will be used to generate the input either on a magnetic tape cassette, key it directly into a computer or prepare it for OCR processing. However, it is more possible that the author will either dictate it to a peripheral for voice recognition processing or his manuscript will be fed into a handwriting recognition device. Elements other than text will be input by CIM [computer input microfilm] routine, plotters, or their successors. (p. 87)

Cuadra (1972) suggests that part of the library's holdings will consist of digital and analog data bases, including such things as census data, and that the library will provide new information media, such as holograms and video cassettes, before these things become cheap enough for sale to a mass audience. Scarfe (1975), discussing the future of libraries within commerce and industry, has referred to "the decisive move away from the printed document as a source of data or information towards less easily conceptualized sources embodied in the *data banks* or *management information systems*" (p. 87).

Burchinal (1977), too, mentions a "substitution of non-print forms of distribution for our present paper-oriented system"; the full text of articles will be available on-line, from remote sources, through a variety of technologies.

Home Delivery of Library Service

Libraries also seem to be moving into the fourth phase listed: delivery of library service directly to homes and offices. Of course, books-by-mail programs (Kim and Sexton [1973] and Jordan [1970]) and the delivery of printed materials to faculty offices (Dougherty [1973]) have been around for some time. Increasingly, however, technological achievements permit more direct forms of service delivery. Library catalogs can already be searched in the home (e.g., the OCLC Home Delivery of Library Service Program) or in the office, and terminals can be used to place orders for materials to be supplied by libraries, booksellers, or other agencies. As more complete text becomes accessible in digital form, delivery of various kinds of materials can be made directly to domestic television receivers or other terminals. In fact, some libraries have already used cable television facilities as a means of transmitting pages to the home (e.g., Dowlin [1970]).

More extensive home-delivery capabilities have been forecast by a number of writers. The System Development Corporation, in an appendix to Knight and Nourse (1969), refers to dial-up reference service and the use of slow-scan television to deliver from libraries to homes. The American Library Association (1963) offers a scenario that includes home libraries linked to external institutional libraries or other resources:

The home library will contain a wall-hung television display of the reflective or electroluminescent type, which may be used both for "live" entertainment and information as cathode ray tube displays are used now. In addition, other sub-systems, such as tape recorders, audio equipment, etc., will be available in somewhat the same setting as in today's high-fidelity audiovisual grouping.

An additional unit might be a high-speed printer incorporating a fiber-optics faceplate cathode ray tube for direct electrostatic contact printing. . . . (p. 41)

Overhage and Harmon (1965), referring to the work of Project IN-TREX, point out that visits to the library may be circumvented for faculty and students in a university setting. Materials would be delivered directly to the users, some by CRT or hard copy printers. Each faculty member would have a console, and further consoles would be widely available for student use. Communication with library resources would be one component of a broader university-wide intelligence system:

Students and scholars will use the system not only to locate books and documents in the library, but also to gain access to the university's total information resources, through Touch Tone telephones, teletypewriter keyboards, television-like displays, and quickly made copies. The users of the network will communicate with each other as well as with the library, data just obtained in the laboratory and comments made by observers will be as easily available as the text of books in the library or documents in departmental files. (p. 1)

Some form of home delivery of library service has also been mentioned by Platt (1966), Smith (1978), and Cuadra (1972), among others. Smith suggests that the ability to deliver text and pictures to the home may increasingly blur distinctions between library services and other types of information services:

Like many of the other possible technological innovations for the library, video systems do much more than displace a traditional library function; they also could fulfill some objectives of the newspaper and show why it may become progressively more difficult to separate library functions from other mass communication services in the future. (p. 89)

Cuadra predicts that the ability of users to access library resources from the home will affect the image of the library in a positive way.

Bypassing the Library

The ability to access information resources from privately owned terminals suggests that the local libraries of today could be bypassed. Instead, individuals could go directly to data banks maintained by publishers or by some form of national information center (perhaps a national library). This capability is implicit in the fifth category of forecast.

In its most ambitious form, this type of prediction is concerned with a single encyclopedic data base or with a network of resources that collectively form such a source. The encyclopedic approach, as best exemplified in Wells' (1938) World Brain, has the ultimate objective of making *all* information in *all* forms accessible to *all* persons in *all* locations. Wells saw his World Brain as

A double-faced organization, a perpetual digest and conference on the one hand and a system of publication and distribution on the other. It would be a clearinghouse for universities and research institutions; it would play the role of the cerebral cortex to these essential ganglia. (pp. 70–71)

Wells also advanced a conceptually "modern" view of the physical nature of a library-like institution. In his view, the World Brain–World Encyclopedia was not to be a static institution, not

. . . a row of volumes printed and published once and for all, but . . . a sort of mental clearinghouse for the mind, a depot where knowledge and ideas are received, sorted, summarized, digested, clarified, and compared. It would be in continual correspondence with every university, every research institution, every competent discussion, every survey, every statistical bureau in the world. (p. 69)

The World Brain need not be located in a single place or center: "It might have the form of a network . . . it would centralize mentally but perhaps not physically" (p. 70).

A somewhat similar picture of a single, comprehensive source was painted by Von Foerster (1972):

With computer terminals at all universities, medical centers, industrial research laboratories, etc., being connected with a centrally located full-fledged cognitive memory, no books and no survey articles will have to be written. The original findings and the arguments that led to them can be entered directly into the cognitive memory system's data base, and are available in any connection and relation to other findings to a user who wishes to explore such connections and relations without being frustrated by the needs of crossing the boundaries of disciplines, journals, books, and departments. (p. 27)

Davis (1965) also looked forward to the emergence of some type of universal brain in the form of "one big library" or "one great journal," while De Grazia (1965) proposed a world reference system for the social sciences and Churchman (1965) a world center indexing ongoing research projects to avoid needless duplication of effort.

The idea of a single automated reference library was put forward by Kemeny et al. (1962). His national research library, from which any desired item could be obtained easily, inexpensively, and within a matter of minutes, could house 300 million volumes. Pages would be photographically transmitted (he visualized ultramicrofiche storage) primarily by television or microwave to a device in the home that Kemeny saw as something "like a Xerox machine." Bolt, Beranek and Newman, Inc. (1964) also presented a plan for an automated library holding a substantial portion of the world's literature.

Direct access to extensive networks of information was predicted by Licklider (1965) and Schlesinger (1967). Licklider urged the rejection of the "scheme of the physical library — the arrangement of shelves, card indexes, and check-out desks" and the replacement of these by "procognitive systems":

By the year 2000, information and knowledge may be as important as mobility. We are assuming that the average man of that year may make a capital investment in an "intermedium" or console — his intellectual Ford or Cadillac — comparable to the investment he now makes in an automobile, or that he will rent one from a public utility that handles information processing as Consolidated Edison handles electric power. (p. 33)

Licklider imagined that this would completely change the desk from a passive piece of furniture to an active and essential tool: ". . . a desk may be primarily a display-and-control station in a telecommunications-telecomputation system — and its most vital part may be the cable (umbilical cord) that connects it, via a wall socket, into the *procognitive utility net*" (p. 33). Schlesinger presents a somewhat similar view:

. . . a system of information retrieval operated by a keyboard (the more poetic engineers speak of "remote interrogation consoles") at the scholar's desk. The written text as such will play a waning role. Instead, bibliographic technicians will have already broken the book down into fragments suitable for storage in giant computers and for transmission through a variety of audio-visual systems. (p. 121)

The capabilities of microphotography, electronics, or a combination of these technologies have led others to suggest the existence of vast, individually tailored, personal libraries that, in effect, permit any individual to own anything he might need. Hays et al. (1968), for example, went so far as to suggest that ultramicroforms could allow such a great reduction in both volume and unit cost that all books could eventually be given away free.

The most-cited view of the "personal library approach" comes from Bush (1945, 1967). Bush's Memex was seen as a personal device for the efficient retrieval of information, structured as closely as possible to conform to human cognitive processes. Originally conceived of as based on microphotography, Memex could house a million volumes in a desk complete with screens, keyboards, levers, and buttons. It would allow an individual to store "all his books, records, and communications" on microfilm and to have access to all the records of "mankind since the invention of moveable type." Memex was more than just a storage device; it was seen as a type of associative processor that would permit the user to index and link stored items by a personal scheme of "associative trails." Whenever a user selected any item from this personal store, Memex would automatically and immediately link together all other items of potential interest.

The decline in importance of the librarian, or other information specialist, as an intermediary between those seeking information and the stored resources is implicit in many of these views of direct user access to sophisticated information sources. Schiller (1977), however, has referred to "librarians subsidizing their own demise." She suggests that the future of the librarian, if any, lies outside the library:

Ultimately, the signs point to a technology offering search capability at home or office terminals without the aid of librarian intermediaries who perform the searches. But libraries are now serving to lay the groundwork for future use on an expanded scale outside their own institutional setting. (pp. 33–34)

On-line Intellectual Communities

The sixth type of forecast deals with some form of integrated electronic communication system incorporating formal and informal elements: on-line composition, electronic mail, computer conferencing, electronic publishing, personal electronic files, and on-line access to remote information resources, among others. In fact, this particular forecast calls to mind the scenario in Chapter 5. A basic element in many of these forecasts is some form of "on-line intellectual community," a kind of network of electronic invisible colleges.

Turoff (1977) foresees a communication network in which abstracting services, journal and book publication, computer conferencing, and information retrieval facilities evolve into a single system. This idea of a completely automated communication system, essentially paperless, has been covered by Turoff and Featheringham (1979), Kochen (1978), and Roistacher (1978b).

The disappearance of the librarian, or even of the library as an institution, is not necessarily a *sine qua non* of this group of forecasts. Roistacher predicts that librarians "will form their own network-based groups," Kochen foresees an essential role for information specialists, and Turoff and Featheringham see the library as playing a central role in the "information society." These particular viewpoints will be discussed in more detail in Chapter 9.

The National Enquiry (1979), although it seems to accept the inevitability of a future electronic system, presents a more conservative scenario. The "humanistic scholar" will still have pens, pencils, paper, and a typewriter, although the typewriter will be part of a computer terminal. His work will be stored in a computer memory. Revisions will be made by simple instructions from the scholar to the computer terminal. When a problem arises, the scholar can, through the typewriter, ask the computer for a bibliography, which would be printed or displayed on a screen. The scholar would then select an item from the bibliography and summon the national network, which would likely display the requested pages. Or he could telephone the university library for a photocopy or a microfiche. He could go to the library or browse among the books (there will still be books) or microfiche (with greatly improved readers). In conclusion, the National Enquiry believes that the library will have assumed a major function as a link between scholars on the campus and a national or international network of information centers.

New Capabilities

Finally, many forecasts discuss the enhanced information-processing capabilities that on-line networks could provide. One recurrent theme is the evolution from present information-retrieval systems, which indicate a possible source of an answer to a user's question, to more advanced systems that may directly answer such questions.

Wilson (1978), for example, describes the need as follows:

> An ideal retrieval system would provide information, not an unsorted mixture of information and misinformation; more carefully, it would provide content of high epistemic standing, not content of unknown epistemic standing. . . . And, an ideal system would accept as inquiries, not bare descriptions of the content of documents, but descriptions of our problems and our goals, and would supply information useful for solving problems and attaining goals. (p. 23)

Von Foerster (1972) suggests that users of information systems will increasingly shift from asking "*Where* is the answer?" to "*What* is the answer?"

> This means . . . that the users of a future library system will not care for having access to some documents that may or may not contain the answers to their questions, but will request to have direct access to the *semantic content* of these documents, and will not care whether the answer given by this system is a verbatim citation from a particular document, or if it is an equivalent paraphrase. The user wants to know the facts and does not care how they are described as long as the reply is correct and meets his needs. (pp. 4–5)

Bolt, Beranek and Newman, Inc. (1964), however, go beyond this:

> The library of the future will *deduce* answers to questions, not only find answers already stored in the memory. Accepting questions and giving answers in "natural, written English," the library will draw upon deductive principles and associative techniques for organizing information. Also, the library will have checked each new piece of information received, to see whether that piece substantiates, contradicts, or repeats information stored previously. (p. 11)

Marill (1963) suggests that the primary function of the library ought to be the provision of information and not documents. A question-answering system would have the capacity to "comprehend" text and to accept questions in natural language through the use of fairly complex semantic nets. Even earlier, Mooers (1960) predicted future information systems capable of providing essays on any given subject and acting as archives for facts rather than texts.

It has also been suggested that electronic systems may allow a high degree of nonlinearity in the structuring and exploitation of text, freeing users from the linear presentations inherent in the print-on-paper medium. Turoff (1977), for example, points out that "In essence, the electronic form of the printed word would allow our creation and use of text in manners more akin to our cognitive processes which appear to be parallel and associative in nature" (p. 407). Von Foerster (1972) also discussed the need for "user adaptive" cognitive memory systems.

Churchman (1971) goes further than most in identifying the capabilities needed in some "ideal" library of the future:

> The objective of any section of the library is to receive all relevant documents of a given kind, to store these documents in a given place and to retrieve them without distortion. In the case of excellent libraries, the library can compare the document received in one sector with one received in another sector. . . . Thus, the "library" of the future may respond to a request for information by scanning its own memory of documents, and if no adequate answer is forthcoming, the library may automatically launch an empirical investigation and make suitable generalizations. It may also conduct a series of empirical studies on a continuing basis, so that its scientific encyclopedia is forever expanding. Hopefully, it will also be able to forget in a strategic manner so that the proliferation of itemized memory does not become monstrous. Such a library would correspond to what many people would call the "systemized collection of knowledge." (p. 117)

Some of the new capabilities specified in these forecasts already exist, while others are still being developed. On-line data banks now provide question-answering capabilities of at least a limited kind. Systems that will respond to inquiries put to them in English sentence form have been designed and implemented (e.g., Salton [1971], Williams [1969], and Kasarda and Hillman [1972]), and work is proceeding on the construction of interfaces to permit existing systems to be interrogated in plain English (Doszkocs and Rapp [1979]). Systems with self-reorganizing elements or with something resembling Bush's "associative trails" have also been built (e.g., Salton [1968], Stiles [1961], Salisbury and Stiles [1969], Giuliano and Jones [1963], and Spiegel et al. [1962]). It is now possible to replace human indexing by computer indexing (Stevens [1970] and Sparck Jones [1974]); to effect indexing as a partnership between humans and machines (Fangmeyer [1974]); to search complete or partial text without any form of indexing (Lancaster [1972]); to automatically identify which data base to interrogate for a particular information need (Williams and Preece [1977]); and to construct some type of thesaurus or classification structure automatically (Sparck Jones [1971]). The interrogation of computer-based systems through voice input is currently being investigated. In fact, there is evidence of considerable interest in the development of information-retrieval systems having some element of built-in intelligence or learning ability. This area of research — the interface between information retrieval and artificial intelligence — has been reviewed in depth by Smith (1980).

9 The Disembodiment
of the Library

The library of the future will not have a card catalogue. It very well may not even have books. In fact "it" — as a defined location on a specific block or college campus — may not exist at all.
— D. Kleiman, "Futuristic Library Does Away With Books"*

Librarianship is perhaps the most institutionalized of all professions. Physicians are not defined as "those who work in a health-care facility"; attorneys are not described as "those who work in courts of law." But in the eyes of the general public, librarians are seen as "those who work in a library" and librarianship is described as "what goes on in a library." Even the *Oxford English Dictionary* defines "librarian" as "the keeper or custodian of a library."

This rigid association between the professional librarian and a building housing a collection of physical artifacts, for which the librarian has responsibility, has had some unfortunate consequences. Because the most visible of activities within a library tend to be routine and clerical, people assume that this is what librarians do and therefore do not expect a high level of professional expertise from them. In general, the public does not recognize that professional librarians are specialists in the organization and retrieval of information. Therefore, these specialists are rarely asked for the help that they are trained to provide.

Librarians have tried hard to dispel the "custodian" image. Question-answering services have been commonplace for many

* In: *The New York Times,* October 26, 1981, pp. C1, C6.

the specific material or types of materials they need or would like at a particular time. More recently, these basic reference activities have been expanded to include referral services (which may necessitate the compilation of files of local institutional and individual resources) and more sophisticated literature-searching activities through on-line access to machine-readable data bases. Still, the image of the librarian as keeper or custodian of a collection persists.

The entirely institutional character of librarianship has other undesirable consequences. Several studies have shown that physical accessibility is the major determinant of the use of information resources. It is well known that use of a particular library is likely to be directly related to the distance people must travel to it, the availability of parking facilities, and other manifestations of physical accessibility. Apart from answering questions by telephone, the library is not perceived as being easily accessible. Librarians have tried to counteract this by bringing services closer to potential users. More branch libraries—including, perhaps, store-front libraries—are being built; bookmobile service and books-by-mail programs are in effect; and services and materials can be delivered directly to institutionalized users and to faculty offices.

Librarians have also attempted to expand the public library audience beyond the traditional core of the white middle classes, "reaching out" to the handicapped, the limited English speaking, and other minority groups and, in some cases, providing specialized services to particular segments of the community, such as small businesses and local government. At the same time, the library has increased its scope by offering not only conventional books but also records, tapes, films, and other audiovisual materials, as well as materials designed exclusively for such special groups as the blind and the nearsighted.

These efforts have met with only limited success. The populace still tends to think of public libraries as primarily book-lending agencies (Gallup Organization, Inc. [1976]); many citizens seem unaware that question-answering services are provided by most public libraries (Chen et al. [1979]); few people acknowledge the public library as a prime source of information; the population of active users of public libraries is small; and the population of frequent users is insignificant.

On the other hand, evidence exists that many people have everyday information needs and are aware that these needs exist (Chen et al. [1979]), and an overwhelming majority (94 percent) do read, and some 55 percent read books (Yankelovich, Skelly and White, Inc. [1978]).

It would seem, then, that needs for information and for materials to read do exist within the community but that the library, by and large, has not been highly successful in meeting either the reading or the information needs of much of the population.

Although several possible reasons for this apparent failure could be postulated, one is singled out for serious consideration. The hypothesis is that the profession has placed too much emphasis on the library as an institution, including the collection of physical artifacts housed by that institution, and not nearly enough on the major resource that the profession has to offer — the skill of its practitioners. The public, insofar as it thinks of libraries at all, looks upon the library as a *place*, a kind of warehouse. But this warehouse is, or should be, the least important part of what constitutes "library service." Instead of thinking in terms of going to the library (a *place*), the public would do better to think in terms of going to the librarian (a *person*). The librarian should be seen as a technical specialist (in much the same way that physicians, attorneys, and stockbrokers are technical specialists) — a consultant capable of making information available, referring to sources of information, advising on reading and related needs, bringing relevant materials to the attention of potential users, and arranging for the delivery of materials to users.

There are, of course, historical reasons why people think of libraries rather than librarians. Libraries, as collections of materials, existed before there were librarians and well before any real professional services were offered by these librarians. Nevertheless, there is no reason why this situation should persist. True, librarians have chosen to stay in the library. But most of their professional tasks could be performed outside the library (where they would be more likely to benefit the public). In addition, more of these tasks should be deinstitutionalized, and librarians should work more closely (and more visibly) with the constituents they serve, rather than be hidden behind four walls. In fact, the future of library service lies outside the library. This argument is made more persuasive by the impact that technology is having on library service and its potential impact in the future.

Trend Extrapolation

The System Development Corporation (Knight and Nourse [1969]), discussing forecasting relating to libraries, identified two major approaches. The first is "theoretically possible": It projects what could happen "given massive infusions of effort and money and rapid acceleration of technological developments." The second, characterized as "more realistic," is the method of prediction based on the extrapolation of already apparent trends: "The other more realistic approach . . . stresses a linear extrapolation of current trends. It charts the probable direction of future library operations and services as a straightforward extension or growth from the present . . . (p. 320).

In this chapter, a reasonable extrapolation of already apparent trends is presented and the implication of this extrapolation for libraries is discussed. The major trend so far is the growth of electronic publishing and the continuing conversion, within libraries, from capital investment in printed publications to some form of on-line access on demand. This is depicted in Figures 16 through 20.

As discussed in Chapter 6, libraries generally offer three major services to the communities they serve: document delivery, question answering, and literature searching. During 1970 (Figure 16), these services were essentially unaffected by computer technology. Materials were delivered to users in print-on-paper form (or possibly a microimage of print on paper) or, less frequently, in some audiovisual form. User questions were answered almost exclusively from printed reference tools, and literature searching, insofar as it was provided at all, also involved the use of printed sources owned by the library.

When the library was unable to satisfy the user, it might have referred him to another library or, occasionally, to another type of institution. In the case of document delivery, this referral would normally take the form of an interlibrary loan: The actual item (or a photocopy of it) would be shipped from library B to library A. If a question were referred from A to B, it would very likely be answered from a print-on-paper source. This would also apply to literature searching. The point is that all three services were based almost exclusively on print on paper.

This is partly an oversimplification. During 1970, a few libraries

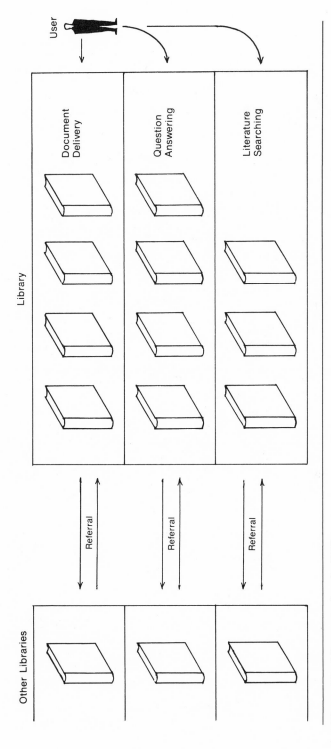

Figure 16 Library services in 1970.

were offering computer searching directly (based on either internal or external data bases), while others were acting as intermediaries between their users and some computer-searching service (e.g., medical libraries referred searches to the National Library of Medicine or to some other center in the MEDLARS network). There was even a minuscule number of libraries (e.g., at the Department of Defense or NASA facilities) having on-line access to some data base. Nevertheless, in terms of the total library picture in the United States, the effect of computers on all three services was still negligible a decade ago. There were very few on-line terminals in libraries. Those that were in place were used for cataloging, circulation control, or other inventory control or technical processing activity.

By 1980, however, the situation had radically changed (Figure 17). On-line terminals had found their way into many — perhaps most — special and academic libraries, and were beginning to reach the public library arena. On-line technology had had obvious impact on the literature-searching service. In fact, it can now be said (for many special libraries at least) that on-line access to remote sources is more important for literature searching than is use of print-on-paper sources within the library itself.

In Figure 17, the external sources are drawn as books. Actually, they are the electronic equivalents of printed books — mainly reference works, indexes, bibliographies, and abstracts journals at the present time. More significantly, these electronic sources, in addition to being shown in their remote locations, are represented as sitting on the library shelves; they are "phantom books." This is intentional and significant. The fact that remote electronic sources are already more important (at least in many special libraries) than print-on-paper sources physically contained within the institution raises the philosophical question, "What exactly constitutes a library's collection?"

An electronic source used regularly on behalf of the library's customers must be considered just as much a part of that library's collection as a print-on-paper source sitting on the library's shelves. When defining "collection," it is irrelevant whether the library chooses to invest in access to a print-on-paper source or to a remote electronic source as the need arises. The electronic source, as a legitimate part of the collection, should appear in the library's catalog. This logic can be carried further. There is little doubt that

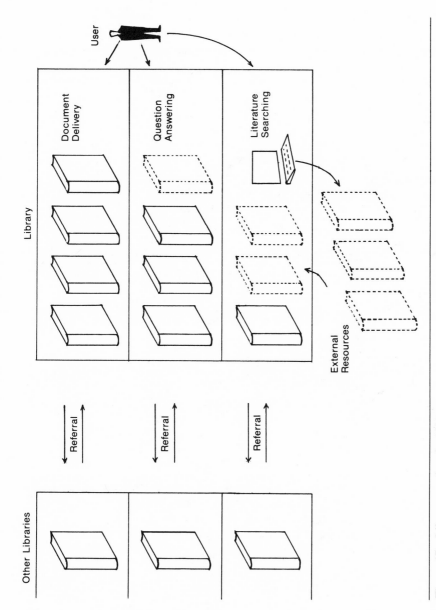

Figure 17 Library services in 1980.

the remotely accessed sources will continue to multiply and gain in importance relative to print on paper. As this happens, *any* remotely accessible source, regardless of whether it has actually been used, can be considered part of each and every library's collection. What is beginning to happen, in fact, is the gradual disembodiment of the library.

It is no longer necessary to think of libraries as large buildings housing extensive resources in print on paper or microform. Indeed, it is no longer necessary to think in terms of defined boundaries around the library's collection. Instead, the collection comprises anything that the library can make accessible to its users. The whole concept of the library's collection thus changes, as does the concept of the catalog. The catalog of *each library* becomes an inventory of all resources that can be accessed, in whatever form they happen to exist and wherever they happen to be located. The library and its collection and catalog become deinstitutionalized or, as just noted, disembodied.

For reasons already discussed, a natural evolution seems to be occurring in the sequence with which the major public services are affected by electronics. At the same time, different types of libraries are affected in another logical sequence. Literature-searching services are affected first. Special libraries adopt on-line access somewhat before the academic libraries, and public libraries follow some years later. This corresponds primarily to a sequence of availability of appropriate data bases: Science and technology are followed by the social sciences, which are followed by the humanities and "general interest" sources.

As Figure 17 shows, on-line access has had some impact on question answering — especially in the case of special libraries — as various data banks and certain kinds of "reference books" have become accessible on-line. Document delivery has been influenced at a negligible level; that is, little delivery to library users of text in electronic form has occurred. (It is true that users of law libraries have had on-line access to substantial bodies of legal text for years, but little complete text has been accessible in other fields, although the text of abstracts has been available in a wide variety of subjects.) Some telefacsimile transmission is now being used within the library field. Moreover, on-line networks can be used as a mechanism for ordering materials from a publisher, another library, or some other type of supplier. In this case, on-line facilities are used to assist conventional acquisition of materials; the materials themselves arrive as paper or microform.

Looking to 1985 (Figure 18), one can see the existing trend continuing at a greatly accelerated pace. More terminals have invaded the library. On-line sources completely dominate print-on-paper sources in literature searching. The question-answering function is now significantly impacted by electronic access, especially in public libraries, and on-line sources are more important than print-on-paper sources for answering factual-type questions. One reason for this is that growing numbers of reference books such as directories, yearbooks, encyclopedias, dictionaries, and concordances have become accessible on-line. Along with news services, the full text of newspapers and magazines, and consumer and other data bases made available through two-way television, these resources have now been widely adopted by all types of libraries. Moreover, a new type of resource sharing has emerged. Libraries have formed an on-line network to support question answering in much the same way that OCLC was formed to support cataloging. Abandoning their card files of "difficult" questions answered, libraries now enter such questions into a cooperatively maintained data base. This data base, which can be searched with keywords in any combination, consists of entries compiled by member libraries in accordance with network standards and protocols. Each entry consists of a narrative statement of a question posed by a library user, the answer supplied, the source of the answer, the date of entry, and the identification of the library submitting it. Various major libraries in the network assume responsibility for updating entries on a regular basis using current news sources. Thus, one library assumes responsibility for entries relating to sports records, a second for government officials, a third for economic indicators, and so on. This network also allows a cooperative approach to question answering. A file of unanswered questions is built up and reviewed regularly by member libraries. In this way, a question for which a public library has been unable to find an answer may, the next day, be fully answered by a special library. The net results are the creation of a kind of "growing encyclopedia," which rapidly becomes the major question-answering tool used in libraries of all types, as well as a substantial improvement in the quality of this aspect of reference service, especially in small public libraries.

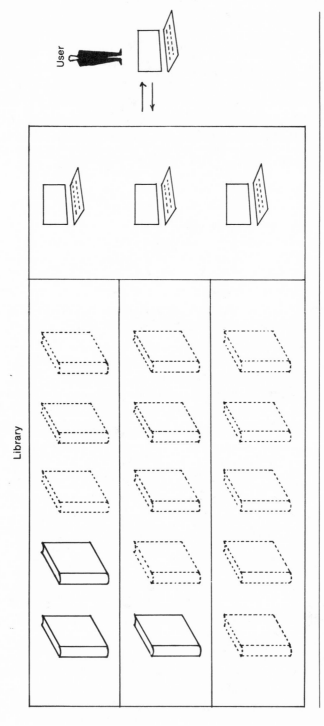

Figure 18 Library services in 1985.

Also by 1985, as increasing quantities of full text become accessible on-line (including the text of newspapers, popular magazines, and scholarly journals), some significant impact of electronics on document delivery can be seen. Libraries are beginning to access the text of certain items on demand, rather than entering subscriptions to these titles in print-on-paper form. Some of these items, of course, are new titles that are only available electronically.

Figure 18 shows another important development. A significant number of potential library users have their own terminals in their offices, homes, or both and can communicate directly with the library. They can search on-line catalogs and other library-built files, confer electronically with information specialists, and have search results, answers to questions, and even text transmitted to their terminals. To some extent, however, the library is being bypassed by a number of users. Simplified search procedures allow these persons a comfortable level of access to a wide range of data bases and data banks, to the question-answering file built up by the libraries, and to an increasingly diverse array of resources in full-text form.

Figure 19, depicting the situation in 1995, shows a continuation of the disembodiment process. The logical conclusion of this trend is the disappearance of the library, which is illustrated in Figure 20, set in the year 2000. Figure 20 can be considered an expansion of one segment of the communication system depicted in Figure 8. The user has access to a vast array of machine-readable resources that can be used to perform literature searches and to answer questions. Moreover, the full text of most reference books and journals is now accessible on-line, so the user no longer needs to subscribe or purchase or to visit a library to obtain access to needed material. There are still occasions, however, when he needs access to earlier material that is not in machine-readable form. On-line catalogs show him where this material is located and allow him to place a request at his terminal. The older print-on-paper resources are stored in various libraries that have become, essentially, archives.

For certain types of literary research involving, for example, the use of rare books, scholars may still need to visit these archives. Other requests for items can be handled by shipping the item to the user. For many requests, however, especially those for short items such as journal articles, the archive will transmit the text electronically to the user's terminal; that is, when the request is received, the

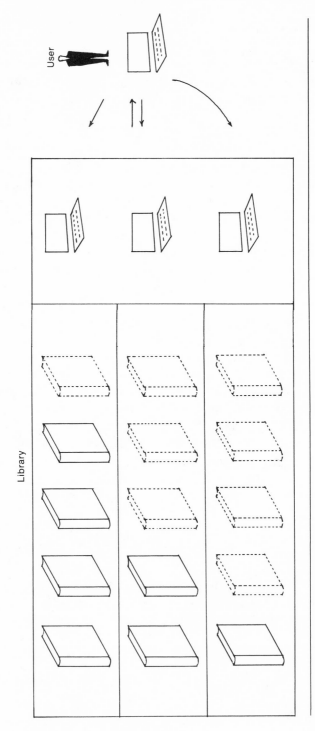

Figure 19 Library services in 1995.

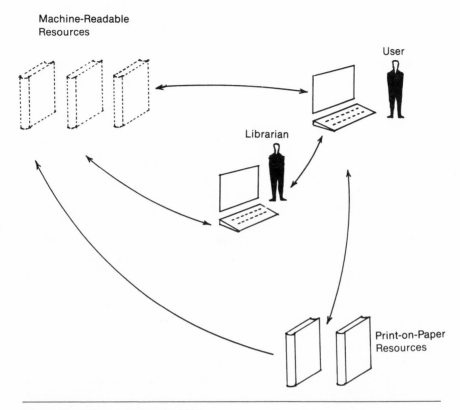

Machine-Readable
Resources

User

Librarian

Print-on-Paper
Resources

Figure 20   Library services in 2000.

item needed is scanned by an optical character reader. The machine-readable text is then transmitted to the requester's terminal in much the same way that store-and-forward telefacsimile systems now operate. The recipient can store the text, on his own storage facilities, and view it at leisure. If he wishes, he can make a paper printout. Once an item has been put into machine-readable form for transmission, the text is also forwarded to one of the machine-readable data bases, so that it will be directly accessible on-line the next time it is needed. In this way, the print-on-paper literature of the past is selectively moved, in response to demand, into more directly accessible on-line storage. (Of course, that literature which is never requested will never be transferred to the electronic medium.)

The impact of electronic delivery on conventional interlibrary loan (ILL) from 1985 through 1995 has been discussed by Arthur D. Little, Inc. (1979):

Somewhere in the decade between 1985 and 1995 direct electronic delivery of some categories of historical materials from suppliers will further negatively impact ILL as we know it today. As publishers move forward in electronic delivery, not only current material but also back material will in time be available through electronic delivery, without a need for retrospective conversion. A journal that cuts over to electronic delivery for current material as an optional alternative in 1983 will have ten years of its backfiles available for electronic delivery in 1993. The incremental cost of keeping and delivering that back material on demand electronically is relatively small, but this will effectively remove such materials from the main ILL flow. (pp. V-9–V-10)

Thus, as Figure 20 shows, the disappearance of the library of today may well be complete in another two decades. All that will remain are a few institutions that preserve the printed records of the past. They will respond to requests in much the same way that a mail-order company now responds to its customers; in other words, they will be passive archives rather than active information services. Note, however, that while the library has disappeared, the librarian has not. This implies an underlying assumption that some type of information professional, roughly equivalent to the present-day librarian, will still be active in the electronic age. This notion, together with that of the disappearance of the library, and the potential role of the library in a period of transition from print on paper to electronics, is examined next.

10   Does the Library Have a Future?

The extrapolation of trends presented in Chapter 9 suggests that the library as an institution may have a limited future, although some kind of librarian will continue to be needed long after the institution has been superseded or bypassed. This hypothesis is now examined in more detail.

It is my belief that electronic communication will continue to substitute for other forms, that electronic publishing will largely replace print-on-paper publishing, and that libraries as we now know them will become obsolete. The only uncertainty relates to the pace of change: How much will have occurred by when? It is reasonable to suppose that the paperless communication system described in Chapter 5 will be substantially in place by the year 2000. Conceivably it could develop more rapidly. On the other hand, the evolution might take longer than now expected.

The Library During a Time of Transition

In the early years of the transition from a paperbound society to one that is electronics bound, libraries will still be places that people visit for access to information resources. In addition to their print-on-paper collections, they will provide the terminals needed to access the electronic resources. More importantly, they will provide the expertise needed to exploit these resources effectively.

Later in the transition, as the electronic sources continue to gain in importance and the paper sources to decline, as terminals become more common in offices and in homes, and as people become familiar and comfortable with the use of on-line resources, the need for visiting libraries will rapidly diminish. When this occurs, the library as an institution will begin its inevitable decline.

Technical services will dwindle rapidly: Electronic sources will not need to be selected, acquired, cataloged (at least by individual libraries), prepared for the shelf, or bound. Likewise, public services within the library can also be expected to decline. When terminals become widely available, potential users will not need to come to the library to consult either information sources or information specialists. Moreover, since large quantities of complete text will be accessible through terminals, there will be no need to visit a library to borrow materials, and interlibrary loan activity will be restricted to older materials that are available only in paper form (although, as suggested in Chapter 9, certain print-on-paper materials may be scanned and transmitted electronically to user consoles).

The role of provider of access to information and materials that the library will play throughout the period of transition—say, the next 20 years—will depend on its willingness to adapt to a radically changing communication environment. At this point, the library performs two important and closely related functions: It facilitates access to printed and other materials for a specific community, and it subsidizes this access. The major functions of the professional librarian are the selection and acquisition of those items most relevant to the community to be served; the control and organization of these resources; and the provision of various services based on these resources.

In the period of transition, libraries could continue to facilitate and subsidize access to resources. But this implies the ability to substitute subsidized access to electronic resources for subsidized access to print on paper to keep pace with changes in publishing. In other words, as electronic sources continue to gain at the expense of print on paper, the library must reallocate its budget, spending progressively less on capital investment in print on paper and progressively more on capital investment in equipment to make electronic resources accessible, subsidized access to these electronic resources, and purchase of distributed electronic forms (such as cassettes, videodisks, and electrobooks). This function will have great social impact during the interim period when terminals are not widely available and/or when their costs are still somewhat prohibitive, and until access to electronic sources becomes cheaper than it is now.

Librarians and, in particular, those responsible for the funding of libraries must therefore be willing to accept less tangible evidence of their expenditures. A library can no longer be judged by the size of its collection or the elegance of its buildings. Instead, it will be evaluated on the effectiveness and efficiency with which it can make needed resources available, in whatever form, when they are needed. At the same time, library administrators must realize that subsidized access to intangible electronic resources is as legitimate an expenditure of public funds as subsidized access to print on paper. Thus, as society moves further into the age of electronics, libraries must incorporate new technology willingly and continue to substitute machine-readable resources for print on paper in literature-searching, question-answering, and document-delivery activities. Moreover, librarians must view electronic sources as an eventual replacement for paper rather than as an added service. Furthermore, they must be prepared to do more than provide access to electronic resources: They must build data bases (e.g., of community resources) to satisfy local needs and must experiment with new methods of information delivery, including the delivery of text and the results of literature searches to user terminals.

This view of the library's role during the next two decades is shared by a number of writers. Smith (1978), for example, sees libraries evolving into information centers, with users sitting at video display units and librarians being available to advise on "how to make best use of the data base."

The OCLC Newsletter (1980), referring to OCLC's Channel 2000 project, suggests that electronics could transform the library into a more dynamic, more highly regarded institution:

The Channel 2000 project, if it is successful, will be anything but transparent to users. It offers the tantalizing prospect that libraries will be able to serve more information to more people in more ways. It can make each library the undisputed information source-of-choice in its community. It could allow libraries to break their physical bonds; in effect to move right into your living room, your office, your dormitory — or whatever — with an array of services and information limited only by the imagination. The potential public benefit from this remarkable coalition of participants is enormous. (p. 5)

The Channel 2000 experiment (Online Computer Library Center, Inc. [1981]) involved 200 selected households in Columbus, Ohio.

Decoders were attached, via the antennae or CATV feeds (in much the same way that an electronic game is attached) to unmodified television sets in these homes. The decoder incorporated an acoustic coupler to permit telephone connection to the OCLC computer, as well as a microcomputer to relay user input from a 16-key keypad. The available services, which could be selected by the user from a list displayed on the TV screen, included

1. Bank One banking transactions
2. Access to the catalog of the Public Library of Columbus and Franklin County (users could select from the catalog and have materials mailed to them)
3. Access to the text of 32,000 articles from the *Academic American Encyclopedia*
4. A Public Information Service, compiled by local volunteer groups, which provided information on employment, human services, parks, sports, and other local matters
5. A Community Calendar, compiled by the Columbus Chamber of Commerce, which gave details on local educational and recreational offerings
6. Two teaching programs developed by Ohio State University, one in reading for preschool children and one in mathematics for kindergarten through sixth-grade level

The home-banking facilities gave users the ability to view the balances in their checking or savings accounts, to look at transaction lists for their accounts, and to pay bills.

Features provided by Channel 2000 included a "bookmark," which allowed users to pick up where they left off, a limited electronic mail facility (e.g., OCLC could communicate electronically with users but not vice versa), and an on-line "help" capability.

Use of the system was evaluated through transaction logs, questionnaires, and group interviews. Although some technical problems and limitations were reported, most of the participants judged the system as easy to use. When evaluated on the basis of usefulness, the services were ranked in the following order: bill-paying, public information, library catalog, bank account balances, bank monthly transactions, encyclopedia access, community calendar, and educational programs. When ranked on the basis of likelihood that the user would pay for the service, the order was encyclopedia access, library catalog, home banking, public information, community calendar, and educational programs. When asked what types of services (hypothetical) they would be most willing to pay for, the following ranking was given: home security, in-home computer facility, video games, library services, catalog shopping, physician-contacting system, adult self-education, encyclopedia, household energy control, and bill paying.

Approximately 17 percent of the participants indicated a willingness to pay for the limited services offered by Channel 2000, but 80 percent indicated a moderate-to-high probability of paying $15 per month for the six most desired services on the hypothetical list. Almost 82 percent of the respondents indicated that public libraries should spend tax money on electronic services.

The OCLC report predicts that such "convenience" services as catalog shopping and bill paying will be the foundation of successful viewdata businesses. Nevertheless, the Channel 2000 experiments seem to offer great encouragement for the further development of home delivery of library services and for the distribution of electronic publications via viewdata-type systems. OCLC will continue to explore the potential in a new project named Viewtel.

Korfhage (1978) predicts that home computers and hand-held intelligent terminals will have a profound influence on the library:

Once a library puts its card catalog behind a computer, and permits public access through terminals in the library, there is little reason to deny such access through remote, dial-up terminals. Given such access, the user may ask for specific items, browse, or ask for subsets of the catalog. Certainly, as home computer memories grow in capacity, it is reasonable to suppose that a user may query the library system, asking for a bibliography on a specific topic to be transferred to his own computer memory for later use. Thus we perceive that there will be some public pressure to augment access to the card catalog with a retrieval service that will increase in sophistication over the years.

The library user generally wishes, of course, not merely reference to available materials, but also to have access to them. Assuming that the user is remotely accessing the catalog system for reference, it is reasonable to further suppose that he or she would like to have the desired materials delivered remotely, rather than needing to go to the library for them. Thus we see the addition of an order and delivery system aimed at getting the desired library materials into customer hands — and retrieving them once the customer is through with them. While some materials, such as paintings, cannot be stored on a computer, other materials of a documentary nature can be. If such materials were stored electronically within the library's computer system, then they could be transmitted to the user's computer, without the need for delay, costly physical transport, or removing them from general circulation. (pp. 10–11)

. . .With more documents being composed, edited, and set for printing with the aid of a computer, there is a wealth of computer-readable full text already available. The inclusion of such materials directly within the library system requires the development of an access method, the availability of reliable mass storage, and the perceived need at the user end of the system. The access method is relatively simple to develop, being an extension of the card catalog system; reliable mass storage is available and increasingly inexpensive; user need will develop as home computers and general computer sophistication become more prevalent.

Extension beyond this requires considerably more work, but already the groundwork for such extension has been laid through the community service work of various types that the libraries are doing. A number of libraries are extending their reference services to include non-traditional information, such as community calendars, and information about community groups, schools, and clubs. Some are also providing reference to non-local services, such as the New York Times Information Bank. With some work—although not necessarily more than is needed to provide such services manually—these services could largely be computerized.

Thus we picture an environment in which a substantial portion of library usage occurs by access to its computer system. The user remotely queries the library to determine the materials he desires, and has the materials displayed at his terminal, or sent to his home computer for later use. Such materials include not only the traditional indexes, books, and journal articles, but also shorter, more fragmentary, and more transient information that applies to his current needs. The speed with which this picture becomes reality depends largely on economics. Technically, we can implement such a remote information service today. Culturally, the populace is becoming sufficiently familiar with computer systems and their uses that this type of information service, if not widely acceptable today, will be widely acceptable by the time we can have it ready for public use. The development, maintenance, and operation of such a system does involve costs; and the major problem in developing the system seems to be a reasonably accurate assessment of these costs, and a determination of the structure of fees and subsidization that will be used to cover the costs.

With the advent of home computers and hand-held terminals, the whole process of information exchange within our society is susceptible to a massive change. As one of the major components in the information structure of society, libraries will be strongly affected by this change. It is therefore appropriate that libraries now study the potential change and prepare for it. For the change will occur, if the history of computing is any guide, before its predicted time. (pp. 12–13)

Kubitz (1980) foresees libraries delivering certain materials directly to home terminals. For longer works, however, the patron may pick up an electronic version at the library:

The eventual extension of high-speed links into the home will make it possible to browse in the library at home and, once a selection is made, have it transmitted to the home computer system where it would be stored to be read whenever desired. Because communication costs are apt to be high, it is not yet clear whether it will be cost-effective to transmit a book such as *Hawaii* to one's home, or whether it would be better to pick it up (on disk) at the library. Another problem is the large amount of *writable* storage that would be needed at home. (p. 150)

Other writers have issued a warning to libraries: adapt or run the risk of being bypassed by the commercial sector. Dowlin (1980), for example, has said,

If the public library does not soon develop a role in the emerging electronic evolution — Toffler's "Third Wave" — we will become irrelevant to the people who require rapid, convenient, and energy conscious access to information and materials. (p. 2265)

Giuliano (1980) is reported as saying that "what is needed . . . is not the document but the information . . . where and when it is needed, the same day, the same hour." Referring to the $32 billion office automation industry, which is growing at 20–30 percent each year, he added that "this revolution is not going to wait for libraries — it's not even going to wait for publishers and publishers are going to have to run to catch up."

Klugman (1980), reviewing the Third International Online Information Meeting (London, December 1979), has also warned that the library may be bypassed by commercial interests:

Viewdata is only one of the several technological innovations which have generated a lot of marketing rhetoric. Other new developments such as videodiscs, the microprocessor, the increased use of home computers and intelligent terminals all seem to point to direct service to the end-user, by-passing the traditional route via vendors and information centers such as libraries. The term "user-friendly systems" kept surfacing as a recurring leitmotif. More than once one was reminded that the information world did not revolve exclusively around libraries but that the information industry was increasingly looking at the extra-library market (home, professional and business) for growth. The library market, due to the "Proposition 13" syndrome, is considered to have a finite information adsorption capacity. (p. 5)

Davinson (1979), referring specifically to Prestel, reinforces this warning:

Librarians who reject Prestel as being principally a non-library, domestic and office system miss the point completely. They do not speculate on what the medium might mean for traditionally conceived librarianship. . . .Without deep and continuous study of the challenges facing librarianship in the new technologies and the burgeoning bureaucracies of the modern world, it is likely that librarians will be replaced in their more traditional roles by other people and systems and will be unable to play their part in the evolution of new ones. (p. 50)

Almost identical sentiments were expressed by Andrew and Horsnell (1980):

By implication, if librarians do not accept the challenge provided by Prestel to make a more up-to-date information service available to residents, somebody else will; but they may not have the skills, the expertise, the impartiality which librarians have. The combined results will be less effective information services and libraries taking a further step backwards into obscurity and irrelevance. (p. 425)

Turoff and Featheringham (1979) believe that the library can play a central role in the "information society." The library, in their view, is the "ideal test bed for exploring and beginning to live the future." It will expand beyond its storage and retrieval roles. Technological advances will allow people to use the library in the creation, organization, and manipulation of information. New services offered by the library might include services to allow the library to support transient information or "lore-oriented" information of its user community; services that will provide mechanisms for people to exchange information among themselves; and services that will establish the library as a learning resources center to develop the skills to use information systems.

Some libraries are already beginning to adapt, at least to a limited extent. Most notably, this has taken the form of fairly wide adoption of on-line access to support literature searching. The Prestel experiments in libraries in the United Kingdom provide another notable example. Carr (1980), describing the experience with Prestel at Aston University Library in the *Journal of Librarianship*,* makes some cogent observations on the advantages it has to offer:

Even in the past twelve months, with Prestel in this very sluggish phase, the system has made a number of positive contributions to our information services at Aston. To begin with, we have been able to offer our readers a certain amount of information not otherwise available on the library premises. One example out of many is the *Shipstats Weekly Report*, to which the library does not subscribe. This is the sort of

---

*The *Journal of Librarianship* is a quarterly journal of The Library Association, the professional body for librarians in the United Kingdom.

area where Prestel could be of considerable value in a smaller academic library, giving fairly cheap, on-demand access to external sources of information. Prestel has also given us access to material not available in the same form anywhere else at all — that is, material specially written for Prestel as, for example, the comment, analysis and forecasting of Phillips & Drew which is of considerable value to students of management and economics. This kind of special Prestel material is fairly widespread, and clearly indicates that Prestel may eventually revolutionize the publishing industry itself, since journalists and authors are now able to write directly on to a potential mass market medium. The mass market has also been opened up to computer-based companies like Datastream, which hitherto have supplied their information to a necessarily restricted section of the business community. By means of a fairly basic computer software package, their tapes have been converted to Prestel format and so have become available to a much wider circle of users, ourselves included. . . . Prestel may well eventually spell the end for the printed version of this, as of other services. It would make economic sense, too, if you only had to pay for the information you actually use. Prestel has also given us access to information available elsewhere but conveniently brought together in an organized and abstracted form. One example of this of particular relevance in an academic library context is *Scitel*, a science magazine mounted specially for Prestel by the Institute for Scientific Information. This provides a modest current awareness service in most of the major fields of science and technology, and has given more than one of our students a convenient lead into new references in his own specialist subject area. (p. 152)

Prestel has also demonstrated to us its ability to provide speedier and more convenient access to material already in the library, but scattered in various far-flung parts of the building. Prestel is capable of serving as a quick-reference collection all in one box and in a very small space. This can be of particular value in a multi-site library. Prestel has already fulfilled the role of a handy, encyclopaedic, quick-reference medium. It does not pretend to have the answer to every query; it may not often give answers in the kind of depth that we as librarians think we would like; but even if we had to accept or reject Prestel as it is, it undoubtedly has a part to play as an additional front-line source of information in the sort of quick-reference general inquiries set-up which we operate from our Ground Floor inquiry point at Aston. If Prestel improves in coverage and in depth with time, so much the better. Meanwhile, it would be wrong to dismiss it with contempt as a one-volume Pear's in a world of Britannicas. If Prestel has not yielded vast amounts of new information to revolutionize the teaching and the research work of our academic community, it has still added an extra line of approach to the retrieval of some useful current data. The system has proved easy to use; a sizeable number of largely untutored staff have been able to master the mechanics of it very quickly; it has slotted into our network of information services with virtually no administrative difficulties; and it has provided a steady source of information on a useful range of topics such as company performance, engineering and manufacturing products, commodity prices, job opportunities, government and local information, courses and conferences, and health and safety matters. It is obviously capable of providing a lot more. In fact, we may not have exploited Prestel's full potential even in its present largely experimental state.

Research studies carried out by Aslib in public reference libraries with Prestel have mentioned the failure of staff to "think Prestel"; there has certainly been a little of that here at Aston. We have tended to use Prestel for information we know to be on the system; and yet it is very difficult even for the keenest Prestel devotee to be familiar with the whole range of its material. There is after all the equivalent of several hundred large reference books available on Prestel now; and none of our staff could claim to know what the contents of them all might be. In a constantly growing and changing database, some form of systematic browsing seems essential. Pressure of other work has prevented this from happening on a large scale with our subject librarians at Aston, and our level of familiarity with the files has obviously suffered as a result. (pp. 152–153)

He goes on to refer to the publicity value of this medium in the library:

This immediate visual impact operates at a number of levels. Television itself is in any case an attractive medium for everybody: the goggle-box syndrome is well-attested in the literature of psychology. But to see a large colour television set in a non-domestic context makes it even more irresistible. The marriage of that automatic attraction with the dissemination of textual information and hard data undoubtedly makes for enhanced packaging both of the printed word and of statistical material. This is true in spite of the obvious limitations on the number of words to a page, and in spite of the feeling (unsubstantiated in our experience at Aston) that people will not be prepared to look at more than a few pages of Prestel in succession because it tires the eyes more quickly than a conventional printed page. At a deeper level, too, many of the better informed members of the university are impressed – as we are – at the unbundling of computer-based information which the Prestel system has achieved. Companies like Datastream, which have been able to convert their computer-based data directly into videotex display format, have already been mentioned. But there is more to it even than that. Computer-based information systems of all kinds have traditionally been, until now, high price, block subscription, narrow audience, specialist media. With Prestel, the computer has entered the mass communications era. Academic libraries are, of course, not really in the mass communication business – but the system itself will certainly have as one of its spin-offs a widespread effect upon people's perception of their use of information. If television is now thought of largely as an entertainment medium, Prestel (or something developed from it) will eventually modify that perception on a very large scale. Meanwhile, in our academic library context the fascination of the televisual display of information is imperceptibly effecting this modification on a specialized section of the wider community. Information handling and the making public of information are the primary business of libraries, and Prestel undoubtedly makes this more obvious to library users. This can be regarded as a very real benefit of the public presence of a Prestel set in an academic library: it can serve as a window on the wider world of information services which any good library has to offer. (pp. 154–155)

The cost of Prestel use at Aston was reported to be £486.49 a year, which certainly seems a modest investment in a new service of this kind. The use of Prestel as a source of business information in a public library is discussed by Marshall (1981).

Andrew and Horsnell (1980) have emphasized that librarians must view Prestel, and similar tools, as an integral component in their information services:

There is insufficient awareness by reference staff of the scope of the Prestel database and a general reticence; the tendency being to regard Prestel as a peripheral information source — rather than an integral part of an up-to-date information service. . . . Remember, Prestel is not a separate information source; it is an integral part of an effective, up-to-date information service. (p. 425)

One library in the United States that seems willing to adapt is the Pikes Peak Regional Library District in Colorado Springs, Colorado. Its director, K. E. Dowlin (1980), recognizes seven major roles for the library in an age of electronics*:

The library could: (1) provide access to complicated or seldom used data bases; (2) provide community conferencing and message center programs; (3) provide online access to information on library resources; (4) provide access to community data and community information locations for referrals; (5) provide access to resources in other libraries via networking; (6) provide access to high demand information and materials via computer or video disk; and (7) provide access to electronic resources for those who cannot afford home computers or terminals. If we examine this seven-point role in detail, it can be seen as a viable role for libraries. (p. 2266)

Dowlin goes on to elaborate on the role of the public library as a community information resource:

Community resource files on clubs, government agencies, adult education, day care centers, career and occupational data bases, and community events will be developed online by libraries that are serious about information and referral. An integrated system that incorporates circulation, inventory, and the catalog system is a powerful tool for indicating materials in the library's collection and their accessibility. If this system also includes community resources and a networking capability, it is the most powerful information access tool in any community. . . . This information could be accessed by the person needing a referral if they appear in person, if they call the library, or if they have access via a home computer. This function would provide the library with a key element for demonstrating that it is serious about information and

---

* Reprinted from *Library Journal,* November 1, 1980. Published by R. R. Bowker Co. (a Xerox company). Copyright © 1980 by Xerox Corporation.

referral to the community and to other agencies. Even the minutes of city council meetings could be included if the offices producing them adopt word processing systems into their regular operations and provide them to the library. It may be possible for the public to add their comments to such "publications" if the dial-up access is provided. Agendas could be incorporated in advance along with the background information, so that the public could input their feedback before decisions are made. The information generated by the online conferencing could be stored for historical purposes if it appears relevant. (p. 2267)

The Pikes Peak Library has already gone a long way toward implementing Dowlin's ideas:

The library currently provides access to the complete inventory file of books and serials. In addition the club file, the adult education and recreation index, the community events calendar, the day care directory, the Colorado Occupation and Career Information file, and the carpooling system for the metropolitan area are online in the Pikes Peak Library's computer. The library expects to have the complete public catalog online in 1981 with full records and subject access. . . . The library has been using an elementary conferencing system that is being expanded at the present time and it serves as a model for the community conferencing system via terminal. When it has been developed further, it will be moved into the public access menu and the home users will be able to communicate with the library through the library's computer. (p. 2268)

The Pikes Peak Library is also experimenting with a public access terminal located in a supermarket. The terminal can be used to access the library's catalog, a listing of local classes, and a calendar of events. It can also be used to link patrons with a librarian.

Dowlin goes on to identify some other libraries that have been "adventurous enough to reach out":

The Natrona County Library in Casper, Wyoming has the first video reference service. The San Francisco Public Library makes extensive use of video tape and cable. The Memphis and Shelby County Public Library is conducting cable experiments. The Washington, D.C. Public Library; the Tri-County Library in Rome, Georgia; the Milwaukee Public Library; the Port Washington Public Library, N.Y.; and the most ambitious current project of using cable television to increase access at the Columbus and Franklin County Public Library, Ohio through Qube system exemplify the growing library involvement in video. There is not yet much activity using the computer to increase access outside the library facilities, but it will come. The Lexington Public Library in Kentucky has specified that their circulation system must interface with the local cable television system. There are libraries that have used cable television, computers, books by mail, telephones, information and referral, but we are still a minority. We need to take pride in what we have done, what we are doing now, and in what we could do in the future. We need to spend less time on introspective discussions and to reach out. Our motto should be "access." (p. 2269)

Sweeney (1981) identifies three major reasons why public libraries should involve themselves with videotext:

1. In the long run, such systems will deliver information to users more cheaply than libraries do today.
2. Videotext can be used to deliver "information to the right place and at the right time"; it is more convenient than present methods of information seeking and information delivery.
3. Through networking, videotext has the potential to make available more information than the world's largest libraries can at present.

Sweeney goes on to describe a model for a public videotext system, the Shared Free Public Information Computer Network (Figure 21).

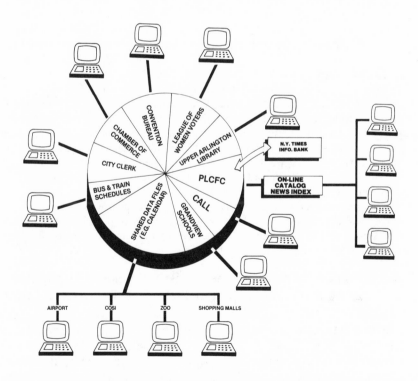

Figure 21 Conceptualization of a free public information system. (Reprinted from Sweeney [1981] by permission of the author.)

The system envisioned would supply to the public, at no cost, information provided by "owner" agencies. It would be exclusively owned and governed by local metropolitan area nonprofit groups.

Sweeney's proposed network would allow local authorities to provide free access to data bases of local information (i.e., built by local agencies), as well as to fee-based services (e.g., The New York Times Information Bank), provided that one or more owner agencies would agree to fully subsidize such access. The network would provide terminals in public locations such as shopping malls, the airport, or the zoo, as well as in all outlets of the public library. Access through the home would also be possible (see Figure 22) through two-way cable television. Sweeney stresses that there is a need for such a network and that public libraries should lead the effort to establish it.

Interestingly a glimpse of the library as a future automated information resource was given, perhaps tongue in cheek, by Dana (1916) as far back as 1907:

Inquirers will not expect libraries to fit them out with thoughts any quicker than a ready-made clothing store can fit them out with clothes. Questions of importance will be answered by persons equal to the task. But many hundred carefully selected inquiries, made repeatedly at all libraries and evidently passed on by inheritance from parent to children, always heretofore fully and courteously answered by attendants, will be replied by the "automatic Who, What, and Why Machine." On the front of an attractive case are several hundred push buttons; below each button is a little label, bearing a question; all the questions are arranged under subjects and then subdivided under the words, Who, What, Which, Why, etc. The inquirer finds the question he wishes to ask, pushes the proper button, and at once a card rises above the case bearing the complete and accurate answer. Many will come to scoff at this machine; all will stay to use it.

Another more elaborate machine answers more difficult, delicate and even quite personal questions; but is actuated only when a penny is dropped in a slot before a button is pushed. This is the famous Pay-Collection of Complete Answers of which you will soon have heard. (pp. 150–151)

Dana may not have predicted the precise technology likely to make his prophecy a reality, but conceptually he may not be too far from the truth.

The predictions of Wisconsin schoolchildren regarding the library of the future, specifically in the year 2028, as reported in *American Libraries* ("A Library That Can Read Your Mind" [1979]) also show some remarkable prescience. For example, they have envisioned a library capable of delivering books "automatically"; a library that

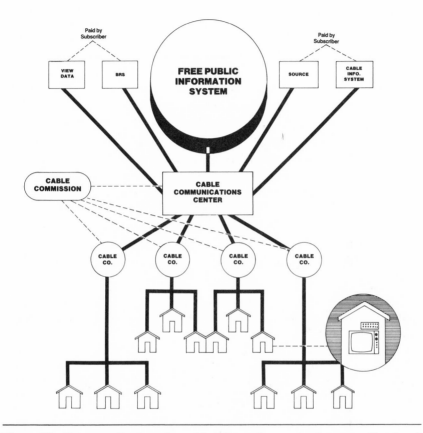

Figure 22 Conceptualization of a cable information retrieval system. (Reprinted from Sweeney [1981] by permission of the author.)

can convert printed text into speech (already made possible by the Kurzweil equipment mentioned earlier); battery-operated "newspads" (a kind of flat, portable TV set capable of displaying graphic or textual material recorded on tapes); the replacement of printed books with "cassettes"; a computer terminal capable of reading to children and showing them pictures; and another device capable of reading out a definition and the correct pronunciation of any word input.

A recently completed Delphi study undertaken in Minnesota (Weingand [1980]) has yielded several predictions regarding the impact of home computers, cable television, satellite communication, and other technologies on the public library. Libraries are seen as potential "electronic interfaces." The electronic delivery systems will fundamentally alter libraries before the end of this century:

Major changes will include provision of computer terminals and audiovisual equipment in the library, and software for home computers and video. This software will be available either in the library or via telecommunications lines to the home, where computer and cable TV systems will be commonplace in the 1990s . . . As libraries attempt to adapt within this electronic revolution, several modifications of operations are likely to occur: restructuring of architecture to accommodate electronic delivery systems; some decentralization into convenient neighborhood locations, such as supermarkets, airports, gas stations . . . the library will become an electronic entity . . . probably against its will . . . . (pp. 187–188)

Weingand concludes that, if the 1990s find electronic publishing in general use, then libraries must use the 1980s to prepare for this phenomenon.

A meeting with far-ranging implications was held in Columbus in March 1981. Organized by the Public Library of Columbus and Franklin County and by OCLC, the meeting's theme was Public Libraries and Remote Electronic Delivery of Information. An important outcome of this meeting was that the American Library Association was approached on establishing an Electronic Library Membership Initiative Group. This action could lead to the formation of an Electronic Library Association.

So far in this chapter, it has been shown that libraries have an important role to play in the transition from print on paper to electronics. They will be needed to provide access to a wide range of information resources. They must be willing to gradually substitute electronic access for access to materials in conventional printed form. Indeed, unless libraries move in this direction, they are very likely to find themselves bypassed by direct delivery from producer to consumer. Some libraries are already moving, albeit cautiously, in the right direction.

It is likely that libraries supporting research will change more rapidly than other types of libraries. But this latter group, including public libraries, will be forced to adapt. In the long term, electronics could have a profound impact on what we now think of as "recreational reading." Although there seems little advantage to reading a printed novel on some type of video display, there is no real reason to suppose that the novel in its present form will survive. One could argue that the novel is an artifact of the print-on-paper era. It seems entirely possible that new forms of literary expression, more suited to the electronic medium, may emerge and eventually replace the present forms. By the same token, electronic art may gradually replace paint on canvas. The future will probably bring about a blurring of the distinctions among types of libraries. In effect, public, school, special, and academic libraries will all have access to the same universe of information and other resources. The differences will relate more to the characteristics of the librarians in these various institutions and to the techniques used by these professionals to serve their various communities of users. This brings us to the role of the librarian in an electronic society.

The Librarian in an Age of Electronics

Earlier in the chapter, three major functions of the professional librarian were identified: selection and acquisition, organization and control, and provision of various services. In a largely electronic world, the first two functions decline substantially in importance. Electronic sources, at least those remotely accessible, do not need to be acquired, nor do they need selection. Rather, the selection activity is of a different kind: Librarians select what to access to satisfy a known demand rather than what to purchase in anticipation of future demands. The organization and control activities also decline, since remotely accessible sources will presumably be cataloged, indexed, and abstracted by some central source rather than the local library. This frees the librarian to focus on service.

Rapid growth of information resources in electronic form may greatly reduce the value of the library, but, by the same token, it may greatly increase the value of the librarian. The magnitude and diversity of the electronic resources available will tend to ensure that skilled information specialists are in great demand, at least in the foreseeable future. Kochen's (1978) view of this future professional seems very close to the point:

. . . This information professional is likely to be employed as a facilitator or linker, as a kingpin in a network in which control is shared by service providers and their clients in jointly coping with complex tasks. It will be an occupation of great responsibility, requiring correspondingly high standards of admission to and training for the profession. (p. 6)

Somewhat similar sentiments have been expressed by others. Reintjes (1967), for example, has said,

In future integrated information-transfer networks, librarians will be the most valuable human resource of the network. Their detailed knowledge of the contents of the network and their ability to employ retrieval techniques that will extract the maximum amount of information from it will create intense demand for their expert services. (p. 9)

Roistacher (1978b) groups librarians with "transfer agents" and visualizes both groups operating through on-line conferencing networks:

These are people whose primary interest is in providing services to network clients. Reference librarians would be able to act much as they do now, but would have better access to potential clients and better knowledge of current issues. The term "transfer agent" applies to someone who would be part organizational development specialist and part extension agent. The transfer agent would act as reference service, social director, and spreader of information. Transfer agents will become increasingly necessary as the demand for information and the complexity of information sources both increase. (p. 20)

It is my belief that professional information specialists will still be valuable in the age of electronics. Indeed, their value could be greatly enhanced as the community at large becomes increasingly conscious of the importance of access to information in all walks of life. They will be needed to

1. Act as information consultants, showing people the best sources for solving their information needs
2. Train people in the use of electronic information sources
3. Search sources that are unfamiliar to particular users
4. Provide an "information analysis" function; that is, synthesize the results of searches in several sources and present evaluated and selective results to the requester, possibly directly to the requester's terminal
5. Assist in constructing effective user interest profiles for use with on-line SDI facilities
6. Assist in organizing personal electronic information files

7. Keep researchers up-to-date on new information sources and services

These will all be important activities in the electronic age, but, interestingly enough, not one needs to be performed within the four walls of the library. This leads to the following hypotheses, implied earlier but not precisely stated:

1. The library, if it is willing to adapt, can play a significant role in facilitating a smooth transition from a print-on-paper society to an electronic society.
2. Nevertheless, libraries, as we know them now, have a limited life expectancy. In the long term, they will become museums or archives, repositories of the records of the past, serving warehouse and delivery functions but offering little service.
3. The librarian, as a skilled information professional, will have a much longer lived function.
4. The future of the librarian depends on his ability and willingness to move out of the library.

In Chapter 9, a failure on the part of the library profession to place emphasis on the librarian as a technical specialist rather than on the physical institution of the library was noted. This results in low visibility of professional expertise and a level of actual service to the community that is well below its potential in a world becoming increasingly dependent on information. It seems clear that it is not only desirable for the librarian to get out of the library and work more directly and visibly with the public, but that technology is making it increasingly possible to free the librarian from a particular building and collection of artifacts. At the same time, developments in publishing and in the distribution of publications and information — with electronic access increasing in importance and access to printed resources declining — threaten the entire *raison d'être* of the library. If librarians do not do something different from what they have traditionally been doing, they run the risk of being replaced by the "information industry" and by the provision of services directly to the home by nonlibrary agencies.

It seems evident that the survival of the library profession depends on its ability and willingness to change its emphasis and image. Since physical facilities and material resources in physical form must inevitably decline in importance, the profession can only survive if its focus shifts to an emphasis on the technical expertise of its practitioners. The library, as a collection of physical artifacts, becomes, then, merely one resource that the information professional uses, in much the same way that the resources available in a pharmacy are just one resource that supports the technical expertise of the physician.

This view is shared by Giuliano (1979):

My main message is that it is time now for librarians to shift context — to start looking at the situation from the other end of the telescope. The shift has to be away from libraries and their institutional structures as the main focal point, towards providing contemporary and needed information services to their constituents, using whatever means, media, or structures that are appropriate. For some, the shift in perspective may mean working outside a library; for many, it may mean transforming a library institution. (p. 1838)

Scarfe (1975) has referred to the fact that the information manager of the future must "integrate his own staff into positions in the corporate structure." The positions will exist in every major corporate division or project team. The actual operational information unit, or library, will be very small. Lower priority will be assigned to the acquisition and provision of information from external sources. The information manager will be responsible for coordinating the activities of numerous information workers within a corporation. These information workers will be directly responsible to their particular divisions or project teams. Their primary objective will be to determine the precise information requirements of their particular units. It will also be the responsibility of the information workers to encourage the use of large remote data bases by the eventual recipient of the information.

It is highly desirable that the librarian of the future should work more closely with the public outside the library. Thus, I expect to see a deinstitutionalization/reinstitutionalization process in the profession, with librarians affiliated directly with academic departments, working as equal members of research teams in academia, health care, industry, and elsewhere. I also expect to see greatly increasing numbers of free-lance librarians, forming, perhaps, small group practices resembling present-day medical and legal practices. Addressing this point, Neill (1981) has suggested that

Close to 60% of the graduates of library schools in 2010 will be self-employed or will work out of libraries under contract to small businesses, community groups, city halls, and even individuals willing to pay for special search services. The growth of the information broker business will be the result of the need to access the mass of information produced, to sort it, and to weigh it for a specific use. (pp. 47–48).

Librarians of the future (maybe once they leave the library they should be given a new name) are likely to have responsibilities far beyond those they have at present. For example, in commerce and industry, they may control the organization of a company's complete electronic files, including its electronic mail files.

Some deinstitutionalization has already occurred. In fact, the idea of library service offered outside the library seems to have originated in German universities at the beginning of the century. There, bibliographers, affiliated with the university library, function as information specialists in academic departments corresponding to their own areas of expertise. The idea of an information specialist as an integral component of an academic department has been slow to catch on elsewhere, although Borden, in 1935, made reference to a "roving professor" who would apply an interdisciplinary knowledge of bibliography to provide information support outside a faculty's regular research area. The work of "floating librarians," operating within the academic community, was later discussed by Hernon and Pastine (1972), King et al. (1971), and Knapp (1966).

Ashworth, writing in 1939, referred to the need for "information officers" in academia. Ashworth's information officer would have no responsibility for the operation of the library and would be completely independent of the university librarian. The information needs of the academic researcher would be the prime focus of his activities.

Orne (1955) referred to a similar type of professional, operating in the United States university environment as a "bibliographic assistant." While using the library as a base, this individual would spend most of his time outside the library. Indeed, he would be most useful to the academic community when not in the library.

An information officer was introduced, on an experimental basis, at Bath University in 1969 (Bath University [1970, 1971] and Line [1971, 1974]). Information officers have also been introduced at other universities in the United Kingdom: Belfast, Newcastle, Reading, Sheffield, Southampton, Birmingham, Cardiff, Imperial College, Salford, Strathclyde, Sussex, Durham, and Manchester (Hall [1972]). In some cases, as in the Bath experiments, the information officer provides current-awareness and search services directly to a faculty. In other cases, he is used more to promote library resources and to introduce new information services to library users.

Somewhat similar to the information officer is the clinical medical librarian (Claman [1978], Roach and Addington [1975], Farmer [1977a, b], Noback and Byrd [1977], Marshall and Hamilton [1978], Algermissen [1974], Colaianni [1975], Cornelisse [1978], Cummings [1978], Greenberg et al. [1978], Lamb [1976], Schnall and Wilson [1976], and Byrd and Arnold [1979]). While working from a medical library, the clinical medical librarian is intended to function as a full professional member of a health-care team. The information needs of the team are brought to the librarian's attention through an intimate association with the health-care process, including attendance during patient rounds in hospitals and participation in clinical conferences.

There has been some experimentation with floating librarians in the public library setting. Penland (1970), for example, described the use of a floating librarian to serve culturally disadvantaged groups who do not have ready access to library services or who are not familiar with the use of library resources. This librarian is essentially an "information agent," working in close cooperation with community agencies and individual citizens. Project Aurora, operated by the Elyria Public Library (1973), was an experiment in door-to-door library service. The itinerant librarians used were not actually professionals, they concentrated almost exclusively on book materials for reading, they were not concerned with reference service, they included children in the service, and their primary objective was to increase library usage.

More recently, the idea of "team librarianship" has emerged within the public library movement in the United Kingdom (Major [1979], Major and Judd [1979], and Hinks [1977]). In essence, this implies that the library is operated by nonprofessionals, while the professionals work outside the library in the community. As described by Major (1979),

> The basis of the system is that non-professional assistants are placed in day-to-day charge of service points and they assume responsibility for the basic services which do not require professional expertise. So, professional and non-professional duties are fairly rigidly divided; librarians "visit" the service point to undertake readers' advisory and bookstock work. In most cases, the non-professional staff report to a Senior Library Assistant and not to a professional member of staff, so librarians are also free from supervision of staff. This arrangement enables librarians to concentrate on professional duties; usually a mixture of community work (i.e., making contact with local groups, community profiles, displays, etc.), bookstock work, and readers' advisory work. Thus, the emphasis is switched from library-based activities to a mixture involving community-based activities. (p. 155)

Another manifestation of information service provided outside the library is the "information broker," an organization or individual providing service for a fee. The origin of the information broker has been traced, oddly enough, to a telephone information service provided by the Budapest Telephone Newspaper in 1923 (Kalba [1977]), although more people might accept the French S'il Vous Plait (SVP), established in 1948, as the real forebear of modern fee-based information services (Gaffner [1976]). The company still operates in France and in the United States as FIND/SVP, and has affiliates throughout the world.

The growth of fee-based information services of this type gained momentum in the late 1960s. There now seem to be at least 170 such services in North America alone (Warnken [1978]). So important have these services become that they now have their own journal, *The Journal of Fee-Based Information Services*. Useful surveys of the subject have been prepared by Maranjian and Boss (1980) and Warnken (1981).

Fee-based services have found a market in the academic community. Library school graduates have had success in establishing freelance services within academia (Bellamy [1977] and Hickey [1974]) and faculty members have been willing to bypass the university library and contact professional information brokers to satisfy literature-searching and document-delivery needs (Finnigan [1976] and Herther [1978]).

Some fee-based services have also emerged in public and academic libraries. One example is INFORM, a service operated by the Minneapolis Public Library for the business community (Shannon [1974]). Examples of special services to the industrial sector offered by academic libraries can be seen at the Colorado Technical Reference Center (Broward [1978]) and at the Georgia Institute of Technology (Dodd [1974]). An information broker serving as a full member of a health planning team has been described by Valdez (1974).

Most of these examples refer to information professionals providing library-type services outside the traditional library setting. This is as it should be. The information professional needs to work in the community to be served and not hide away inside a decaying institution. As has been said before, *the future of the librarian depends on his willingness to leave the traditional library and to look on the library as merely a collection of physical artifacts that is one element in an armory of available resources.*

The deinstitutionalization of the librarian will probably continue at a greatly accelerated pace during the next few years, if for no other reason than that electronic publishing will allow increased freedom from the library as an institution. More precisely, the process will be one of reinstitutionalization, with librarians working as team members throughout industry, academia, health care, law, and other professional environments, or as members of fee-based enterprises. This movement of library service into the community is essential to the survival of the profession, a notion similar to the team librarianship concept mentioned earlier and in line with recommendations made by Smith (1974) for the university environment.

The need to move the librarian out of the library has been emphasized, at least by implication, by several writers. Nelson (1975), for example, has said that meaningful information services based on sound subject competence require that academic researchers be met on their own ground. Cheney (1971) and Harmon (1975) have both spoken of the need for the information profession to reach out to the research community by infiltrating its laboratories and offices, while Foskett (1964) has claimed that the information specialist must play a more active role on the research team. Major (1979) has put the situation in a nutshell:

The librarian of the next generation should be able to take his place in a team serving the community alongside community workers, social workers, teachers, etc. If the general public has been educated to have a limited concept of what a librarian offers we will not correct this by staying quietly in our buildings. As more and more professional tasks either become automated or provided by a central institution, the emphasis in public librarianship will shift away from conservation to a more active exploitation of our resources. (p. 156)

In summary, the information profession must take advantage of the opportunities presented by the new technologies to free itself from its present institutional straitjacket. If it does, it could survive prosperously long after the institution itself has outlived its usefulness. In this respect alone, I am in disagreement with Lewis (1976, 1980), who can see little future for the library or the librarian. In the long term, as the population becomes increasingly comfortable with the use of terminals and as retrieval systems become simpler to use, Lewis may be proved right. On the other hand, there may always be a need for the unique expertise that information specialists can provide. As Line (1969) has pointed out,

This . . . argument ultimately comes down to a value judgment; it is on par with the feeling that researchers ought to do their own programming, repair their own electron microscopes, or for that matter, darn their own socks. If a necessary job can be done far more efficiently by someone else, you don't do it yourself. (p. 219)

Good information specialists have the opportunity to make themselves indispensible to the research community. Recipients of their services have expressed this as follows (Byrd and Arnold [1979]):

How easy it was to research the literature. It really made you lazy. . . . as long as such people are available, I'm not interested in being proficient in library work. (p. 311)

Hiltz and Turoff (1978) hedge on the future of the information specialist. On the one hand, they view computer conferencing as the appropriate medium for interlibrarian communication:

Given the availability of computer terminals in public libraries for public access and use, and for online searches of computer based bibliographic and abstract files, a computer conferencing system might be used by librarians themselves to form what Manfred Kochen calls a "referential consulting network." (p. 203)

This network would be used for the referral of questions that cannot be answered by the library in which they are received. It would be a "large network of reference librarians and 'on-call' experts utilized to share their resources." Later, however, Hiltz and Turoff express some doubts on whether such professionals will be needed at all:

On the other hand, it may be that libraries and librarians as intermediaries between the public and stored information will be replaced to a large extent by the computer based systems that give access directly to the public. (p. 203)

Turoff and Featheringham (1979) describe the librarian of the future as an information specialist who is a full member of an electronic discussion group consisting of scientists, scholars, and practitioners. When a particular query is posed from within the group, the information specialist relays that query to an information brokerage house for processing against specific data bases. The accessed information is then "analyzed, organized, and distributed back to the users through the message/conferencing system."

They also claim that this information specialist will have the responsibility of teaching people how to use the technologies applicable to information access. The information specialists will probably not be institution-based. Rather, they will be "reference and referral librarians" working in the comfort of their own homes.

Cuadra (1972) predicts the growing importance of the information broker as an intermediary between those who need information and the information sources themselves:

The average library or information center user will not wish to subscribe to one SDI service covering one type of literature and another service covering a different type. He will want, instead, to tell someone nearby—an information broker—what he needs and let the information broker serve as a middleman in the necessary transactions. (p. 475)

Saunderson (1977) believes that intermediaries will not be needed for quick reference searches of on-line data bases or for searches performed for current-awareness purposes. The information professional may still be needed for comprehensive retrospective searches and the handling of complex questions. The devolution of the decision making, with more people involved in the process, the need for more diverse information to support decision making, and the growth of available information all point to the need for analysis and synthesis before information is presented to those who are to use it. Saunderson sees a need for the reinstitutionalization process alluded to earlier in this chapter:

Aided and abetted by technological advance the wheel would turn full circle. The information function of the future will return to where it was before information units and libraries were established. The information function will be within "user departments" . . . where there is a "need to know." (pp. 89–90)

Brown (1980), a consultant on strategic planning and the management of change, has claimed that "Today's tidal wave of change is terrifying many people who have depended upon institutions that now are crumbling" (p. 23). He goes on to say that "As history shows us, during such transformations the institutions that comprise the framework of the dying society crumble and fall apart, a necessary pre-condition to the construction of the new institutions of a new society. Old institutions impede the development of a new age, which has new needs and new people" (p. 23). Through the deliberate de-emphasis of the library as a building and collection of artifacts and a deliberate promotion of the technical expertise of its trained practitioners, the library profession has the ability to construct the type of new institution that Brown refers to. Moreover, this new institution could be considerably stronger than the one it replaces.

The Education of the Librarian

It has become something of a cliche to say that we live in an Age of Information, or that we are witnessing an Information Explosion. However, although the terminology has entered easily into our language many of our institutions (including schools) have yet to respond to the challenges that such an age confronts us with. The ability to locate, retrieve, select, organize, evaluate and communicate information will increasingly become a major component of what we understand the term "literacy" to mean; consequently such abilities will be crucial to each individual's quality of life. New developments in information and communication technologies are rapidly expanding our "information environments," and also the range of skills required to exploit them; however, many pupils are still leaving school unable to manipulate even our most basic and traditional information sources.

This quotation, extracted from an information sheet prepared by the Inner London Education Authority (1980), provides a useful springboard to a discussion of needs for education within the library profession. Not only has education in general failed to come to grips with the implications of the information age, but library education itself has lagged behind technological developments in many ways.

There is no doubt that librarianship is becoming more complex and more demanding than it was even a decade ago. Machine-readable data bases and on-line access to them have greatly increased the capability of libraries to provide a high level of literature-searching service. But these new capabilities demand more from the modern librarian. It is no longer enough for him to be familiar with the information sources physically present within one institution. A single on-line terminal can now give access to several hundred data bases. The effective exploitation of these vast on-line resources depends on the librarian's knowledge of their scope and on his ability to search them. This ability, in turn, requires some knowledge of indexing policies and practices and of procedures for vocabulary control, as well as a familiarity with alternative searching strategies.

Moreover, technology does not stand still — far from it. In data processing and in telecommunications, new capabilities and applications constantly emerge, one on the heels of another. Many of these developments, including satellite communication, interactive television, computer conferencing, and electronic mail, offer exciting new opportunities for rapid and efficient information transfer, including transfer across international boundaries. The librarian of today cannot afford to ignore such developments. Indeed, he should be constantly alert to their potential for increasing the quality and efficiency of information services.

The library science curriculum of 10 years ago is no longer adequate to prepare information professionals to adapt to the evolutionary forces converting us from a print-on-paper society to an electronic society. Yet, the curricula of library schools change slowly, and some schools have changed little in the past decade. It is time for a complete recasting of these curricula. As Giuliano (1969) pointed out some years ago, the focus of professional education must be changed. It should no longer be the library as an institution. Instead, the whole field of human communication, formal and informal, and the role of the information professional in facilitating effective communication must be considered. The focus, then, shifts from the institution to the individual — to the information professional as a technical specialist removed from a particular institutional environment. This change in emphasis is needed now because on-line networks are rapidly bringing about a deinstitutionalization process. Certain professional activities previously performed within the library can now be handled outside the library, and an increasing number of activities could become deinstitutionalized in the near future.

The developments occurring in technology and their application in innovative approaches to communication make it imperative that librarians continue their education throughout their professional careers. Continuing education is becoming increasingly important in all branches of human activity. Universities, national libraries, professional societies, and international organizations have the responsibility to develop courses, workshops, seminars, and congresses to ensure that the librarian understands and applies appropriate new techniques, instead of continuing to rely on the traditional methods of the past. Librarians themselves must accept some responsibility in this area by convincing the appropriate organizations that such continuing education courses are necessary and by identifying their own specific needs for further education and training.

Conclusion

The probable long-term effect of technology on the library profession is a matter of controversy. Some believe that technology strengthens the professions. Others, however, see a danger that technology will lead to a "deprofessionalized" society (Haug [1975]). Nielsen (1980) has presented these various viewpoints within the context of librarianship.

It is my belief that, in the long run, the process of deinstitutionalization/reinstitutionalization will be very beneficial to the profession. The librarian of the electronic age could become a valued professional colleague of chemists, physicists, physicians, attorneys, educators, and other professionals. The profession has been institutionalized far too long. The deinstitutionalization process of the electronic age, by focusing on the information professional as an expert in a technical field, rather than on the institution in which he operates, could greatly improve the librarian's image, status, and rate of compensation.

The decline of the library does not imply the decline of the librarian. As society moves further into the information age, the fact that "information is power" will become more widely recognized, as will the great potential value of professional persons familiar with the multitude of information resources available in electronic form and capable of exploiting these resources efficiently and effectively. The future of the professional information specialist appears very secure.

11 Conclusion

Two scenarios are presented in this book. The first, in Chapter 5, depicts a possible future system in which formal publication is one component within a larger electronic network of interpersonal and intergroup communication. The second, in Chapter 9, builds on the first. It depicts the gradual disembodiment of the library in the last two decades of this century.

Both scenarios are personal interpretations. They encapsulate the views of the author on what the future is likely to hold for formal and informal channels of human communication and for libraries and librarians caught up in a tumultuous period of rapid technological and social change. They are, however, logical extrapolations from the technological trends of the past decade. Moreover, they lean in the direction of conservatism rather than "blue sky" speculation. They are based on existing technological capabilities and on reasonable forecasts of future technological and economic trends. They are not dependent, in any way, on technologies and capabilities yet to be developed. In fact, all the activities performed by the hypothetical scientist in Chapter 5 are being performed now, in one form or another. They just have not been pulled together into a single system.

The scenario of Chapter 5 is derived from an extrapolation of developments in on-line information retrieval, publishing, computer conferencing, electronic mail, interactive television, and related technologies within a period of approximately 20 years (1959–1979). The second scenario is entirely dependent on the first in that the changes forecast for libraries and librarians will come about only if the broader changes in human communication patterns, as forecast in Chapter 5, actually occur.

Of course, both scenarios will undoubtedly be more accurate in general content than in specific detail. In other words, it is more definite that the communication developments predicted will occur than that they will be implemented in the particular mode described here.

Alternative Scenarios

While examining alternative scenarios in studies performed in other areas, it became apparent that many alternative scenarios are not really alternative at all. Instead, they are a series of very similar scenarios having different time scales associated with them; that is, one alternative is optimistic in terms of when particular events will occur, one is pessimistic on these same events, and a third is middle of the road. This is true, for example, of the alternative future information systems (expected, accelerated, and conservative) described by King Research, Inc. (1978). In the King study, however, even the optimistic (accelerated) forecast seems conservative. The position adopted here is as follows: If, many years from now, one could look back over the long history of human communication, it is likely that the print-on-paper era would form a rather short segment of this history—a little over 500 years. This print-on-paper era is now evolving into an electronic era, an evolution that I regard as inevitable. In substance, the developments described earlier will occur. The exact time at which they occur, however, is less clear. I adopted the year 2000 as the setting of the scenario in Chapter 5 and as the end point of the developments described in Chapter 9 and presented a picture of what I consider likely to have been achieved in this evolutionary process by that date. I recognize, however, that the dates of specific occurrences are much less certain than the occurrences themselves. The scenario set in the year 2000 might more appropriately be set in 2010 or 2020. On the other hand, it might be completely appropriate to 1995.

It has been suggested to me that I should produce an alternative "disaster scenario," but "disaster scenario" is an imprecise term. No doubt many people will regard the developments forecast in this book as a disaster. In this context, however, the term "disaster scenario" refers to a situation in which economic, political, or other impediments prevent an otherwise plausible chain of events from taking place.

Cornish (1980) refers to three types of future scenarios: standard (an extrapolation of current trends), optimistic, and pessimistic. In his view, these alternatives have the following general characteristics:

Standard scenario: World population will grow; but living standards will remain about the same. Many advances will occur in technology, especially electronics and communications but the economic benefits of these advances will be largely offset by the shrinking in the amount of prime natural resources. . .

Pessimistic scenario: The world economy will deteriorate badly in the 1980s. . . . The developed countries will face soaring unemployment; the developing countries will experience mass famines. Major wars—both civil and international—will occur, and there is the possibility of World War III.

Optimistic scenario: New communications devices will spearhead a parade of new technological devices that will solve most of the pressing problems of the 1970s. Microprocessors will vastly increase the efficiency with which energy is used, enabling people to keep their homes warm and drive their automobiles with far less expenditure of fuel than is now required. Breakthroughs in energy production will substantially free the world from its enslavement to petroleum and natural gas. New birth control methods will curb population growth in the developing countries, thus preventing starvation and making it possible for them to advance economically. Artificial intelligence will provide an exciting new alternative for decision-making, and increasingly, electronic devices will be entrusted with arbitrating differences among nations. At the same time, human wishes will be expressed on a mass basis through computer-communications devices hooked up to homes everywhere. As the nations move toward an anticipatory democracy mode, with huge electronic "town meetings" involving millions of people, the world will move rapidly toward peace and prosperity. (p. 5)

The developments described in this book assume a situation that is close to Cornish's optimistic scenario. At the very least, they assume a world scenario somewhere between the standard and the optimistic—that is, an expanding world economy, freedom from world war, and an international climate favorable to the exchange of information. If these presumptions are incorrect, developments could take a different turn or be delayed far beyond the dates predicted.

Turoff (1979) has suggested additional situations that would greatly reduce the credibility of the scenarios presented in this book:

1. Government funding and regulatory policies drive up the cost of information.

2. Regulatory mechanisms applied to electronic networks reflect a premise that these will only be used by industry and government,

leading to high entry costs and other constraints discouraging the use of such systems by the private citizen.

3. An "information elite" (e.g., large corporations) emerges that can afford access to information products with the concomitant emergence of an "information underprivileged" class.

4. Lack of adequate copyright protection for authors of electronic publications leads to a decline in the publication process.

5. Home computers and interactive television do not develop significant markets. Cheap terminals do not emerge.

6. A multitude of on-line networks, without adequate control or interface mechanisms, springs up. Lack of adequate integration and planning leads to an "information nightmare."

And so on. It is easy to see that a "disaster" situation could occur. But rather than developing a disaster scenario that would, perforce, be based on a whole host of imponderables, it seems sufficient to identify some of the dangers that could lead to a disaster situation or, at least, greatly reduce the rate of progress predicted.

Assumptions

Some basic assumptions underlie the scenarios presented in this book. One is that, in the long run, an electronic communication system will be less expensive than one that is primarily based on paper. According to the data of Senders et al. (1975), Folk (1977), and Roistacher (1978a), electronic publishing may already be the cheaper alternative, and it can be expected that the cost of electronic processing will continue to decline relative to the more conventional methods.

It is also assumed that the terminal infrastructure needed to support a paperless communication system will be in place before the end of the century. Again, the technological forecasts referred to in Chapter 2 indicate that this is likely. Another, perhaps more important, underlying assumption is that a substantial shift away from print-on-paper toward electronic access will occur in the consumer market for publications. Before this is considered further, it may be useful to review the basic economic differences between print-on-paper access and electronic access.

In the print-on-paper world, a library must purchase a publication in order to make it accessible to its users. The purchase cost, plus cost of processing it for use, is a form of capital investment. The capital investment is a capital investment in *accessibility.* The only way to make a print-on-paper publication conveniently accessible is to buy it and place it on the library's shelves. The return on the investment is the amount of use the publication receives. If it costs $210 per year to subscribe to and maintain a particular journal that is used 30 times per year, the library's cost per use is $7.

In the print-on-paper environment, then, accessibility is primarily a two-level phenomenon, the publications that a library owns being considerably more accessible to its users than those it does not own. Presumably, a library will try to acquire those materials that are likely to yield the greatest return (in use) for the investment. The expected return is related to the cost of purchase: The more expensive items require more use in order to be justified from a cost-effectiveness point of view.

Thus, in the library of a pharmaceutical company, it might be very easy to justify a subscription to *Chemical Abstracts*, even at a cost in excess of $5,000 per year, because of the volume of expected use. In the library of an engineering organization, on the other hand, it might be difficult to justify this subscription. If only 50 searches a year are conducted with this tool, the cost per search for data base access alone (i.e., excluding all librarian and user costs) would exceed $100.

It is clear that in the electronic world a completely different economic environment exists. To gain access to a publication, a library no longer needs to make a capital investment in that publication. Instead, it pays for access when such access is needed. It is entirely an on-demand, "pay-as-you-go" situation. Thus, the engineering library, which could not justify a subscription to *Chemical Abstracts,* could certainly afford to access the equivalent electronic data base, perhaps at a cost for data base access of less than $20 per search. In the electronic environment, the capital investment is made in equipment to make a multitude of data bases accessible rather than in the data bases themselves.

This situation favors the potential user of information products. Because the library pays for only what it uses, it is taking no investment risks. Consequently, the library can afford to access very many data bases that would be inaccessible in a print-on-paper situation. From the point of view of the publisher, however, publication only in electronic form is less attractive. The publisher of a print-on-paper periodical receives income "up front"; payment for a subscription is made before any issues are received. In the case of the electronic journal, however, the publisher is paid only when his product is used.

On the other hand, it seems reasonable to assume that in the long run the market for many publications in electronic form is potentially much greater than the market for these same publications in paper form. It seems highly unlikely, for example, that there are many individuals and institutions waiting to subscribe to *Chemical Abstracts* at $5,000 per year. For all intents and purposes, the market for this publication is probably already saturated. Indeed, subscriptions to this and many other secondary services are declining. It seems probable, however, that there is a vast market of individuals and institutions able and willing to pay for on-line access to this data base when the need for this access arises. The surface of this market has hardly been scratched.

It seems equally evident that the cost of electronic access, to this or any other data base, will continue to decline rapidly relative to the cost of access to the print-on-paper product (unless the publisher deliberately inflates the cost of electronic access in order to subsidize the paper publication). This does not mean that the cost of *producing* a data base for electronic access is less than the cost of producing a data base for publication in printed form (although it may be; for example, for efficient use, a printed index may have to use a controlled vocabulary assigned by human indexers, whereas human indexing and the maintenance of a controlled vocabulary may be dispensed with in an electronic equivalent) but, rather, that the cost of distributing it—that is, making it accessible—is likely to be less.

For data bases that currently exist in dual form, income from the electronic version is likely to be only a fraction of income from the paper version. The paper version is bearing most, if not all, of the costs of producing the data base. It is, in effect, subsidizing electronic access. For reasons mentioned earlier, it can be expected that this situation will change and that, for those publications accessible in both forms, income from electronic access will increase relative to income from the paper products. A point will be reached when the income from electronic access begins to subsidize the production of publications in paper form. Eventually, it will no longer be economically feasible to produce the latter and electronic distribution will take over completely. There will, of course, be a difficult transition period in which income from paper products may decline more rapidly than the complementary increase in income from the electronic products, resulting in temporary cost increases for both until the electronic access market grows large enough to maintain low costs.

It is difficult to predict when this market transition is likely to occur for those publications (mostly indexing and abstracting services) already available in both modes. It is even more difficult to foretell when it will occur for primary journals, reference works, and other publications for which no dual-mode experience has yet been accumulated. Participants in the Delphi study reported by Lancaster et al. (1980) predict that approximately 25 percent of existing reference books could have converted to exclusive electronic access by 1990. Availability of journals exclusively in electronic form, even in science and technology, is expected to lag behind this date. In fact, most panelists forecast that it will be after 2000 before even one-quarter of existing journals have converted completely to electronic access. (Note, however, that this prediction was for the worldwide situation. It is very likely that the conversion process will be much more rapid for the North American journals.)

Barwise (1979) examined this market transition for the International Council of Scientific Unions Abstracting Board (ICSU/AB). The Barwise investigation, which is based on somewhat limited statistical data plus a survey of expert opinion, concludes that on-line searching has had little impact on sales of printed services as yet but that the likely impact from 1978 through 1985 is very uncertain. A cost-strategy model, applied to a hypothetical publisher of an abstracts journal, suggests that on-line royalties are now low relative to the price of printed products and that on-line user charges could increase by a factor of 2 to 2½, relative to print prices, in the next five years. The author points outs, however, that better data are needed on on-line usage and its impact on print subscriptions.

There seem to be some basic assumptions underlying the Barwise study. One is that the cost of creating a data base will be the same, whether it is produced for electronic or print access. Thus, the question becomes one of pricing strategy: How much of this cost should be assigned to the purchasers of electronic access and how much to print-on-paper subscribers? The study assumes that both means of access will continue and does not consider the possibility that, at some future date, the electronic access will completely replace the paper access. As pointed out earlier, abandonment of the paper product could substantially reduce the costs of preparing some data bases since it may mean that publishers could dispense with costly, labor-intensive human indexing and the maintenance of controlled vocabularies.

Another simplifying assumption is that a data base will exist in essentially a noncompetitive market environment. In the Barwise models, income from on-line royalties is traded against income from subscriptions to print on paper. No consideration is given to possible competition from new data bases that are made accessible only in the electronic mode. Although it may seem unlikely that strong competitors to the large discipline-oriented services will emerge, it is entirely possible that "electronic only" competitors to some of the smaller services will appear. If this occurs, a dual-mode publisher may find itself competing for on-line royalties with a newer on-line–only service. This would presumably alter the entire market picture, with print subscriptions threatened from two sides rather than one.

There is another imponderable, touched on in the scenarios in Chapters 5 and 9. If, as I have predicted, the trends in primary publication parallel the trends in secondary publication, we can expect to see the full text of journals becoming accessible on-line in the next few years. When a substantial number of these journals are accessible electronically, will it make any sense to continue to publish secondary guides to this literature in print-on-paper form? Viewed another way, is it not reasonable to suppose that, as primary journals become accessible on-line, a substantial demand for on-line access to guides to this primary literature will occur, causing a pronounced shift in demand for secondary services toward on-line access and away from subscriptions to print on paper?

To carry this further, if the full text of journals is accessible through on-line networks and if on-line SDI services can be "fed" from, say, titles and abstracts of this text, is there any need for "conventional" secondary publications in electronic or paper form?

The next 20 or 30 years may see the complete disappearance of most, if not all, secondary services, or at least the disappearance of such services as they are known today. The justification for this assertion can be illustrated by a simple hypothetical example. Imagine a secondary service a number of years old, that deals with a highly specialized subject area, such that only 50 journals are covered. When first established, the service wrote abstracts for most articles in each journal and indexed each article by use of a controlled vocabulary. As the years went on, however, this service prepared fewer and fewer abstracts; since most of the journals were already carrying abstracts, it was content to accept these intact. The service then moved into the dual-mode phase and began to issue a machine-readable data base. By this time, all 50 periodicals included acceptable abstracts. The task of "abstracting," then, involved nothing more than putting the author abstracts into machine-readable form. After the data base had been used for some time, it was recognized that the indexing activity was becoming redundant, since acceptable searches could be done on the text of titles plus abstracts. The human indexing was retained solely to produce a usable printed tool. As the years went by, however, subscriptions to this printed tool declined to the point where on-line income was actually subsidizing the printed product. The printed tool was then abandoned. When this occurred, the role of the secondary service, regarding the 50 periodicals, consisted solely of putting bibliographic references plus abstracts into machine-readable form. By this time, however, many of the journals were already accessible in full-text form through on-line networks. A few years later, all 50 were accessible in this way. It was then recognized that the secondary service served no useful purpose. All 50 periodicals were stored in a single on-line service center that not only provided access to full text, but also was able to build a searchable data base of abstracts. The secondary service was thus replaced by the on-line service center.

This projection is oversimplified in a number of respects. First, it assumes that all journals carry acceptable abstracts. Although this is not the case at present, it could well be in the future should it be made a condition for acceptance of a journal by an on-line service center. Second, it takes no account of the language problem. This may not be a problem later. The recent resurgence of interest in machine translation may lead to the automatic reduction of all abstracts to a common language. The greatest oversimplification is one of scale. To speak of 50 journals is one thing, but to speak of 100,000 is something else. Nevertheless, in principle, there is no reason why

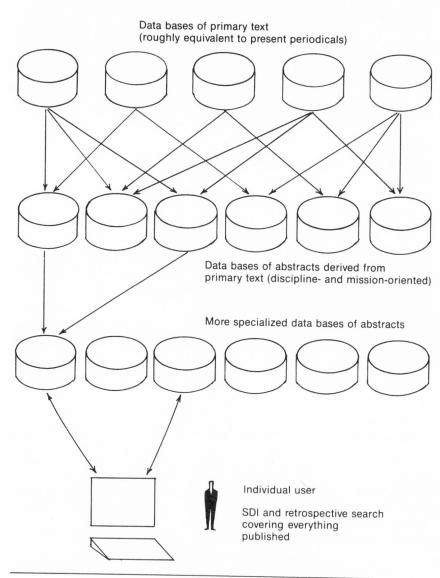

Figure 23 Filtering levels in a paperless publishing environment.

acceptable "accessing data bases" could not be built directly from the primary literature, assuming that the journals exist in machine-readable form and include abstracts. A series of filters (really subject profiles) would be necessary to form major discipline-oriented and mission-oriented data bases from all items newly added to all data bases (i.e., not restricted to a particular set of journals). More refined filters would form more specialized data bases from the first-level data bases. User-interest profiles could then be applied to the second-level data bases. An individual user would log onto some system and be informed that X number of items, matching his profile of interests, have been published since he last used the system. He could then view abstracts and, if required, get on-line access to the complete item. Rather than "subscribing" to any one electronic journal, the filters would keep him informed of everything matching his interest, wherever published. At various levels, data bases of abstracts would be available for searching when specific information needs arise.

The situation envisioned is illustrated in Figure 23. The diagram does not imply any particular number of data bases or the use of any particular technology. Nor does it imply any particular institutional configuration. Those organizations that now produce secondary services might still play an important role in the total system (e.g., in building and maintaining subject profiles), but it will be a different role from that played today. The diagram does imply that the need for organizations to abstract and index the literature will disappear, assuming that primary sources in print-on-paper form will eventually be replaced by equivalent sources in machine-readable form. Instead, the equivalent organizations of the future will be concerned with building the various levels of filters and searching aids (synonym tables, text-based "thesauri") that will be needed to provide effective current-awareness and literature-searching services at the user level.

Some Economic Considerations

Collier (1978) has presented some hypothetical data on economic aspects of the use of on-line services compared with subscriptions to printed services in libraries. Collier's view of the economics of on-line searching seems misleadlingly pessimistic because

1. It looks only at *costs* and not at *effectiveness* in comparing the two modes of access and searching. An analysis combining cost and effectiveness aspects (i.e., a cost-effectiveness analysis) would give a completely different picture.

2. The way the cost data are presented is grossly unfair to the on-line mode of access and use.

Collier's data are presented in Table 11, which represents a hypothetical data base under varying conditions. The cost of producing and distributing the data base is assumed to be $3 million. The total cost for on-line access, taking all elements into account, is assumed to be $80 per hour, a realistic figure for the U.S. situation.

In situation *A*, there is no on-line use. At a subscription rate of $2,500 annually, 1,200 library subscribers would be needed for the publisher to recover the $3 million investment. The total cost to the "library community," Collier points out, is $3 million. Actually, it would be more than this, perhaps over $3.6 million, if the cost of storage and handling in 1,200 libraries is taken into account. Studies at the University of Pittsburgh (Kent et al. [1979]) suggest that the real cost of owning a serial publication could be at least 20 percent more than the subscription cost alone. In situations *B, C, E,* and *F,* there is no income from printed subscriptions. The variables are the per-hour royalty charges and the number of hours of on-line use. Total on-line cost per hour also varies in *E.* In *B,* with royalties set at $20 per hour, 150,000 hours of access would be needed for the publisher to recover his investment. Since the total cost of on-line access is $80 per hour, Collier is correct in stating that the total cost to the library community would be $12 million per year. Clearly, as the royalty rate is increased, the number of hours of access needed to recover data base costs declines. In *C,* at a royalty of $40 per hour, 75,000 hours of access would be needed. In *E,* with royalties of $100 per hour, and total on-line costs of $150 per hour, only 30,000 hours of access are needed. Total annual costs to the library community are $6 million and $4.5 million respectively. The total cost to the library community is brought down to $3 million per year in alternative *F.* But, with royalties set at $30 per hour and access hours set at 37,500, this option would bring a loss to the publisher of almost $2 million per year. Situation *D* is a mixed-income situation. With the cost of an annual subscription set at $3,000 and royalties at $30 per hour, 700

Table 11 Alternative Pricing Strategies for Print-on-Paper and On-line Access

	A	B	C	D	E	F
Cost of producing and distributing data base ($)	3,000,000	3,000,000	3,000,000	3,000,000	3,000,000	3,000,000
On-line royalty income ($)		3,000,000	3,000,000	900,000	3,000,000	1,125,000
Royalty charge per hour ($)		20	40	30	100	30
Number of hours of on-line use		150,000	75,000	30,000	30,000	37,500
Total on-line cost per hour ($)		80	80	80	150	80
Number of subscribers to printed index	1,200			700		
Cost of one annual subscription ($)	2,500			3,000		
Subscription income ($)	3,000,000			2,100,000		
Total cost to library community ($)	3,000,000	12,000,000	6,000,000	4,500,000	4,500,000	3,000,000

SOURCE: Adapted from Collier (1978).

subscribers plus 30,000 hours of on-line access would be needed for the publisher to recover his $3 million investment. Different figures could be plugged into Collier's framework to assess the economic effects of declining subscriptions, increasing subscription costs, increasing royalty charges, and increasing levels of on-line access.

Collier does not explain how in alternatives *B, C, D,* and *F* it is possible for on-line royalties to vary from $20 to $40 per hour without a concomitant variation in total on-line cost per hour. But since this does not affect the argument presented here, Collier's figures are used as he presented them.

Collier's analysis is certainly interesting, and his figures, while hypothetical, accurately depict the difficult pricing decisions facing publishers who issue a data base in both paper and electronic forms. Nevertheless, his conclusions about the impact on the library community are misleading for the following reasons:

1. The cost to a library of owning the printed service is more than the cost of the subscription. Storage, handling, and other costs could add another 20 percent or more to the cost of the subscription.

2. A printed service that costs $2,500 per year for a subscription plus $500 per year for other costs, represents an annual cost of $3,000 per year to the library for data base access alone; that is, the cost to the library is $3,000 per year even if the printed service is never used. The data in situation *A,* then, can be considered costs incurred, even if no searches are undertaken. This is not true of the on-line situation, in which access is paid for only when necessary.

3. Collier's $80 hourly costs to the library include $10 for "equipment, training and terminal operator." In other words, Collier is charging personnel costs of searching the data base to the on-line situation but not to the print-on-paper situation. Assume that the librarian conducting on-line searches is paid $8 per hour (Collier's $10 minus $2 for training costs plus terminal use) and that four on-line searches can be done in one hour of access. Looking at option *C* in Table 11, 75,000 hours of access would represent 300,000 searches. It seems reasonable to assume that these searches, if conducted in the printed data base, would take much longer to perform. A conservative estimate is that each search would take twice as long in the printed tool, but this ratio might be as high as 8:1. In this case, a 2:1 ratio is used. In other words, the 300,000 searches would take

150,000 hours of librarian time at $8 per hour, for a total of $1.2 million. Therefore, a more realistic cost of situation A to the library community, assuming 300,000 searches each year and taking storage and handling into account, is $4.8 million. This is a more valid comparison of situation A with situation C because C takes into account all costs of 300,000 searches (excluding printout or photocopying costs and time taken for "negotiation" with the requester, which is assumed to be equal in the two situations), whereas A represents only subscription costs, assuming no level of use. It is easy to see that if the average time taken to search the printed tool is three times that needed to search the on-line data base, the cost to the library community of alternative A, assuming 300,000 searches, would be $5.4 million, which is close to the $6 million in situation C. If the average time taken to search the printed tool is eight times greater, the cost to the library community of alternative A would be $8.4 million.

4. Collier's analysis considers costs but not effectiveness of the two modes of literature searching. Thus it is a cost analysis but not a cost-effectiveness analysis. If effectiveness is taken into account, the situation changes completely. To achieve the same level of effectiveness in a search of a printed data base that is achieved in a search of the on-line equivalent (e.g., measured in terms of recall), it could easily take eight times longer (if, indeed, it would ever be possible to reach the same level of effectiveness). If cost-effectiveness is accounted for, then, the costs in situation A could easily be around the $8 million level, if not more.

These figures are largely hypothetical. The most complete and realistic comparison of the cost of on-line searching versus searching of printed tools is, I believe, that performed by Elchesen (1978). According to Elchesen's data, which are based on 80 searches conducted in both modes, a print search takes about 4½ times longer, on the average, than an on-line search (119.5 minutes versus 26.7 minutes). If only searching time (i.e., excluding time for question negotiation, photocopying, output processing and distribution, etc.) is considered, however, a print search takes nearly eight times longer than an on-line search (89.6 minutes versus 11.6 minutes). Elchesen computed the average cost of an on-line search to be $26.05, whereas the average cost of a print search was computed at $30.15. These are true cost figures that take into account all the following factors: personnel costs (professional and clerical), data base access costs (including subscription costs for the printed services and connect time plus royalties for the on-line mode), reproduction costs, costs of equipment purchase or rental, space costs, and telecommunications costs. Overhead is built into the personnel costs and the space costs.

The appropriate cost-effectiveness measure to use in the comparison is the cost per relevant reference retrieved. This is computed by dividing the total cost of the search by the number of retrieved references judged relevant by the initiator of the search. In the Elchesen analysis, the average number of references retrieved per search was 35.2 for print and 47.1 for on-line. The average number of *relevant* references retrieved was 35.2 and 39.8, respectively. The computed recall ratios were 43 percent and 57 percent. The precision ratios were 100 percent for print (hardly surprising since the searcher is making relevance decisions continuously as the search is conducted) and 84 percent for on-line. The cost per relevant reference retrieved was $0.86 for print and $0.65 for on-line.

Plugging Elchesen's data* into alternative *B* of Table 11 shows that 150,000 hours of on-line time will account for 750,000 searches per year, which will cost the library community $26.05 × 750,000, or approximately $19.5 million. In contrast, 750,000 searches conducted in print will cost $30.15 × 750,000 or approximately $22.6 million. This is a much fairer comparison than that provided by Collier, who charged total costs to the on-line side of the comparison but not to the print side. In Table 11, it is meaningless to compare situation *A* with situation *B*, since *B* represents 750,000 searches, and no searches at all are present, explicitly or implicitly, in *A*. As mentioned earlier, the costs for alternative *A* are incurred even if the printed tools are never opened.

Even on the basis of cost alone, then, the on-line mode of operation compares favorably with the print mode when realistic values are used in the analysis. If cost-effectiveness is considered, the comparison favors the on-line mode even more strongly, since Elchesen's

---

* While it may seem dangerous to extrapolate from 80 searches to 750,000 searches, I believe such extrapolation is entirely reasonable in this case. If 5,000 libraries each perform 150 searches per year, there is no reason to believe that the average cost and level of effectiveness per search will vary widely from Elchesen's data.

data indicate that on-line searching is about 33 percent more cost-effective than print searching ($0.65 versus $0.86 per relevant reference retrieved). Thus, at 750,000 searches per year, the cost to the library community for searching the printed tool is $22.6 million, whereas it is $19.5 million for on-line searching. To raise the level of *effectiveness* of the printed tool to the level of effectiveness implicit in the $19.5 million expenditure for the on-line mode, the $22.6 million value for the printed tool must be multiplied by 1.33. Therefore, the library community would have to spend approximately $30 million per year in the print mode to achieve a cost-effectiveness equal to that of the on-line mode.

It is evident from the Barwise and Collier analyses that the dual-mode publishers, lacking competition from organizations producing publications in electronic form only, can, through their pricing policies, favor the on-line customers or the print-on-paper subscribers, or adopt a neutral policy in which the electronic publication competes with the paper publication in the marketplace. Since it is likely that, in the long term, the on-line access market is potentially much larger than the paper market, it seems misguided for publishers to adopt pricing strategies that deliberately restrict the growth of the on-line market.

In 1981, subscriptions to printed indexing and abstracting services were generally on the decline, partly due to the accessibility of equivalent data bases on-line. Through ever-increasing subscription prices, publishers have so far been able to maintain or slightly increase their revenues (*Chemical Abstracts* reported a 10 percent increase in revenues from subscriptions in 1979 despite fewer subscribers). Income from on-line royalties, on the other hand, was increasing rapidly in 1981. *Chemical Abstracts* noted a 25 percent yearly gain, and some other secondary services reported increases as much as 40 percent.

Additional assumptions underlie the scenarios in Chapters 5 and 9. It is assumed that *paperless* means *electronic*. Microforms are deliberately ignored. The reason is that, although microform may retain its value for many years as an inexpensive and compact storage medium for infrequently used material, it probably has no long-term future within the dynamic communication environment described in Chapter 5. In fact, it may be that microform is merely an "interim" medium in the transition from paper to electronics. For example, it seems highly unlikely that computer-output-microform (COM) catalogs will be in use for very many years. It is more likely that they merely represent an interim stage in the evolution from card or printed book catalogs to catalogs in on-line form. This sentiment has been echoed by Croxton (1981), who suggests "that the days of microfilm as the medium of choice for preserving the contents of paper copy are nearly fulfilled" (p. 15).

The same is probably true for facsimile transmission; that is, the transmission of hard copy, by whatever form, will eventually be bypassed by the distribution of electronic soft copy, and, therefore, facsimile transmission has no long-term future. According to a recent Arthur D. Little, Inc. (1979) report on the National Periodicals Center (NPC): "The one electronic information delivery option available to NPC, facsimile, will probably remain expensive, labor-intensive and not in major use" (p. 9).

Characteristics of the Electronic Communication System

The communication system depicted in Chapter 5 has several characteristics that distinguish it from present systems. Perhaps the most significant difference is that in the system projected the distinction between formal and informal communication will be much less clear. At present, the formal and informal channels are distinct, although there are many examples of interaction between the two (e.g., formal publications distributed informally; verbal answers based on information from a published source; and annual conferences, which combine formal and informal communication elements). In the electronic world, the interaction will, presumably, be greater, and the distinction will become increasingly blurred. For one thing, a single device — the on-line terminal — will provide the main entry point to both formal and informal channels. Thus, a user will send and receive mail, confer with groups, write and distribute reports, receive SDI notifications, search data bases, request and receive text, build and search personal files, and so on, all within a common communication environment.

Problems of Implementation

The transition from a paper-based communication environment to a paperless one will not be free from problems. The economic difficulties of the transition have already been alluded to, and the technological problems seem less serious. Nevertheless, if the livelihood of a large portion of the population is dependent on communication networks, these networks must be considerably more reliable and responsive than those currently used. All resources will need to be backed up, so that if one computer or network goes down, the services and facilities normally offered will be assumed by another computer or network. There are additional problems that make electronic systems more vulnerable than paper-based systems. Power failures are the most obvious threats. While emergency generators now protect health care and other essential services from shutdown due to power outages, it seems unlikely that emergency power supplies would be available to protect all levels of a diffuse communication system. It seems equally unlikely that public power supplies would be completely protected against electrical storms and other natural hazards within the foreseeable future. (Of course, adverse weather conditions do not affect electronic systems alone. Severe weather can completely disrupt our present communication patterns. Indeed, business enterprises that make extensive use of electronic communication may suffer less disruption from such conditions than those that rely heavily on staff travel to and from a fixed place of business.)

Doubt has sometimes been voiced about the energy required to power electronic networks in an electronic future. There is concern whether sufficient power will be available. It is not known today what alternative power sources will exist 20 years from now, but it does seem clear that petroleum could continue to be both expensive and scarce in the United States. Insofar as electronic communication systems will reduce the need for commuting to and from a fixed place of work, they will reduce vulnerability to disruptions in the supply of this energy source. Concerns about future energy requirements to power electronic networks are valid. But equally valid are concerns regarding future requirements for the energy and raw materials needed to support a rapidly expanding communication system that is based predominantly on paper.

In addition to the technological and economic problems, there are social problems that will impede the evolution from paper to electronics. Social acceptance will lag behind economic viability, which will, in turn, lag behind technological feasibility. Ten years from now, an electronic publication system may be completely acceptable to society, since by that time, computer terminals will most likely pervade all segments of society and all branches of human activity.

Regarding social acceptance of the inevitability of a paperless society, attitudes seem to be changing rapidly. Seven years ago, when I first began to lecture on the evolution from a print-based society to one that is based on electronics, the reaction was one of skepticism or incredulity from virtually all audiences. This is now much less evident. Indeed, the impending paperless society seems to be taken for granted in many quarters today. A recent Arthur D. Little, Inc. (1979) report views a largely paperless communication system as inevitable:

> For many of the data base publications, a shift in usage from print-copy form to data base access form will have occurred in enough instances (including legal documents, government economic statistics, abstract journals) that major publishers will have decided that the handwriting is on the wall for most professional, scientific and technical journals, and they will be pursuing plans for unbundling of articles and/or for electronic delivery. (p. V-6)

Even "conventional" publishers and academic librarians are taking the transition seriously. As mentioned earlier, J. William Baker (1979), president of Macmillan of Canada, has said,

> First to disappear will be scientific journals and certain types of reference works. Books which consist largely of data, especially data subject to change, will become obsolete. The Macmillan *Dictionary of Canadian Biography*, recently released in its fourth edition, is unlikely to appear in book form in its fifth edition. (p. 265)

In a similar vein, Rutherford D. Rogers (1979), Librarian of Yale University, is reported as saying,

> The researcher-writer will type and edit his copy electronically and transmit it directly to his publisher. . . . By the year 2001, the University Library will be the user and producer of enormous data banks of information stored in computers, transmitted worldwide by satellite. . . . It is possible that much of the intellectual content of books and articles will be stored on computers. (p. 1)

In Europe, too, the profound implications of electronic networks for the publishing industry have been recognized. For example,

Davies (1980), Education Director of the Publishers Association (London), reviewing developments in EURONET and its operational element DIANE (Direct Information Access Network for Europe), has warned,

The development of this network for direct information access has wide-ranging implications for the role of the primary publisher of scientific and technical journals. It is likely that, very soon, he will find himself no longer a primary publisher, distributing his publications directly to the customer, but an "IP" (information provider) for the network. In the long-term, his role may evaporate entirely, with authors submitting their material directly to the system, and governments, information scientists, librarians or professional societies may then become the main disseminators of scientific information. (p. 5)

Raben (1979), describing the advantages of computers within the existing publishing environment, goes on to raise the obvious question of whether or not we still need to print out on paper:

While all this activity is designed to produce conventional printed pages which will not reveal in their appearance that they derive from a totally new technology, there must arise the inevitable question: if so much can be accomplished without paper, why must it be employed in the final step? If the author can compose on a terminal, the editor edit, the referees referee, why must the ultimate user hold in his hand a bound book or journal? Why cannot this reader, too, turn on a terminal and receive what he wants when he wants it? Why must he receive an entire journal in order to obtain a single article? Why purchase an entire book in order to read one chapter or essay? Shouldn't he be able to scan a list of abstracts (on his terminal, of course), and then call up for immediate inspection the works which seem most apposite to his interests at the moment?

In these matters, as in most others, our actions and attitudes will be part of a syndrome, not isolated and autonomous. Some scholars who telephone ahead for motel reservations, fly by jet to Los Angeles, and drive in a high-speed rented car along the freeways to Pasadena may then relish the luxury of abandoning twentieth-century technology for a rich enjoyment of Elizabethan books or even older manuscripts. Others, however, may feel that each age has its appropriate mechanisms, and ours are electronic. If editors are fully exploiting the new technology to gather, prepare, and store material, then perhaps we should also achieve access to it by the same (or similar) means. For the very same terminals, linked by the same telephones to the same central data bases, can provide readers with the selected information they require. Terminals, it is true, cannot be carried into the subway or to bed; they cannot be tucked into pockets; they are not in Harold Wooster's term, cuddly. Neither, of course, were the first books, which were chained to library walls to prevent theft. How soon miniaturization will take effect here is a trivial problem, for the digital watch, the dashboard computer, the desk-top terminal were all fantasies only a few years ago. Long before another generation has elapsed, the pocket terminal will be as commonplace as the pocket radio. (pp. 206–207)

One aspect of acceptability seems particularly important, namely the willingness of the academic community to view publications in electronic form as equivalent to publications in paper form when evaluating candidates for promotion, tenure, and the like. A survey on this subject, reported by Seiler and Raben (1981), presents some preliminary evidence to suggest that the academic community may not be as conservative in this regard as previously feared. Moreover, the survey also seems to indicate an unexpectedly high level of acceptance of the inevitability of the transition to the electronic publication.

Beyond acceptability, there are many other social problems that could prove to be obstacles to a smooth transition from a paper-based to a paperless society. One of these is copyright. The present copyright laws are not entirely adequate to deal with the relatively static paper environment. How much less adequate will they be to deal with a more dynamic situation in which text can be rapidly transferred from store to user and store to store, read and disposed of, put into personal files, updated and annotated, and incorporated into other reports? Protecting the rights of authors and publishers may be very difficult in this situation, although it will be much easier to monitor many kinds of uses than it is now.

Still, this monitoring capability raises problems of its own. The privacy issue is one that generates widespread concern. There are already those who fear that even the limited computer conferencing systems now in existence are routinely monitored by the CIA, the FBI, the KGB, or some other such presence. The question of privacy is a real concern. Electronic networks must offer reasonable levels of security to protect users and their files from unlawful intrusion. But electronic systems are not 100 percent secure; indeed, they will always be as vulnerable as the individuals who program and manage them. On-line networks can be as secure as the telephone or the mail service, both of which are now used without excessive paranoia, although both are vulnerable communication channels.

Another problem relates to possible loss of revenue from advertising. Even though many scholarly journals eschew advertising, others receive substantial income from this source. It remains to be seen whether an effective and acceptable form of advertising can be used with electronic journals. As discussed in Chapter 3, electronic delivery systems are seen as offering great new advertising opportunities (Ris [1980] and Powell [1980]).

There are political problems and barriers to the implementation of electronic communication systems on an international scale. Telephone and other communications lines are owned or regulated by governments. The experience of EURONET suggests that securing agreements of government bodies on tariffs and on regulatory mechanisms controlling transborder data flows is, at best, a tedious and time-consuming process. There are also monopolistic practices that provide additional barriers. The U.S. Postal Service, for example, has a near monopoly on conventional mail delivery but has no such control over electronic message switching. Monopolies on transatlantic communication are already impeding effective computer conferencing at an international level. George Orwell's warning in *1984*—that technology can give governments frightening power to control many aspects of life and to crush any opposition—still haunts many minds.

Some Dangers

It is believed that a system in which the generation and distribution of paper is largely replaced by electronics is one that offers tremendous potential for improving both formal and informal communication processes. But such a system has its associated dangers. An electronic world could serve to democratize human communication, making information more readily available to all segments of society than it has ever been before. On the other hand, it could have the reverse effect, promoting the establishment of "information elites." Which of these events occurs partly depends on how rapidly changes take place, on the type of information available on-line, on how this information can be accessed (e.g., domestic television receivers versus special-purpose terminals), on pricing strategies, and on institutional attitudes (e.g., whether or not libraries consider it their duty to subsidize access to electronic sources in the way in which they subsidize access to print on paper). In the history of technological innovation, the normal pattern of development is one in which initial elitism does occur, with the development filtering down gradually to much larger segments of the population. For example, the automobile and the telephone reached only the elite for a number of years after their introduction.

It seems reasonable to expect, then, that paperless communication systems will also reach an elite long before they spread to the public. Actually, this is already the case. Computer conferencing, for example, is now serving a small elite in the United States, although its use is spreading.

In terms of access to publications, on the other hand, the elitist stage may be very brief. In fact, one could argue that "conventional" access is an elitist situation and that on-line services are already democratizing access. In the print-on-paper environment, the information elite consists of those individuals affiliated with or having ready access to fine libraries (i.e., collections of physical artifacts). Thus, a physician associated with a small community hospital in Tennessee is disadvantaged compared to a physician affiliated with a large teaching hospital in New York City. This particular form of elitism is already being greatly reduced: Through relatively inexpensive terminals, both physicians have equal access to a wide array of on-line information resources made available by the National Library of Medicine and various other institutions. If this is not an antidote to elitism, what is?

Still, other dangers must be recognized and guarded against. The "invisible college" structure of science already provides an elitist environment, since those not well integrated into an informal communications network (because of lack of years in a field, political barriers, language barriers, or whatever) are disadvantaged in terms of access to information. The disadvantage, in this case, is largely one of delay. Through formal publications (prepared, perhaps, more for "publish or perish" reasons than to satisfy a strong desire to communicate), the disadvantaged will learn of new developments much later than their better-integrated colleagues.

Suppose that, in the electronic age, promotion, tenure, and salary increases are based on considerations other than formal publication. If scholars no longer need to publish to earn "brownie points," a great danger arises. It is easy to visualize the emergence of closed "invisible colleges" in specialized areas, the members communicating with each other through computer-conferencing networks but feeling no need to transfer information beyond the immediate, elite circle. It would be very difficult for new researchers to break into such a group; information accessibility would deteriorate rather than improve; cross-fertilization among research areas would decline rapidly; and, in the long term, progress in all research areas would slow down, and much more duplication of research would be likely.

There is another facet of elitism. It is assumed that, by the turn of the century, satellite communication will have greatly improved the accessibility of information resources in the developing world. Several of my colleagues in developing countries have expressed their concern that the electronic publication and distribution of information products will put them at a great disadvantage. This would certainly be true today. Not only would there be economic barriers, there would also be technological (telephone and even electric power systems inadequate to support communications networks) and cultural barriers. On the other hand, these countries are already in an information-disadvantaged position. Fine libraries are few, publications are expensive and increasing in price, and currency-exchange regulations restrict importation of needed publications into many countries. Moreover, even when publications are imported, they are available in such small numbers as to be virtually inaccessible to most researchers. This situation is unlikely to improve significantly as long as publications continue to be distributed as print on paper.

In point of fact, improvements are more likely to be made through electronic networks. For reasons of national prestige alone, governments of developing nations may be more likely to invest in electronic communication than in building up conventional library services. Furthermore, the establishment of communications networks would be a highly visible manifestation of technology transfer from the developed to the developing world. It is probable, then, that foreign-aid programs would support the establishment of networks in the developing world that are similar in scope and purpose to EURONET. It seems entirely possible that EURONET may be followed by AFRONET, ASIANET, and so on. In fact, work is already under way to give the developing countries electronic access to the data bases of the developed world. For example, PADIS (the Pan African Documentation and Information System), which is already being implemented under the auspices of the United Nations, includes a component, PADIS/NET, designed to make data bases accessible to African countries through a sophisticated telecommunications network.

Bourne (1977) believes that computer-based operations provide the most cost-effective option available for the improvement of information services in developing countries. Woodward (1980) sees problems but agrees that on-line services could offer considerable benefits to these countries.

The danger to the developing world actually has little to do with electronics. It has to do with attitudes in the developed world toward information and information products. These attitudes are beginning to change as information services pass more and more out of the hands of government into the hands of the "information industry." This is seen clearly in the professional literature (see, for example, Brenner [1979] and Zurkowski [1979]) in the form of exhortations to protect the interests of commercial information services. Information products are now seen as big business; they are no longer considered products that can be distributed to the developing world at minimum cost. Indeed, as society becomes more postindustrial (i.e., less goods-producing and more information-producing), the pressure to sell information products "at true cost" will intensify. In fact, Zurkowski has already suggested that "information" may be the most exportable product that the United States has to offer and that information products should be priced to reflect their true value (related to the cost of the research that they encapsulate) rather than the cost of producing the information package itself. It is these ideas that the developing world must fear. Perhaps the best form of protection it can give itself is greater participation in international information systems, such as INIS and AGRIS, which reduce outright dependence on the most developed nations.

The rate of progress in the conversion to electronics will depend largely on what Cawkell (1980) has referred to as the "convergence of telephone, data transmission and computer technologies." This convergence, in turn, will be strongly affected by political, social, technological, and commercial factors. Cawkell believes that the political and social factors, which greatly influence demand, will tend to retard the rate of change, whereas technological and commercial factors will accelerate it. The next decade will reveal how quickly the technological and commercial factors are able to overcome the inertia that the political and social climate may impose. Will the paperless society be in place by the end of this century? It seems highly likely that it will. But only time will tell.

Bibliography

Algermissen, V. "Biomedical Librarians in a Patient Care Setting at the University of Missouri-Kansas City School of Medicine." *Bulletin of the Medical Library Association, 62*(4):354–358, October 1974.

American Library Association. *The Library and Information Networks of the Future.* Chicago, 1963.

Andrew, G., and V. Horsnell. "The Information Source Libraries Cannot Ignore." *Library Association Record, 82*(9):424–425, September 1980.

Arthur D. Little, Inc. *A Comparative Evaluation of Alternate Systems for the Provision of Effective Access to Periodical Literature.* Cambridge, Mass., Acorn Park, 1979.

Ashworth, W. "The Information Officer in the University Library." *Library Association Record, 41*:583–584, December 1939.

Aspen Systems Corporation, and Westat Research, Inc. *Editorial Processing Centers: Feasibility and Promise.* Rockville, Md., 1975.

Baer, W. S. *Interactive Television: Prospects for Two-Way Service on Cable.* Santa Monica, Calif., Rand Corporation, 1971.

Bagdikian, B. H. *The Information Machines: Their Impact on Men and the Media.* New York, Harper & Row, 1971.

Bair, J. H. "An Analysis of Organizational Productivity and the Use of Electronic Office Systems." *Proceedings of the American Society for Information Science, 17*:4–9, 1980.

Baker, J. W. "Will Public Libraries Be Obsolete in the 1980's?" *Canadian Library Journal, 36*(5):262–266, October 1979.

Bamford, H. "A Concept for Applying Computer Technology to the Publication of Scientific Journals." *Journal of the Washington Academy of Sciences, 62*(7): 306–314, October 1972.

Baran, P. *Potential Market Demand for Two-Way Information Services to the Home 1970–1990.* Menlo Park, Calif., Institute for the Future, 1972.

Barnes, R. E. "An Educator Looks Back from 1996." *The Futurist, 12*(2):123–126, April 1978.

Barwise, T. P. *Online Searching: The Impact on User Charges of the Extended Use of Online Information Services.* Paris, International Council of Scientific Unions Abstracting Board, 1979.

Bath University of Technology. *Experimental Information Officer in the Social Sciences.* Report to Office of Scientific and Technical Information, London, on work carried out in 1969. February 1970.

―――. *Experimental Information Service in the Social Sciences.* Report to Office of Scientific and Technical Information, London, on work carried out in 1970. January 1971.

Bell, D. *The Coming of Post-Industrial Society.* New York, Basic Books, 1973.

Bellamy, F. W. "The Information Brokerage Scene in America." In: *First Online Information Meeting, London, England.* New York, Learned Information, 1977, pp. 215–223.

Bernstein, L. M., E. R. Siegel, and C. M. Goldstein. "The Hepatitis Knowledge Base." *Annals of Internal Medicine, 93*(1) Part 2: 169–181, July 1980.

Best, F. "Recycling People: Work-Sharing Through Flexible Life Scheduling." *The Futurist, 12*(1):5–16, February 1978.

Bolch, J. "Thinker Toys." *American Way, 13*(4):24–30, April 1980.

Bolger, W. F. "Electronic Mail: Room for a Partnership." *Telephony, 197*:28–30, July 16, 1979.

Bolt, Beranek and Newman, Inc. *Toward the Library of the 21st Century: a Report on Progress.* Cambridge, Mass., 1964.

Borden, A. K. "The College Librarian and Research." *Bulletin of the American Library Association, 29*(7):412–416, July 1935.

Bork, A. "Books Versus Computers―Learning Media." *Proceedings of the American Society for Information Science, 17*:13–16, 1980.

Bourne, C. P. "Computer-Based Reference Services as an Alternative Means to Improve Resource-Poor Local Libraries in Developing Countries." *International Library Review, 9*(1):43–50, January 1977.

Branscomb, L. M. "Information: The Ultimate Frontier." *Science, 203*:143–147, 1979.

Brennan, R. "The Automobile's Endangered Future." *The Futurist, 13*(5):317–323, October 1979.

Brenner, E. H. "Opinion Paper: Euronet and Its Effects on the U.S. Information Market." *Journal of the American Society for Information Science, 30*(1):5–8, January 1979.

Broward, M. "To Pay or Not to Pay?" *LASIE, 9*:13–16, November/December 1978.

Brown, A. "The Age of Osiris: Tumult and Transformation." *The Futurist, 14*(2): 23–27, April 1980.

Brown, J. S. Remarks before the Committee on Science and Technology, U.S. House of Representatives, October 12, 1977. In: *Computers and the Learning Society: Hearings Before the Subcommittee on Domestic and International Scientific Planning, Analysis and Cooperation of the Committee on Science and Technology, U.S. House of Representatives, Ninety-Fifth Congress, First Session.* Washington, D.C., U.S. Government Printing Office, 1978, pp. 288–312.

Burchinal, L. "Impact of On-Line Systems on National Information Policy and on Local, State and Regional Planning." In: *The On-Line Revolution in Libraries.* Edited by A. Kent and T. J. Galvin. New York, Dekker, 1977, pp. 75–84.

Burns, J. C. "The Evolution of Office Information Systems." *Datamation, 23*(4): 60–64, April 1977.

Bush, V. "As We May Think." *Atlantic Monthly, 176*:101–108, 1945.

———. "Memex Revisited." In: *Science Is Not Enough.* Edited by V. Bush. New York, Morrow, 1967, pp. 75–101.

Byrd, G. D., and L. Arnold. "Medical School Graduates' Retrospective Evaluation of a Clinical Medical Librarian Program." *Bulletin of the Medical Library Association, 67*(3):308–312, July 1979.

Carr, R. "Prestel in Test Trial — an Academic Library User Looks Back." *Journal of Librarianship, 12*(3):145–158, July 1980.

———. "Prestel: What's in It for Librarians." *Assistant Librarian, 74*(1):13–16, January 1981.

Cawkell, A. E. "The Paperless Revolution." *Wireless World,* July 1978, pp. 38–42; August 1978, pp. 69–74.

———. "Electronic Information Processing and Publishing — Problems and Opportunities." *Journal of Information Science, 2*(3/4):189–192, October 1980.

Chabay, R., and S. G. Smith. "The Use of Computer-Based Chemistry Lessons." *Journal of Chemical Education, 54*(12):745–747, December 1977.

Chen, Ching-chih, et al. *Citizen Information Seeking Patterns: A New England Study.* Boston, Simmons College, School of Library Science, 1979.

Chen, K. "Future Trends in Microcomputers." *Technology Tomorrow, 3*(1):1, 10, February 1980.

Cheney, A. G. "Information Dissemination in a Research Establishment." *The Information Scientist, 5*:66–75, June 1971.

Cherry, S. S. "Telereference: The New TV Information Systems." *American Libraries, 11*(2):94–98, 108–110, February 1980.

Churchman, C. W. "Toward a Mathematics of Social Science." In: *Mathematical Explorations in Behavioral Science.* Edited by F. Massadrik and P. Ratoosh. Homewood, Ill., Irwin, 1965, pp. 29–36.

———. *The Design of Inquiring Systems; Basic Concepts of Systems and Organization.* New York, Basic Books, 1971.

Claman, G. G. "Clinical Medical Librarians: What They Do and Why." *Bulletin of the Medical Library Association, 66*(4):454–456, October 1978.

Clark, D. "Viewdata Strains the Entente Cordiale." *Teleclippings,* December 11, 1978, p. 548.

Clarke, A. C. "Electronic Tutors." *Omni, 2*(9):77–78, 96, June 1980.

Clayton, A., and N. Nisenoff. *The Influence of Technology upon Future Alternatives to the Scientific and Technical Journal.* Arlington, Va., Forecasting International Ltd., 1975.

———. *A Forecast of Technology for the Scientific and Technical Information Communities.* 4 Vols. Arlington, Va., Forecasting International Ltd., 1976. PB 253 937.

Colaianni, L. A. "Clinical Medical Librarians in a Private Teaching-Hospital Setting." *Bulletin of the Medical Library Association, 63*(4):410–411, October 1975.

Collier, H. R. "Long Term Economics of On-Line Services and Their Relationship to Conventional Publishers Seen from the Data Base Producers' Viewpoint." *Aslib Proceedings, 30*(1):16–24, January 1978.

Cornelisse, L. "A Clinical Reference Program in the Department of Medicine, Tufts-New England Medical Center Hospital." *Bulletin of the Medical Library Association, 66*(4):456–458, October 1978.

Cornish, E. "An Agenda for the 1980's." *The Futurist, 14*(1):5–7, February 1980.

Costigan, D. M. *Electronic Delivery of Documents and Graphics.* New York, Van Nostrand, 1978.

Creps, J. E., Jr. Remarks made at the National Information Conference and Exposition, NICE III, Washington, D.C., April 1979.

Criner, K., and M. Johnson-Hall. "Videotex: Threat or Opportunity." *Special Libraries, 71*(9):379–385, September 1980.

Croxton, F. E. "Libraries in the Year 2000." Paper presented at the Conference on Science and the Information Onslaught, Los Alamos National Laboratory, Los Alamos, N.M., June 1–5, 1981.

Cuadra, C. "Computer Technology and Libraries of the Future." In: *Computer Communications: Impacts and Implications. Proceedings of the First International Conference on Computer Communications.* Edited by S. Winkler. Washington, D.C., International Conferences on Computer Communication, 1972, pp. 472–476.

Cummings, P. "Health Sciences Libraries and Education: Heritage and Horizons. *Catholic Library World, 50*:28–29, July/August 1978.

Dana, J. C. *Libraries: Addresses and Essays.* White Plains, N.Y., H. W. Wilson Co., 1916.

David, L. "What's Ahead in the 1980's?" *Mechanix Illustrated, 75*(619):21–24, December 1979.

Davies, J. "EURONET—a Trap for the Unwary?" *Earth and Life Science Editing, 10*:5–6, January 1980.

Davinson, D. *Reference Service.* London, Bingley, 1979.

Davis, W. "The Universal Brain: Is Centralized Storage and Retrieval of All Knowledge Possible, Feasible, or Desirable?" Paper delivered to the National Microform Association, Cleveland, Ohio, May 13, 1965.

De Grazia, A. "A Theory of Encyclopedism." *American Behavioral Scientist, 6*(1): 38–40, September 1962.

———. "The Universal Reference System." *American Behavioral Scientist, 8*(8):3–14, April 1965.

Dodd, J. B. "Pay-As-You-Go Plan for Satellite Industrial Libraries Using Academic Facilities." *Special Libraries, 65*(2):66–72, February 1974.

Doll, D. R. "A Data Communications Forecast for the '80s." *Computerworld, 13*(53):8–9, December 31, 1979; continued in *14*(1):78–81, January 7, 1980.

Dordick, H. S., et al. "Network Information Services: The Emergence of an Industry." *Telecommunications Policy, 3*(3):217–234, September 1979.

Doszkocs, T. E., and B. A. Rapp. "Searching MEDLINE in English: A Prototype User Interface with Natural Language Query, Ranked Output, and Relevance Feedback." *Proceedings of the American Society for Information Science, 16*: 131–139, 1979.

Dougherty, R. M. "The Evaluation of Campus Library Document Delivery Service." *College and Research Libraries, 34*(1):29–39, January 1973.

Dowlin, K. E. "Broadcasting Reference Service Over a Community TV System." *Library Journal, 95*(15):2768–2770, September 1, 1970.

———. "The Electronic Eclectic Library." *Library Journal, 105*(19):2265–2270, November 1, 1980.

Drucker, P. F. *The Age of Discontinuity.* New York, Harper & Row, 1969.

———. "The 'Re-Industrialization' of America." *Wall Street Journal,* June 13, 1980. p. 10.

Dunn, S. L. "The Case of the Vanishing Colleges." *The Futurist, 13*(5):385–393, October 1979.

Elchesen, D. R. "Cost-Effectiveness Comparison of Manual and On-Line Retrospective Bibliographic Searching." *Journal of the American Society for Information Science, 29*(2):56–66, March 1978.

Elyria Public Library. *Project Aurora: An Experiment in Expanding Library Awareness.* Columbus, Ohio Library Foundation, 1973.

Emery, J. C. "The Status of Information Processing Technology." In: *Report on the Conference on Cataloging and Information Services for Machine-Readable Data Files.* (Airlie House, Warrenton, Va., March 29–31, 1978.) Arlington, Va., Data Use and Access Laboratories, 1978.

Engelbart, D. C. "NLS Teleconferencing Features: The Journal, and Shared-Screen Telephoning." *Comp Con Fall 1975, 11th IEEE Computer Society International Conference,* 1975, pp. 173–176. 75 CH 0988-6C.

Epstein, E. J. "Good News from Mr. Bad News." *New York, 9*(32):34–44, August 1976.

Fangmeyer, H. *Semi-Automatic Indexing: State of the Art.* Paris, Advisory Group for Aerospace Research and Development, 1974. AGARD-ograph Report AD-776642/IGA.

Farmer, J. "Does the Librarian Have a Place on the Clinical Team?" *Proceedings of the Library Association Centenary Conference.* London, Library Association, 1977a, pp. 86–88.

———. "Full Members of the Team: Medical Librarians in the Patient Care Setting." *Library Association Record, 79*(2):81–85, February 1977b.

Fedida, S., and R. Malik. *The Viewdata Revolution.* London, Associated Business Press, 1979.

Finnigan, G. "Nontraditional Information Service." *Special Libraries, 67*(2): 102–103, February 1976.

Folk, H. "The Impact of Computers on Book and Journal Publication." In: *The Economics of Library Automation.* Edited by J. L. Divilbiss. Urbana, University of Illinois, Graduate School of Library Science, 1977, pp. 72–82.

Foskett, D. *Classification and Indexing in the Social Sciences.* Washington, D.C., Butterworths, 1964.

Freeman, M., and G. P. Mulkowsky. "Advanced Interactive Technology: Robots in the Home and Classroom." *The Futurist, 12*(6):356–361, December 1978.

Gaffner, H. B. "The Demand for Information-On-Demand." *Bulletin of the American Society for Information Science, 3*(2):39–40, February 1976.

Gallup Organization, Inc. *The Role of Libraries in America.* Frankfort, Kentucky Department of Library and Archives, 1976.

Gershuny, J. I. "Post-Industrial Society: The Myth of the Service Economy." *Futures, 9*(2):103-114, April 1977.

Giuliano, V. E. "The Relationship of Information Science to Librarianship—Problems and Scientific Training." *American Documentation, 20*(4):344-345, October 1969.

_____. "A Manifesto for Librarians." *Library Journal, 104*(16):1837-1842, September 15, 1979.

_____. Remarks made at the Annual Conference of the American Library Association, New York, June 28-July 4, 1980, as reported in *Information and Data Base Publishing Report, 1*(13):9-10, August 13, 1980.

Giuliano, V. E., and P. E. Jones, Jr. "Linear Associative Information Retrieval." In: *Vistas in Information Handling.* Vol. 1. Edited by P. W. Howerton and D. C. Weeks. Washington, D.C., Spartan Books, 1963, pp. 30-54.

Goldstein, C. M. "The Potential Impact of Optical Disc Technology." In: *Telecommunications and Libraries.* White Plains, N.Y., Knowledge Industry Publications, 1981, Chapter 7.

_____. "Optical Disk Technology and Information." *Science, 215*:862-868, February 12, 1982.

Gordon, T. J. *The Future.* New York, St. Martin's Press, 1965.

Grayson, L. P. Personal communication, 1980.

Greenberg, B., et al. "Evaluation of a Clinical Medical Librarian Program at the Yale Medical Library." *Bulletin of the Medical Library Association, 66*(3):319-326, July 1978.

Gregory, N. "The U.S. Congress—Online Users as Policymakers." In: *Second International Online Information Meeting, London, 1978.* Oxford, Learned Information, 1979, pp. 1-8.

Guillaume, J. "Computer Conferencing and the Development of an Electronic Journal." *Canadian Journal of Information Science, 5*:21-29, May 1980.

Haiman, R. J. "An Interview with Robert J. Haiman." *National Forum, 60*(3):5-8, Summer 1980.

Hall, J. "Information Services in University Libraries." *Aslib Proceedings, 24*(5): 293-302, May 1972.

Harmon, G. "The Invisible Manpower Market for Information Scientists." *Proceedings of the American Society for Information Science, 12*:59-60, 1975.

Haug, M. R. "The Deprofessionalization of Everyone?" *Sociological Focus, 8*(3): 197-213, August 1975. Also in: *Libraries in Post-Industrial Society.* Edited by L. Estabrook. Phoenix, Oryx Press, 1977, pp. 67-84.

Hays, D. G., et al. *A Billion Books for Education and the World.* Santa Monica, Calif., Rand Corporation, 1968. Memorandum RM-5574-RC.

Heckel, P. "Designing Translator Software." *Datamation, 26*(2):134-138, February 1980.

Hernon, P., and M. Pastine. "The Floating Reference Librarian." *RQ, 12*(1):60-64, Fall 1972.

Herther, N. K. "Free-Lancing: A Personal Experiment." *RQ, 18*(2):177–179, Winter 1978.

Hickey, D. J. "Room for Library Students?" *American Libraries, 5*(10):527, November 1974.

Hiltz, S. R., and M. Turoff. *The Network Nation: Human Communication Via Computer.* Reading, Mass., Addison-Wesley, 1978.

Hinks, J. "Leicestershire Libraries: a Team-Based Organization Structure." In: *Studies in Library Management.* Edited by G. Holroyd. Vol. 4. London, Bingley, 1977, pp. 67–84.

Hirsch, P. "Videotex Seen Changing Social Behavior in the '80s." *Computerworld, 14*(15):64, April 14, 1980.

Hogan, C. L. "The Challenges of the Microelectronic Era." *Progress: The Fairchild Journal of Semiconductors, 6*:3–10, October 1978.

Holt, P. "Publishing the 'Paperless Book.'" *Publishers Weekly, 217*(6):51, April 25, 1980.

Hooper, R. S., and S. Henderson. "The Status of 'Paperless' Systems in the Intelligence Community." In: *The Role of the Library in an Electronic Society: Proceedings of the Sixteenth Annual Clinic on Library Applications of Data Processing.* Edited by F. W. Lancaster. Urbana, University of Illinois, Graduate School of Library Science, 1980, pp. 94–105.

Inner London Education Authority. "Information Sheet." London, 1980.

Jones, G. E. " '1984,' How Close to Reality?" *U.S. News and World Report, 86*: 49–50, February 5, 1979.

Jordan, R. T. *Tomorrow's Library: Direct Access and Delivery.* New York, Bowker, 1970.

Joseph, E. C. "Longterm Electronic Technology Trends: Forecasted Impacts on Education."*Journal of Cultural and Educational Futures, 1*(2):14–17, July 1979a.

———. "1990: A Vision of the Future." *Computerworld, 13*(53):4–5, December 31, 1979b; continued in *14*(1):68–77, January 7, 1980.

Josephine, H. B. "Electronic Mail: The Future Is Now." *Online, 4*(4):41–43, October 1980.

Kahn, H., and W. M. Brown. "The Optimistic Outlook." In: *Handbook of Futures Research.* Edited by J. Fowles. Westport, Conn., Greenwood Press, 1978, pp. 455–477.

Kalba, K. "Librarians in the Information Martketplace." In: *Libraries in Post-Industrial Society.* Edited by L. Estabrook. Phoenix, Oryx Press, 1977, pp. 307–319.

Kane, D., and B. Sherwood. "A Computer-Based Course in Classical Mechanics." *Computers and Education, 4*:15–36, 1980.

Kasarda, A. J., and D. J. Hillman. "The LEADERMART System and Service." *Proceedings of the Annual Conference of the Association for Computing Machinery.* New York, 1972, pp. 469–477.

Kemeny, J. G., et al. "A Library for 2000 A.D." In: *Management and the Computer of the Future.* Edited by M. Greenberger. Cambridge, Mass., MIT Press, 1962, pp. 134–178.

Kent, A., et al. *Use of Library Materials: The University of Pittsburgh Study.* New York, Dekker, 1979.

Kim, C. H., and I. M. Sexton. *Conference on Books by Mail Service: A Report.* Terre Haute, Indiana State University, Department of Library Science, 1973.

King, D. W., et al. *Statistical Indicators of Scientific and Technical Communication: 1960-1980.* Vol. 1. Rockville, Md., King Research, Inc., 1976.

King, J. B., et al. "What Future Reference Librarian?" *RQ 10*(3):243-247, Spring 1971.

King Research, Inc. *Systems Analysis of Scientific and Technical Communication in the United States.* Rockville, Md., 1978. (A report to the National Science Foundation.)

Kleiman, D. "Futuristic Library Does Away With Books." *The New York Times,* October 21, 1980, pp. C1, C6.

Klugman, S. "Variations on Popular Online Themes." *CU News, 35*(2):5-6, January 17, 1980.

Knapp, P. *The Monteith College Library Experiment.* New York, Scarecrow Press, 1966.

Knight, D. M., and E. S. Nourse, eds. *Libraries at Large: Tradition, Innovation and the National Interest.* New York, Bowker, 1969.

Kochen, M. "On-Line Intellectual Communities." Paper presented at the Annual Meeting of the Society for General Systems Research, Denver, Colo., February 22, 1977.

———. "Alternative Futures of the Library and Information Professions in a Post-Industrial Age." Louisiana State University, School of Library Science, 1978. Lecture Series #40.

Korfhage, R. R. "The Impact of Personal Computers on Library-Based Information Systems." *Forum: A Publication of the ACM Special Interest Group on Information Retrieval, 12*(4):10-13, Spring 1978.

Kotler, P. "Educational Packagers: A Modest Proposal." *The Futurist, 12*(4): 239-242, August 1978.

Krall Management, Inc. *The Viability and Impact of Electronic Storage and Delivery of Handbook-Type Information.* Radnor, Pa., 1977. PB 278 072.

Kubitz, W. J. "Computer Technology: A Forecast for the Future." In: *The Role of the Library in an Electronic Society: Proceedings of the Sixteenth Annual Clinic on Library Applications of Data Processing.* Edited by F. W. Lancaster. Urbana, University of Illinois, Graduate School of Library Science, 1980, pp. 135-161.

Kupperman, R. H., and R. H. Wilcox. "EMISARI: An On-Line Management System in a Dynamic Environment." In: *Computer Communication: Impacts and Implications. Proceedings of the First International Conference on Computer Communications.* Edited by S. Winkler. Washington, D. C., International Conferences on Computer Communication, 1972, pp. 117-120.

Lamb, G. "Bridging the Information Gap." *Hospital Libraries, 1*:2-4, November 15, 1976.

Lancaster, F. W. *Vocabulary Control for Information Retrieval.* Arlington, Va., Information Resources Press, 1972, Chapter 16, pp. 135-152.

———. *Toward Paperless Information Systems.* New York, Academic Press, 1978.

Lancaster, F. W., L. Drasgow, and E. Marks. *The Impact of a Paperless Society on the Research Library of the Future.* Urbana, University of Illinois, Graduate School of Library Science, 1980. (Final report to the National Science Foundation.)

Larson, E. "What's an Office Without Paper?" *Wall Street Journal,* July 30, 1980, p. 21.

Lea, P. W. "Alternative Methods of Journal Publishing." *Aslib Proceedings, 31*(1): 33–39, January 1979.

Lecht, C. P. "The Next 20 Years in DP." *Computerworld, 13*(53):23–26, December 31, 1979; continued in *14*(1):65–67, January 7, 1980.

Lewis, D. A. "There Won't Be an Information Profession in 2000 AD." Paper presented at meeting of Aslib, London, October 1976.

———. "Today's Challenge—Tomorrow's Choice: Change or Be Changed, or, the Doomsday Scenario MK 2." *Journal of Information Science, 2*(2):59–74, September 1980.

Licklider, J. C. R. *Libraries of the Future.* Cambridge, Mass., MIT Press, 1965.

Line, M. B. "Information Services in University Libraries." *Journal of Librarianship, 1*(4):211–224, October 1969.

———. "Information Services in a Technological University: Plans and Prospects." *The Information Scientist, 5*:77–88, June 1971.

———. "The Case for Information Officers." In: *Educating the Library User.* Edited by J. Lubans. New York, Bowker, 1974, pp. 383–391.

Lipinski, H. M., and R. H. Miller. "FORUM: A Computer-Assisted Communications Medium." In: *Computer Communication Today and up to 1985. Proceedings of the Second International Conference on Computer Communications.* Edited by the ICCC-74 Secretariat. Stockholm, International Conferences on Computer Communication, 1974, pp. 143–147.

Lorenzi, N. M. "Information to Patient Care Areas via Television: A New Program." *Biosciences Communication, 2*(10):362–370, October 1976.

Loveless, B. "KSL-TV Fuels Teletext Interest with Successful On-Air Tests." *Teleclippings, 558:*8–10, 1978.

MacLeod, A. "Britain's Turn-On Newspapers." *Christian Science Monitor,* April 9, 1979, p. 20.

Magarrell, J. "Computer Links Stanford Officials in Test of Electronic Mail System." *The Chronicle of Higher Education,* October 6, 1980, p. 5.

Major, R. "Team Librarianship." *Assistant Librarian, 72*(12):154–157, December 1979.

Major, R., and P. Judd, eds. *Team Librarianship.* Bradford, England, Association of Assistant Librarians, Northern Division, 1979.

Maranjian, L., and R. W. Boss. *Fee-Based Information Services: A Study of a Growing Industry.* New York, Bowker, 1980.

Marill, T. *Libraries and Question-Answering Systems.* Cambridge, Mass., Bolt, Beranek and Newman, Inc., 1963. Report 1071.

Marshall, J. G., and J. Hamilton. "The Clinical Librarian and the Patient: Report of a Project at McMaster University Medical Centre." *Bulletin of the Medical Library Association, 66*(4):420–425, October 1978.

Marshall, P. "Guiding Business—Via Prestel." *Library Association Record, 83*(2):78–79, February 1981.

Martin, J. *The Wired Society.* Englewood Cliffs, N.J., Prentice-Hall, 1978.

Martino, J. P. "Telecommunications in the Year 2000." *The Futurist, 13*(2):95–103, April 1979.

Martyn, J. "Prestel and Public Libraries: An LA/Aslib Experiment." *Aslib Proceedings, 31*(5):216–236, May 1979.

Marvin, C. "The Impact of Technology on the Production and Distribution of the News. Part 2. Delivering the News of the Future." In: *The Role of the Library in an Electronic Society: Proceedings of the Sixteenth Annual Clinic on Library Applications of Data Processing.* Edited by F. W. Lancaster. Urbana, University of Illinois, Graduate School of Library Science, 1980, pp. 36–47.

Maury, J. P. "Plans and Projections for the Electronic Directory Service." In: *Viewdata and Videotext, 1980–81: A Worldwide Report.* White Plains, N.Y., Knowledge Industry Publications, 1980, pp. 39–50.

McHale, J. "The Future of Art and Mass Culture." *Futures, 10*(3):178–190, June 1978.

McKean, J. M. "Facsimile and Libraries." In: *Telecommunications and Libraries.* White Plains, N.Y., Knowledge Industry Publications, 1981, Chapter 6.

Mooers, C. "The Next Twenty Years in Information Retrieval: Some Goals and Predictions." *American Documentation, 11*(3):229–236, July 1960.

Moray, N., and J. Stocklosa. "Electronic Journals, an Editor's View." In: *EURIM 4.* Edited by L. J. Anthony. London, Aslib, 1980, pp. 17–18.

National Enquiry into Scholarly Communication. *Scholarly Communication: the Report of the National Enquiry.* Baltimore, Md., Johns Hopkins University Press, 1979.

Negroponte, N. "Books Without Pages." *Conference Record,* pp. 56.1.1–56.1.8. IEEE International Conference on Communications, Boston, Mass., June 10–14, 1979.

Neill, S. D. "Libraries in the Year 2010." *The Futurist, 15*(5):47–51, October 1981.

Nelson, J. "Comment on Communication and Systems Compatibility." *Catholic Library World, 46:*390–391, April 1975.

Nelson, T. H. "As We Will Think." *Online 72 Conference Proceedings.* Vol. 1. Uxbridge, England, Online Computer Systems Ltd., 1972, pp. 439–454.

———. *Computer Lib.* South Bend, Ind., T. H. Nelson, 1974.

———. "Electronic Publishing and Electronic Literature." In: *Information Technology in Health Science Education.* Edited by E. C. DeLand. New York, Plenum Press, 1978, pp. 211–216.

Nielsen, B. "Online Bibliographic Searching and the Deprofessionalization of Librarianship." *Online Review, 4*(3):215–224, September 1980.

Nisenoff, N., et al. *Costs and Benefits of Some Alternative Information Delivery Systems of 1985.* Arlington, Va., Forecasting International Ltd., 1977.

Noback, R. K., and G. D. Byrd. *Developing Clinical Information Needs and Systems.* Bethesda, Md., National Library of Medicine, 1977. ED 145 864.

Nora, H. "French Policy on Videotex." In: *The Impact of New Technologies on Publishing.* London, Saur, 1980, pp. 59–64.

Nora, S., and A. Minc. *The Computerization of Society.* Cambridge, Mass., MIT Press, 1980.

*OCLC Newsletter, 127:*5, February 6, 1980.

Oettinger, A. G. "Educational Technology." In: *Toward the Year 2018.* Edited by the Foreign Policy Association. New York, 1968, pp. 75–86.

Olson, S. "Prospects for the Automobile: Sputtering Toward the Twenty-First Century." *The Futurist, 14*(1):27–34, February 1980.

Ong, W. J. "Literacy and Orality in Our Times." *Profession '79:* Selected articles from the bulletins of the Association of Departments of English and the Association of Departments of Foreign Languages, New York, Modern Language Association of America. 1979, pp. 1–7)

Online Computer Library Center, Inc. *Channel 2000 Project Report.* Columbus, Ohio, 1981.

Orne, J. "An Experiment in Integrated Library Service." *College and Research Libraries, 16*(4)353–359, October 1955.

Outman, J. "Information Services for Cable to Be Delivered via Satellite by Reuters." *TV Communications, 15*(5):122–123, January 1978.

Overhage, C. F. R., and R. J. Harmon. "The On-Line Intellectual Community and the Information Transfer System at MIT in 1975." In: *The Growth of Knowledge: Readings on Organization and Retrieval of Information.* Edited by M. Kochen. New York, Wiley, 1967, pp.77–95.

———, eds. *INTREX: Report of a Planning Conference on Information Transfer Experiments.* Cambridge, Mass., MIT Press, 1965.

Panko, R. R., and R. U. Panko. "An Introduction to Computers for Human Communication." *Communications News, 14:*32–34, December 1977.

Papert, S. Remarks before the Committee on Science and Technology, U.S. House of Representatives, October 12, 1977. In: *Computers and the Learning Society: Hearings Before the Subcommittee on Domestic and International Scientific Planning, Analysis and Cooperation of the Committee on Science and Technology, U.S. House of Representatives, Ninety-Fifth Congress. First Session.* Washington, D.C., U.S. Government Printing Office, 1978, pp. 257–272.

Parker, E. B. "Background Report." In: *Conference on Computer Telecommunications Policy: Proceedings of the OECD Conference, February 4–6, 1975.* Paris, Organization for Economic Cooperation and Development, 1976, pp. 87–129.

Penland, P. R. *Floating Librarians in the Community.* Pittsburgh, Pa., University of Pittsburgh, 1970.

Pfaffenberger, A., and S. Echt. "Substitution of SciSearch and Social SciSearch for Their Print Versions in an Academic Library." *Database, 3*(1):63–71, March 1980.

Phillips, D. "A Review of Telidon Development." *Online Review, 4*(2):169–171, June 1980.

Phillips, K. P. *Mediacracy.* Garden City, N.Y., Doubleday, 1975.

Platt, J. R. *The Step to Man.* New York, Wiley, 1966.

Porat, M. U. *The Information Economy.* Washington, D.C., U.S. Department of Commerce, Office of Telecommunications, 1977.

Powell, C. "Prestel: The Opportunity for Advertising." In: *Viewdata and Videotext,*

1980-1981: A Worldwide Report. Knowledge Industry Publications, 1980, pp. 233-246.

Raben, J. "The Electronic Revolution and the World Just Around the Corner." *Scholarly Publishing, 10*(3):195-209, April 1979.

Rada, J. *The Impact of Microelectronics.* Geneva, International Labor Organization, 1980.

Radolf, A. "Knight-Ridder to Test Home Electronic Info System." *Editor and Publisher, 113*(15):7-8, April 12, 1980.

Ranganathan, S. R. *The Five Laws of Library Science.* 1931. Reprint. Bombay, Asia Publishing House, 1963.

Reintjes, J. F. " 'Instant' Librarians." *Christian Science Monitor,* August 3, 1967, p. 9.

Rinder, R. "ACS Is Coming." *Datamation, 24*(12):95-99, December, 1978.

Ris, C. "Electronic Newspapers Could Alter Shape of the $4.6 Billion Classified Ad Market." *Wall Street Journal,* August 11, 1980, p. 15.

Roach, A. A., and W. W. Addington. "The Effects of an Information Specialist on Patient Care and Medical Education." *Journal of Medical Education, 50:* 176-180, February 1975.

Rogers, R. D. Remarks reported in the *Yale Weekly Bulletin and Calendar,* November 5-12, 1979.

Rogoff, M. "The Case for Electronic Mail." *Modern Data,* December 1974, pp. 34-37.

Roistacher, R. C. "The Virtual Journal." *Computer Networks, 2*(1):18-24, January 1978a.

———. "The Network-Based Scientific Community Economic Climate and Social Structure." *IASSIST Newsletter, 2*(1):19-22, Winter 1978b.

———. "The Virtual Journal: Reaching the Reader." In: *The Role of the Library in an Electronic Society: Proceedings of the Sixteenth Annual Clinic on Library Applications of Data Processing.* Edited by F. W. Lancaster. Urbana, University of Illinois, Graduate School of Library Science, 1980, pp. 16-22.

Rolland, J. "The Microelectronic Revolution: How Intelligence on a Chip Will Change Our Lives." *The Futurist, 13*(2):81-90, April 1979.

Rout, L. "Many Managers Resist 'Paperless' Technology for Their Own Offices." *Wall Street Journal,* June 24, 1980, p. 117.

Sackman, H., and N. Nie. *The Information Utility and Social Choice.* Montvale, N.J., AFIPS Press, 1970.

Saffady, W. "Facsimile Transmission for Libraries: Technology and Application Design." *Library Technology Reports, 14:*445-531, September-October,1978.

Salisbury, B. A., Jr., and H. E. Stiles. "The Use of the B-Coefficient in Information Retrieval." *Proceedings of the American Society for Information Science, 6:*265-268, 1969.

Salton, G. *Automatic Information Organization and Retrieval.* New York, McGraw-Hill, 1968.

———. *The SMART Retrieval System: Experiments in Automatic Document Processing.* Englewood Cliffs, N. J., Prentice-Hall, 1971.

———. "Proposals for a Dynamic Library." In: *Libraries in Post-Industrial*

Society. Edited by L. Estabrook. Phoenix, Oryx Press, 1977, pp. 272–305.

Saunderson, M. "The Information Function in Relation to User Departments: An Excursion into the Future." *Aslib Proceedings, 29*(2):77–90, February 1977.

Savage, M. "Beyond Film: A Look at the Information Storage Potential of Videodiscs." *Bulletin of the American Society for Information Science, 7*(1):26–29, October 1980.

Scarfe, D. "The Future Patterns of Information Services for Industry and Commerce." *Aslib Proceedings, 27*(3):80–89, March 1975.

Schiller, A. R. "The Potential of On-Line Systems and the Librarian's Role." In: *The On-Line Revolution in Libraries.* Edited by A. Kent and T. J. Galvin. New York, Dekker, 1977, pp. 31–37.

Schlesinger, A., Jr. "Is Gutenberg Dead?" *PLA Bulletin, 22*:121–128, February 1967.

Schnall, J. G., and J. W. Wilson. "Evaluation of a Clinical Medical Librarianship Program at a University Health Sciences Library." *Bulletin of the Medical Library Association, 64*(3):278–283, July 1976.

Schuyler, J. A., and R. Johansen. "ORACLE: Computerized Conferencing in a Computer Assisted Instruction System." In: *Computer Communication: Impacts and Implications. Proceedings of the First International Conference on Computer Communications.* Edited by S. Winkler. Washington, D.C., International Conferences on Computer Communication, 1972, pp. 155–160.

Seiler, L. H., and J. Raben. "The Electronic Journal." *Society, 18*(6):76–83, September/October 1981.

Seligman, L. "Putting the Pieces Together." *Computerworld, 14*(1):45–52, January 7, 1980.

Selim, R. "Health in the Future: In the Pink or in the Red?" *The Futurist, 13*(5):329–342, October 1979.

Senders, J. W. "An On-Line Scientific Journal." *The Information Scientist, 11*(1):3–9, March 1977.

_____. "The Electronic Journal." In: *EURIM 4.* Edited by L. J. Anthony. London, Aslib, 1980, pp. 14–16.

Senders, J. W., C. M. B. Anderson, and C. D. Hecht. *Scientific Publications Systems: An Analysis of Past, Present and Future Methods of Scientific Communication.* Toronto, Toronto University, 1975. PB 242 259.

Shackel, B. "The BLEND System: Plans for the Study of Some 'Electronic Journals.' " (In press)

Shackleford, P. "Planning for Tourism Research Needs in a Growth Industry." *Futures, 2*(1):32–43, February 1979.

Shannon, Z. J. "Public Library Service to the Corporate Community." *Special Libraries, 65*(1):12–16, January 1974.

Sheils, M., et al. "And Man Created the Chip." *Newsweek,* June 30, 1980, pp. 50–56.

Siegel, E. R. "Validating and Updating the NLM's Hepatitis Data Base: the Role of Computer Conferencing." *Proceedings of the American Society for Information Science, 16*:124–130, 1979.

Sigel, E., ed. *Videotext: The Coming Revolution in Home/Office Information*

Retrieval. White Plains, N.Y., Knowledge Industry Publications, 1980.

Singleton, A. "The Electronic Journal and Its Relations." *Scholarly Publishing, 13*(1):3–18, October 1981.

Smith, E. "The Impact of the Subject Specialist Librarian on the Organization and Structure of the Academic Research Library." In: *The Academic Library*. Edited by E. I. Farber and R. Walling. Metuchen, N.J., Scarecrow Press, 1974, pp. 71–81.

Smith, L. C. "Artificial Intelligence Applications in Information Systems." *Annual Review of Information Science and Technology, 15*:67–105, 1980.

Smith, R. F. "A Funny Thing Is Happening to the Library on Its Way to the Future." *The Futurist, 12*(2):85–91, April 1978.

Smith, S. G., and B. Sherwood. "Educational Uses of the PLATO Computer System." *Science, 192*:344–352, April 23, 1976.

Sobel, D. S., ed. *Ways of Health: Holistic Approaches to Ancient and Contemporary Medicine*. New York, Harcourt Brace Jovanovich, 1979.

Sparck Jones, K. *Automatic Keyword Classification for Information Retrieval*. Hamden, Conn., Archon Books, 1971.

———. "Automatic Indexing." *Journal of Documentation, 30*(4):393–432, December 1974.

Spiegel, J., et al. *Statistical Association Procedures for Message Content Analysis*. Bedford, Mass., Mitre Corporation, 1962.

Stanley, W. G. "Changing Revenue Patterns from Online Use." Paper presented at the National Information Conference and Exposition, NICE III, Washington, D.C., April 1979.

Stetten, K. J. *TICCIT: A Delivery System Designed for Mass Utilization*. Washington, D.C., Mitre Corporation, 1971a.

———. *Interactive Television Software for Cable Television Application*. Washington, D.C., Mitre Corporation, 1971b.

Stevens, M. E. *Automatic Indexing: A State-of-the-Art Report*. Washington, D.C., National Bureau of Standards, 1970. NBS Monograph 91.

Stewart, J. "Computer Shock: The Inhuman Office of the Future." *Saturday Review, 6*(13):14–17, June 23, 1979.

Stiles, H. E. "Machine Retrieval Using the Association Factor." In: *Machine Indexing, Progress and Problems*. Washington, D.C., American University, 1961.

Sweeney, R. T. "Model for a Free Public Information System." Paper presented at the Public Libraries and Remote Electronic Delivery of Information meeting, Columbus, Ohio, March 23–24, 1981.

Thursh, D., and F. Mabry. "An Interactive Hyper-Text of Pathology." *Proceedings of the Fourth Annual Symposium on Computer Applications in Medical Care*. 1980, pp. 1820–1825.

Timour, J. A. "Use of Selected Abstracting and Indexing Journals in Biomedical Resource Libraries." *Bulletin of the Medical Library Association, 67*(3): 330–335, July 1979.

Toffler, A. *Future Shock*. New York, Random House, 1970.

———. *The Third Wave*. New York, Morrow, 1980.

Trubkin, L. "Migration from Print to Online Use." *Online Review, 4*(1):5–12, March 1980.

Turoff, M. "PARTY LINE and DISCUSSION Computerized Conference Systems." In: *Computer Communication: Impacts and Implications. Proceedings of the First International Conference on Computer Communications.* Edited by S. Winkler. Washington, D.C., International Conferences on Computer Communication, 1972, pp. 161–171.

———. "An On-line Intellectual Community or 'Memex' Revisited." *Technological Forecasting and Social Change, 10*(4):401–412, December 1977.

———. Informal communication distributed within the Electronic Information Exchange System (EIES), 1979.

Turoff, M., and T. Featheringham. "Libraries and Communication Information Technology." *Catholic Library World, 50*:368–373, April 1979.

Turoff, M., and S. R. Hiltz. "The Electronic Journal: A Progress Report." (In press)

Urrows, H., and E. Urrows. "Around the World with Videotext." *Microcomputing, 5*(11):84–93, November 1981.

Vail, H. "The Automated Office." *The Futurist, 12*(2):73–78, April 1978.

Valdez, M. "An Information Broker as a Member of a Health Service Planning Unit." *Aslib Proceedings, 26*(12):473–476, December 1974.

Vallee, J., et al. *Group Communication Through Computers.* 5 Vols. Menlo Park, Calif., Institute for the Future, 1974–1978.

Veith, R. H. "Informatics and Transborder Data Flow: The Question of Social Impact." *Journal of the American Society for Information Science, 31*(2):105–110, March 1980.

———. "Videotex—the New Information Systems." Paper presented at the Eighteenth Annual Clinic on Library Applications of Data Processing, University of Illinois, Graduate School of Library Science, April 26–29, 1981.

Volk, J. *The Reston, Virginia Test of the Mitre Corporation's Interactive Television System.* Washington, D.C., Mitre Corporation, 1971.

Von Foerster, H. *Technology: What Will It Mean to Librarians? (A Response).* Urbana, University of Illinois, Department of Electrical Engineering, 1972.

Wagschal, P. H. "Illiterates With Doctorates: The Future of Education in an Electronic Age." *The Futurist, 12*(4):243–244, August 1978.

Warnken, K. *The Directory of Fee-Based Information Services 1978-1979.* New York, Dover Publications, 1978.

———. *The Information Brokers.* New York, Bowker, 1981.

Wedemeyer, D. J. "New Communications Services for the Future." *World Future Society Bulletin, 14*(1):1–6, January–February 1980.

Weingand, D. *Reflections of Tomorrow: Lifelong Learning and the Public Library.* Minneapolis, Derby Associates, Inc., 1980.

Wells, H. G. *World Brain.* New York, Doubleday, 1938.

White, R. B. "A Prototype for the Automated Office." *Datamation, 23*(4):83–90, April 1977.

Wicklein, J. "Wired City, U.S.A.: The Charms and Dangers of Two-Way TV." *Atlantic, 243(2):*35–42, February 1979.

Williams, J. H., Jr. *BROWSER: An Automatic Indexing On-Line Text Retrieval System.* Gaithersburg, Md., IBM Federal Systems Division, 1969. Annual Progress Report. AD 693 143.

Williams, M. E., and S. E. Preece. "Database Selector for Network Use: a Feasibility Study." *Proceedings of the American Society for Information Science,* *14*:34, 1977.

Wilson, P. "Some Fundamental Concepts of Information Retrieval." *Drexel Library Quarterly, 14*(2):10–23, April 1978.

Woodward, A. M. *Editorial Processing Centres: Scope in the United Kingdom.* London, British Library Research and Development Report 5271, 1976.

———. "Future Information Requirements of the Third World." *Journal of Information Science, 1*(5):259–265, January 1980.

Yankelovich, Skelly and White, Inc. *The 1978 Consumer Research Study on Reading and Book Purchasing.* New York, 1978.

Zurkowski, P. G. "Misconceptions about Information Are Costing the United States a Bundle." *Publishers Weekly,* July 9, 1979, pp. 37–38.

INDEX

Accessibility of materials, 100–102
Addington, W. W., 172
ADONIS, 74–75
Advertising via electronic media, 49,
    202–203
Algermissen, V., 172
Alternative scenarios, 182–184
American Library Association,
    128–129, 166
Andrew, G., 110, 158, 161
Antiope, 41
Arnold, L., 172, 175
Arthur D. Little, Inc., 150, 198, 200
Artificial intelligence, 136
Art in the future, 11–12, 73
Ashworth, W., 171
Aspen Systems Corporation, 55
Assumptions underlying move toward
    a paperless society, 184–190

Baer, W. S., 50
Bagdikian, B. H., 48
Bair, J. H., 31
Baker, J. W., 16, 61, 200
Bamford, H., 55
Baran, P., 47–48
Barnes, R. E., 9
Barwise, T. P., 187–188
Bath University, 171–172
Bell, D., 1
Bellamy, F. W., 173
Bernstein, L. M., 71

Best, F., 11
Bolch, J., 73
Bolger, W. F., 29
Bolt, Beranek and Newman, Inc., 127,
    131, 134
Book-centered education, 9–10
Books in electronic form, 45–46,
    56–60, 63–64, 70–74
    see also Electrobooks
Borden, A. K., 171
Bork, A., 10
Boss, R. W., 173
Bourne, C. P., 206
Branscomb, L. M., 16–17, 22
Brennan, R., 9
Brenner, E. H., 206
Brokers, 173–174
Broward, M., 174
Brown, A., 177
Brown, J. S., 72
Brown, W. M., 9
Burchinal, L., 128
Burns, J. C., 29–30
Bush, V., 132
Bypassing the library, 130–132,
    147–150, 157–158
Byrd, G. D., 172, 175

Cable television, *see* Interactive
    television
CAPTAIN, 44–45
Carr, R., 39, 158–161